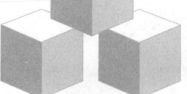

Hands On
Visual C++®
for Web
Development

Send Us Your Comments:

To comment on this book or any other PRIMA TECH title, visit Prima's reader response page on the Web at **www.primapublishing.com/comments**.

How to Order:

For information on quantity discounts, contact the publisher: Prima Publishing, P.O. Box 1260BK, Rocklin, CA 95677-1260; (916) 632-4400. On your letterhead, include information concerning the intended use of the books and the number of books you wish to purchase. For individual orders, turn to the back of this book for more information, or visit PRIMA TECH's Web site at **www.prima-tech.com**.

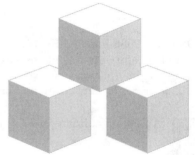

Hands On
Visual C++®
for Web
Development

Dr. Donald Doherty

PRIMA
TECH

A Division of Prima Publishing

A Division of Prima Publishing

Prima Publishing and colophon are registered trademarks of Prima Communications, Inc. Prima Publishing, Rocklin, California 95677.

Publisher: Matthew H. Carleson
Managing Editor: Dan J. Foster
Senior Acquisitions Editor: Deborah F. Abshier
Project Editor: Kevin Harreld
Editorial Assistant: Kim V. Benbow
Technical Reviewers: Dan Wygant, Ben Thompson
Copy Editors: Robert Campbell, June Waldman
Interior Layout: Debbie Lee at CWA, Inc.
Cover Design: Prima Design Team
Indexer: Katherine Stimson

Prima Publishing and the author have attempted throughout this book to distinguish proprietary trademarks from descriptive terms by following the capitalization style used by the manufacturers.

Microsoft, Windows, Windows NT, Internet Explorer, Visual Basic, Visual C++, FoxPro, and Visual Studio are trademarks or registered trademarks of Microsoft Corporation.

Important: If you experience problems running Visual C++ 6, go to Microsoft's Web site at **www.microsoft.com**, or check the online help for technical support information. Prima Publishing cannot provide software support.

Information contained in this book has been obtained by Prima Publishing from sources believed to be reliable. However, because of the possibility of human or mechanical error by our sources, Prima Publishing, or others, the Publisher does not guarantee the accuracy, adequacy, or completeness of any information and is not responsible for any errors or omissions or the results obtained from use of such information. Readers should be particularly aware of the fact that the Internet is an ever-changing entity. Some facts may have changed since this book went to press.

ISBN: 0-7615-1394-9
Library of Congress Catalog Card Number: 98-65161
Printed in the United States of America

98 99 00 01 02 DD 10 9 8 7 6 5 4 3 2 1

To people of all ages and all over the world creatively using the computer, a tool in its infancy, in the service of earth and humanity.
—DD

Contents at a Glance

Contents

Acknowledgments

A book is a team effort. The team behind this book at Prima deserves a huge round of thanks for helping to create this book. Thanks to the technical editors, especially Dan Wygant. Thanks to Tom Barich for doing an excellent job on creating a companion CD for this book. Thanks to the superb editing team at Prima. In particular, thanks to Kevin Harreld, the project editor, and Dan Foster, the managing editor. And, finally, special thanks to my acquisitions editor, Debbie Abshier, for being so supportive, especially through the difficult times when I would have rather been vacationing on a tropical island.

Special thanks go out to the Visual C++ team at Microsoft, especially to Chris Hargarten for fielding questions while hard at work on the final Visual C++ product.

Finally, thanks to Vanessa Keech for her love and support through this project and to my neighbor and friend Shahnaz Denlinger for surprising me with delicious meals while I was working on my porch with my laptop computer into the early morning hours.

About the Author

Dr. Donald Doherty is a neuroscientist and a computer expert. He received his Ph.D. from the Department of Psychobiology at University of California, Irvine. Don's computer experience includes programming large-scale computer models of brain systems. He's written on a wide range of computer topics. His books include *Teach Yourself Borland JBuilder 2 in 21 Days*. Don is a Research Associate in the Department of Neurobiology at the University of Pittsburgh School of Medicine. Visit his Web site at http://ourworld.compuserve.com/homepages/brainstage/.

Introduction

This book takes you far beyond the Visual C++ documentation in a practical step-by-step manner. It teaches you to create substantial full-featured applications for the Web and the entire computing enterprise with surprising ease.

Using the powerful tools that make up the Visual C++ integrated development environment (IDE), this book simplifies many apparently difficult programming problems—once you know how the IDE works. That's the catch.

This book takes you through major software projects in which you create software using the latest and most important technologies such as ActiveX components, COM, and DCOM. Along the way, you learn how to use the full power of the Visual C++ IDE. You learn everything from start to finish, including:

- Using wizards to generate the initial code
- Using Visual C++ tools such as ClassWizard to customize code
- Using the Visual C++ debugger to debug and explore your application or component
- Using InstallShield to deploy the finished application or component (InstallShield is included with Visual C++)

When you are finished with this book, you will be able to use the vast potential of Visual C++ to help transform your ideas into actual new applications and software controls for the Web and the entire computing enterprise.

How This Book Is Organized

This book has five parts:

- **Part I: Visual C++ and Internet Primer.** Provides an overview of relevant Internet technologies and the way that the Visual C++ IDE transforms these technologies into a powerful tool for developing applications for the Web and the entire computing enterprise.

- **Part II: Hands On Project 1—Creating QuickBrowse.** Develop the QuickBrowse application, which is a custom Web browser optimized for specific information requirements. Learn how Microsoft's commitment to transform the Windows environment into a collection of software components together with the power of the Visual C++ IDE and the Microsoft Foundation Classes (MFC) library makes it easy for you to create customized applications for your own or your client's specific use. QuickBrowse uses some of the software components used by Internet Explorer, but the QuickBrowse interface includes a tree of destinations, customized to meet the information needs of a specialist, that the user can easily see and click on to load into the browser.

- **Part III: Hands On Project 2—Creating LogoMagic.** Develop the LogoMagic ActiveX control that displays bitmap images from wherever they reside on the computing enterprise. Learn to use the Visual C++ IDE to rapidly create ActiveX controls by utilizing the Microsoft Foundation Classes (MFC) library and the MFC ActiveX ControlWizard. Also, dive below the surface of the code Visual C++ generates to create a control with sophisticated properties that transfer bitmap files from anywhere on the enterprise—from your own computer's hard disk drive or from anywhere on the Internet. Use the LogoMagic control to display your company logo on Web pages, Word documents, Excel spreadsheets, Active Desktops, or anywhere that you can place an ActiveX control.

- **Part IV: Hands On Project 3—Creating InstantPost.** Develop the InstantPost project, an enterprisewide, distributed-message posting system that really consists of two Visual C++ projects: the InstantPost and InstantPostServer projects. Use the Active Template Library (ATL) and the ATL COM AppWizard, which were specifically developed to simplify the process of creating COM-based software components, to program these projects. The InstantPost controls, which can be placed anywhere on the enterprise, enable users to post their own messages and to view messages posted by colleagues. In contrast, the InstantPostServer component runs invisibly on a server, managing the various client connections from deployed InstantPost ActiveX controls and managing the posted messages from those clients. With InstantPost, you take the next step by not only deploying software components across the enterprise, but also virtually wiring the components together from wherever they are deployed. Place is no longer an issue.

- **Part V: Appendixes.** Brush up on the C++ language and object-oriented programming using C++. You also find information on online resources and a glossary containing brief definitions of unfamiliar terms and acronyms. Finally, an appendix outlines what is on the CD-ROM that is included with this book.

Conventions Used in This Book

To make it easier for you to use this book, Prima uses some conventions for consistently presenting different kinds of information. You should review these conventions before moving on in this book:

- Code. Any Visual C++ code discussed in this book is presented in a special typeface to make it easy to distinguish from the rest of the text.
- Text you type. When you need to type some text to complete a procedure, or when I provide an example of text you can enter, the text you need to type appears in bold.

Special Elements

At times, you'll be provided with information that supplements the discussion at hand. This special information is set off in easy-to-identify sidebars, so you can review or skip these extras as you see fit. You'll find the following types of special elements in this book:

Tips provide shortcuts to make your job easier, or better ways to accomplish certain tasks.

Notes provide supplemental information that might be of interest to you, but is not essential to performing the task at hand.

Caution

Cautions alert you to potential pitfalls, or warn you when a particular operation is risky and might cause you to lose some of your work.

Hardware and Software Requirements

You need the following software and hardware to work along with the examples in this book:

- Microsoft Visual C++ 6.0
- Windows 95, Windows 98, or Windows NT
- Internet Explorer 4.0 or more recent
- A connection with the Internet

The Project 2 example requires Windows NT.

CHAPTER 1

Overview of the Internet

You're probably an experienced Internet user, since you want to develop applications for the Internet using Microsoft Visual C++. Nevertheless, you can brush up on some of the technical details that you might have missed by reading, or skimming, this chapter. Internet technology is flourishing, and there is always likely to be some facet that you haven't heard of, that you've only heard of in passing, or that you have yet to learn about in any detail. After a brief look at the Internet as a global organism, reacquaint yourself with some of the Internet's myriad organs of communication.

The Internet Corpus

The Internet corpus is the body of a vast and constantly changing global collection of communication and information tools. The success of the Internet is largely due to the fact that its various organs, or tools, work together in a mostly transparent fashion so that users can glide with ease through its data space. This is particularly true of the World Wide Web (WWW), where users often move between different resources, architectures, and services without the least bit of worry about the acronym jungle waiting for professionals, like yourself, who are concerned with creating Internet content and infrastructure.

Internet Architecture

On one level, the Internet's architecture is simple. The Internet consists of a large number of nodes that are computers of various sorts, including personal computers, workstations, and supercomputers. The nodes are connected together by wires that enable communication between the nodes. The wires can be special high-speed fiber optic cables, slow-speed copper telephone wire, or anything in between. This schematic hardware-level view of Internet architecture displays the physical web of this global network while concealing a dynamic cacophony of hardware and software technologies, and people, constantly flowing throughout its innumerable arteries, veins, and capillaries. The rest of this chapter focuses on the nature of the nodes and the standard ways in which these nodes communicate with each other.

Clients and Servers

When you hear of clients and servers, you might think of restaurants. If you do, you aren't far off the mark. When you sit down at a restaurant, you are a client with the expectation of being served food. You order specific food items from a waiter or waitress, the server, who brings the food items that you order to your table. Likewise, nodes on the Internet, those various types of computing machines, can be roughly divided into clients and servers. A client sends an order of items that it wants to a server. The server cooks up the order and sends the product back to the client.

Most of your experience with the Internet and the World Wide Web is probably as a client. You point your browser to a particular address on the Web and receive content, usually in the form of a page of text and graphics. Behind this scene, what actually happened is that you and your browser, the client, asked the computer at the specified address, the server, for a Web page. The server gathers up the appropriate page and sends it back to the client who ordered it, you and your browser. This process, a client talking with a server, is carried out through common languages defined so that clients and servers can understand one another. These languages are known as protocols.

Protocols

Protocols are essential to the life of the Internet. All communication between the various nodes of the Internet is carried out through protocols, standards defined so that all of the various computing machines connected to the Internet can understand one another. The understanding reached isn't quite the same as your understanding of this sentence. You glean meaning from these concatenations of words. Computers, as far as we know, don't comprehend instructions through meaning. Nevertheless, a computer is able to react to a request from another computer and send the appropriate response to the requesting computer. This is possible largely due to protocols.

There are several Internet protocols in existence, some of which are listed in Table 1.1. In the following chapters you create programs that use many of the protocols in this table, including TCP/IP, HTTP, and others. Visual C++ provides objects that hide much of the low-level implementation of these protocols so that you can use them in your programs without getting down into the gritty details of how they work. Nevertheless, some understanding of how the protocols work does help you to take full advantage of a protocol.

Table 1.1 Internet Protocols

Protocol	Description
File Transfer Protocol (FTP)	FTP, a protocol developed early in the life of the Internet, provides a simple way to transfer files between server and client computers.
Hypertext Transport Protocol (HTTP)	HTTP is the protocol that enables the request and deployment of hypertext files across the Internet. This protocol provides the core mechanisms on which the World Wide Web (WWW) is based.
Network News Transport Protocol (NNTP)	NNTP is the protocol used by some newsgroups on the Internet, including the Usenet newsgroups and the Microsoft newsgroups on the msnews.microsoft.com news server.
Point-to-Point Protocol (PPP)	PPP is one of the protocols that can be used to make TCP/IP connections between client computers and the Internet over a regular telephone line and modem.
Post Office Protocol (POP)	POP is the most commonly used Internet protocol for handling electronic mail (e-mail).
Serial Line Internet Protocol (SLIP)	SLIP is one of the protocols that can be used to make TCP/IP connections between client computers and the Internet over a regular telephone line and modem.
Simple Mail Transport Protocol (SMTP)	SMTP is used to transfer electronic mail between POP servers.
Transmission Control Protocol/ Internet Protocol (TCP/IP)	TCP/IP forms a suite of network protocols that form the foundation of the Internet.

The World Wide Web (WWW)

The projects in this book either use browser technology, the software used for accessing the World Wide Web (WWW), or can be displayed in Web browsers. There are just a few major Web browser providers, but they come in many versions. Typically, you use Microsoft Internet Explorer version 4 or greater, like the copy shown in Figure 1-1, while you develop applications using Microsoft Visual C++ version 6.

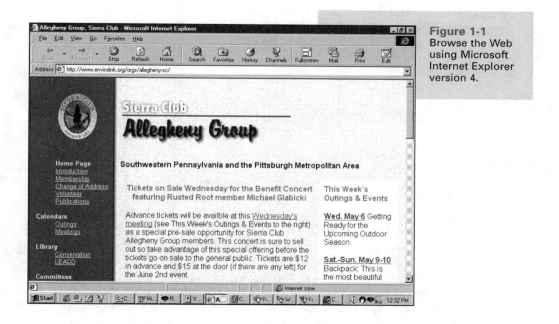

Figure 1-1
Browse the Web using Microsoft Internet Explorer version 4.

Accessing content through Internet Explorer makes it seem as if the Web and the entire computing enterprise are simply parts of your local computer. In fact, they are! Additionally, Internet Explorer makes displaying and even working with data associated with different applications as easy as working with data associated with different machines across the enterprise. For instance, you can open Microsoft Word documents that reside on your computer or somewhere out on a network. Figure 1-2 shows a Word document loaded from the local computer's C: drive and displayed by Internet Explorer 4.

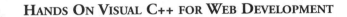

Figure 1-2
Browse the enterprise using Microsoft Internet Explorer 4.

> **Note**
>
> Open an active document such as a Word, Excel, or PowerPoint document by typing in its path and file name into the Address text box in the Internet Explorer Address Bar. (The Address text box displays C:\WINNT\Profiles\ Administrator\Desktop\ADVstocktrader Whitepaper.doc in Figure 1.2.) Alternatively, you can type in a path and file name into the Open text box in the Open dialog box, which you can open by selecting the Open command from the File menu. You can also browse for the file from the Open dialog box by clicking on the Browse button. (When you browse for a file, be sure to select the proper file type in the Files of type drop-down list or select All Files.)

The idea of what the Web is and isn't has become blurred, and its definition can be argued about. Generally, the Web consists of pages created using the Hypertext Markup Language (HTML) that reside on computers running Hypertext Transport Protocol (HTTP) server software. Internet Explorer is able to traverse computer file systems that may not provide Web pages or host an HTTP server, and it displays files that are not necessarily HTML files. In fact, all browsers have been able to do this since the beginning of the Web. They all traverse computers running Gopher and FTP servers, for instance, and display Gopher pages, FTP directories, and text files. The difference is that Internet Explorer has extended the reach of the Web browser far beyond its humble beginnings.

Even though Web browsers can transverse and display much more, it is practical to consider the Web as computers connected with the Internet running HTTP server software and storing HTML files for display. Details of the HTTP server technology are beyond the scope of this book. However, the Hypertext Markup Language (HTML) is examined more closely.

Hypertext Markup Language (HTML)

The Hypertext Markup Language, commonly known as HTML, is the text-based language for creating Web pages. You can create an HTML document in the Visual C++ integrated development environment by selecting the New command from the File menu. The New dialog box appears, as in Figure 1-3.

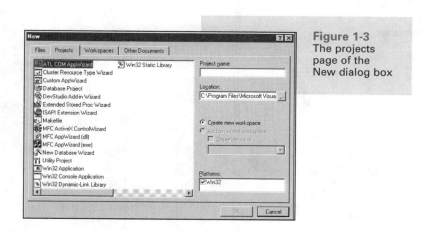

Figure 1-3
The projects page of the New dialog box

Click on the Files tab to open the Files page of the New dialog box, as in Figure 1-4.

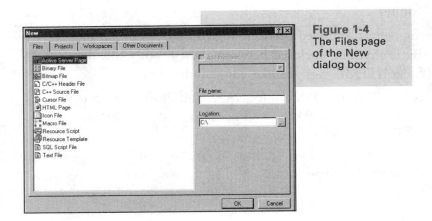

Figure 1-4
The Files page of the New dialog box

Select HTML Page from the list on the Files page of the New dialog box and then click on the OK button. A new HTML document appears in Visual C++, as in Figure 1-5.

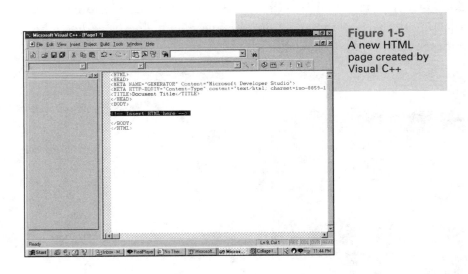

Figure 1-5
A new HTML page created by Visual C++

The Visual C++ editor displays the HTML code in color, highlighting various key words. The first thing you see, the first line of HTML code, is the following:

```
<HTML>
```

The string "HTML" enclosed between angled brackets (<>) is known as a tag. In fact, anything enclosed between these brackets is known as an HTML tag. HTML tags are like commands; they tell Web browsers what to do. The <HTML> tag informs Web browsers that the code that follows, up to the </HTML> end-tag that you see as the last line in the HTML page, is HTML code.

The next line of code displays the <HEAD> tag. The <HEAD> tag marks the beginning of the Web page's heading. Browsers load and evaluate all code in a heading, the code between the <HEAD> tag and the </HEAD> end-tag, before displaying any of the Web page's content. The heading is a particularly useful place to enter script procedures that might be called by a user's action. Procedures must be loaded into a browser and be ready to work before a user is able to click on buttons or other interface elements that call the procedures. Other things go in the heading as well, some of which are included in the HTML source code created by Visual C++.

<META> tags are placed in the heading, for example. The <META> tag provides information about an HTML document to browsers, servers, and other applications. Visual C++ automatically includes two <META> tags: one reveals that the document was generated by Microsoft Developer Studio, and the other gives information about the character set that the document uses.

The title of a Web page, the one displayed in a Web browser's title bar and saved in your Internet Explorer Favorites menu, is also defined in the heading section. Text set between the <TITLE> tag and the </TITLE> end-tag is the page's title. Document Title is the default title of the page created by Visual C++.

Following the heading is the Web page's body. The body is everything between the <BODY> tag and the </BODY> end-tag. This newly created Web page is blank; there is nothing in the body except a comment line. Anything set between <!-- and --> is ignored by the browser's interpreter as a comment for programmers who want to understand the code better. Most of the content that you add to a Web page is added to its body.

Save the Web page just as it was created by Visual C++, by clicking on the Save button on the Visual C++ toolbar or by selecting the Save command from the File menu. The Save As dialog box appears. Type the file name, **Hello.htm**, into the File name text box in the Save As dialog box, as in Figure 1-6.

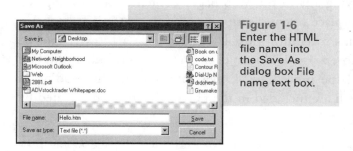

Figure 1-6
Enter the HTML file name into the Save As dialog box File name text box.

Click on the Save button and the file is saved. Open the Hello.htm file in a Web browser. The page is blank, and the browser's title bar displays the default title, Document Title.

Display Text

Display text in a Web page simply by typing the text into the HTML file. Replace the following comment line in the Hello.htm file

```
<!-- Insert HTML here -->
```

with the following text:

```
HTML says "Hello world!"
```

Also, change the title of the page to reflect its content. Type Hello World! between the <TITLE> tag and the </TITLE> end-tag. The HTML code should look like Figure 1-7.

Figure 1-7
The HTML code in the Hello.htm file after a line of text is added.

Save the modified file by clicking on the Visual C++ toolbar Save button or by selecting the Save command from the File menu. Then reload the Hello.htm file into your Web browser. You should see a new title and a message, as in Figure 1-8.

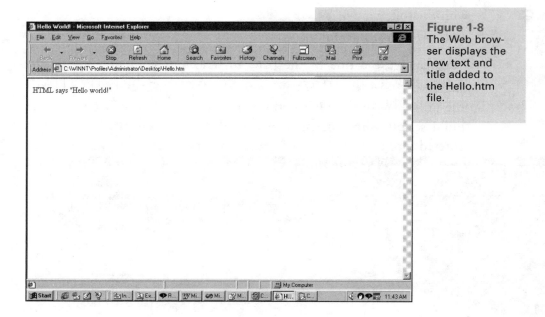

Figure 1-8
The Web browser displays the new text and title added to the Hello.htm file.

That was easy. You type in text and use HTML tags to define the text layout. HTML also provides tags for creating links between different parts of the same Web page or between different Web pages. In fact, it's this latter capability that gives the spider web–like character to the multitude of interlinked HTML pages that make up the World Wide Web. Users interact with Web pages by clicking on links that can result in loading another Web document.

The capabilities that HTML provided, page layout and links between documents, rapidly appeared too limited to Web enthusiasts, especially when it came to the range of user interactions that HTML enabled, which amounted to clicking on links to other documents. Early on in the existence of the Web, Web page builders found that they needed mechanisms to enable more sophisticated user interactions. Scripting languages were developed to fill this need.

Scripts

The Common Gateway Interface, or CGI, was one of the first mechanisms to enable scripting languages to be used on the Web. As the name suggests, CGI gives you a common interface that allows you to extend the utility of your Web page through scripts. Because of CGI, you can build scripts with languages such as Perl or C that take information entered into a form on a Web page, such as a user's name and address, check the information for errors, and then stores it to a file or database for your use. You can build other useful and user-friendly interfaces using CGI scripts: an easy-to-use user interface to a search engine, for example. There are, however, several problems with CGI.

The primary problem with CGI is that the scripts must be kept in a directory on a Web server, and CGI scripts create a lot of "talking" between the Web page displayed in the user's Web browser and the Web server. Furthermore, every person who uses, say, a search engine with a CGI script interface causes a script to run on a Web server. The running script uses up memory and computing resources on the Web server that provides the search engine. The Web server providing the search engine quickly bogs down with too many users running too many scripts at the same time. Clearly, this process is inefficient and unacceptable, since millions of people use the Web.

Note

Some other difficulties are caused by the way CGI scripts must interact with Web servers. CGI assumes that the people who want to build extensions into their Web pages have access to the server. Most people don't have the time or the desire to maintain a server, but they may want to build their own Web pages. People who rent space for a Web site may find it difficult to use CGI scripts. They may even find it impossible, because some system administrators don't want the high overhead on their systems' resources that can result from using CGI scripts.

The JScript and VBScript scripting languages solve these problems, but they go far beyond just that. JScript is the Microsoft version of JavaScript, and VBScript is the pared-down scripting version of the Visual Basic programming language. Three closely related features of these scripting languages resolve some of the problems of CGI scripts and provide powerful Web tools:

1. Interpreters are built into Web browsers.
2. Scripts are written in the HTML document.
3. Clients carry out the processing.

JScript and VBScript are interpreted languages that are typed directly into your HTML document. When a user opens your Web page, his or her Web browser downloads your HTML document. The user's Web browser then interprets your script. The script runs on the client machine after it's downloaded and leaves the server free to do other things!

There is one hitch. A Web browser must have the interpreter for the scripting language to be able to run it. Therefore, to run JScript, your Web browser must have a built-in JScript interpreter. To run VBScript, your Web browser must have a built-in VBScript interpreter. Microsoft Internet Explorer includes both a JScript and a VBScript interpreters.

Comparing JScript and VBScript

JScript and VBScript have a lot in common. Two common features of these scripting languages are particularly important. They both are object based and event driven, as you learn in the following sections.

Object-Based Features

Your key to effective programming in JScript or VBScript is to understand objects and how these scripting languages use them. A large part of your programming task, in either scripting language, is to know what objects to use and how to use them.

JScript and VBScript are object-based languages. This means that they use and manipulate objects, but in contrast to object-oriented languages such as C++, they don't support class libraries or inheritance. You can build objects, but you can't build classes that can be used to create different objects.

Scripting languages use objects that are very similar to objects in the world around you. Because you'll be programming in the virtual world of your computer and the Web, contemplate on what you might consider to be an object in that world. Your browser is an object. It's a thing that you surf the Web with. In fact, the browser is an object to JScript and VBScript. Scripting languages recognize browsers through the Scripting Object Model, which presents them as navigator objects.

Browsers have *properties*. A browser has a name and a version, for instance. Likewise, objects in VBScript and JScript (and in all object-based or object-oriented languages) have properties. Properties are a part of an object. You can observe a property of a software object by calling the object's property by name. To call an object's property, you write the object's name (`objectName`), then a period, followed by the property's name (`propertyName`), like the following in this form:

```
objectName.propertyName
```

You can program your Web page to look up the name of the browser under which it's running by adding the following JScript line:

```
navigator.appName
```

The browser object, `navigator`, has an `appName` property that holds the name of the browser. The name may be Netscape or Microsoft depending on the browser being used. You might also find another `navigator` object property useful. The `appVersion` property returns the version of the browser.

Objects can be made up of other objects. A computer is an object that is built from other objects such as a monitor and a hard disk. Likewise, a Web browser is an object made up of other objects. A Web browser is composed of a window, for instance. Both JScript and VBScript recognize window objects presented as `window` in the Scripting Object Model.

Like browser objects, window objects have properties. They also do things. You can get a software object to do something by calling on the object's *method* of doing it. A method is actually a function that is a part of the object. To call an object's method, you write the object's name (`objectName`), then a period, followed by the name of the object's method (`methodName`), like the following:

```
objectName.methodName (parameters)
```

For example, a window can open and close. The window object `window` has a method to open a new browser window named `open`. To open a new browser window, you add the following code in JScript:

```
window.open("URL", "windowName", ["windowFeatures"])
```

> **Note** The parameter list between parentheses is method specific. These issues are addressed when you actually write JScript and VBScript code later in the JScript and the VBScript sections of this chapter.

A window object is, of course, made up of other objects. A window object can contain a document (usually an HTML document); the document can be made up of forms, anchors, links, and so on. The list of objects makes up an object hierarchy. Figure 1-9 presents a chart of the object hierarchy provided by the Scripting Object Model. Refer to this chart often while you're learning the objects provided by the Scripting Object Model.

> **Note** Each object can have many properties and methods—far too many to cover in this chapter. You can look them up in the Scripting Object Model documentation provided in Visual C++ help.

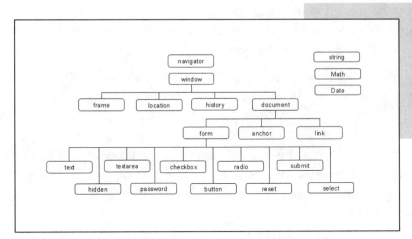

Figure 1-9
The object hierarchy provided by the Scripting Object Model allows easy manipulation of browser-related objects.

Event-Driven Features

You now understand that JScript and VBScript are object-based languages that recognize objects that encapsulate methods for doing things. But how do you initiate those methods? How do you get an object to do something? The short answer is that JScript and VBScript also are event-driven languages.

Something happens, usually a user action, which triggers an object to activity. That is the essence of event-driven languages and, for that matter, event-driven environments.

Today's operating systems, including Microsoft Windows, Mac OS, and UNIX X Windows, are event-driven environments. They sit and wait for you to click on an icon or select a menu option. When you do, you cause a user-initiated event to occur, and the operating system or program can respond to the event.

The event-driven model is reflected in the programming methods used for event-driven environments. You could write a program that just cranks though a procedure and doesn't respond to user-initiated events.

However, the user of your program will be very upset when his or her operating system locks up and he or she is unable to interact with the program until it's done with the procedure.

JScript and VBScript respond to events through event handlers. You can include any of the built-in event handlers to tell your program when a specific event occurs. Your program can then respond in a specific way—maybe with an object's method. For instance, you might want to cause the text "Caution!" to appear in the browser's status bar when a user's mouse pointer is over a sensitive part of your Web page, or you might want to run a sound file that says "Thank you!" when a user submits a form.

Now that you understand that JScript and VBScript are event driven and object based, your main conceptual tasks are accomplished. You can build effective scripts by using objects, methods, properties, and event handlers. You can also extend the power of JScript and VBScript by using Java applets and ActiveX controls. Java applets and ActiveX controls provide new objects for you to manipulate through the scripting languages.

 ActiveX controls are software components that are explained in Chapter 2. You use ActiveX controls throughout this book, and you actually create them in Projects 2 and 3.

JScript

Now you're ready to create a JScript program. Follow tradition and create a script that prints "Hello World!" to the document window in your Web browser. Add or change the highlighted code in Listing 1.1 into the standard Visual C++ HTML page, and save it as JHello.htm.

Listing 1.1 JHello.htm —JavaScript Hello World!

```html
<HTML>
<HEAD>
<META NAME="GENERATOR" Content="Microsoft Developer Studio">
<META HTTP-EQUIV="Content-Type" content="text/html; charset=iso-8859-
1">
<TITLE>JScript Hello World!</TITLE>

<SCRIPT LANGUAGE="JavaScript">
<!--
    document.write("JScript says \"Hello World!\"")
// -->
</SCRIPT>

</HEAD>
<BODY>

<P>
HTML says "Hello World!"

</BODY>
</HTML>
```

View JHello.htm in your Web browser. You should see something like Figure 1-10.

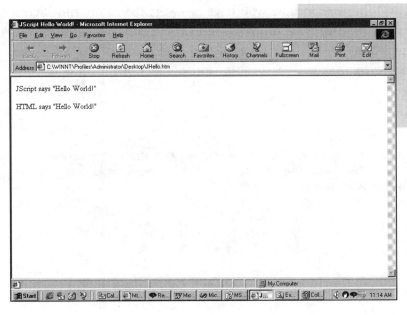

Figure 1-10
Internet Explorer displays both JScript and HTML output from the JScript Hello World! Web page.

Listing 1.1 is mostly standard HTML code. The new JScript-specific code is listed again here:

```
<SCRIPT LANGUAGE="JavaScript">
<!--
    document.write("JScript says \"Hello World!\"")
// -->
</SCRIPT>
```

Even this part is mostly made up of HTML tags. The `<SCRIPT LANGUAGE>` tag signals that the code that follows is a scripting language and, specifically, that the language is JScript up to the closing `</SCRIPT>` tag.

"JavaScript" rather than "Script" is passed to the `<SCRIPT LANGUAGE>` tag argument rather than JScript so that all Web browsers, not only Microsoft browsers, recognize that the script is in some version of the JavaScript language.

The `<!--` after the `<SCRIPT LANGUAGE>` tag and the `// -->` before the `</SCRIPT>` end-tag tell the browser to ignore the script between them if the browser does not recognize JScript. Including these tags is very important; otherwise, people who have browsers that don't run JScript will see what appears to be rubbish, your JScript code actually, on your Web page when they load it. Using the tags enables all users to view your Web page even if they don't get the added functionality provided by your scripts.

You can and should add comments on the same line after `<!--` and between the `//` and `-->`. For example, you can add the following:

```
<!-- Begin hiding JScript
// End hiding JScript -->
```

The key line in Listing 1.1 is

```
document.write("JScript says \"Hello World!\"")
```

This line invokes the document object's `write()` method.

Look at the object hierarchy in Figure 1-9. Notice that the document object is under the window object. This means that a window object can be composed of a document object along with frame, location, and history objects. In fact, the window object is implied in the line of code but is not required in this instance. You could just as well write the following:

```
window.document.write("JScript says \"Hello World!\"")
```

The document object's `write()` method includes a single parameter: the string `"JScript says \"Hello World!\""`. The `write()` method can take any number of expressions between the parentheses and displays them in a document window. If you list more than one expression, you need to separate them with commas. This string includes two `\"` sequences in it: one before `Hello` and one after `World!`. Such a sequence is called an *escape sequence*, and it allows you to include quotations inside the string. The string itself is delimited by the regular quotation marks. The final result is that JScript displays the string `JScript says "Hello World"` in your browser's document window.

VBScript

Write the VBScript equivalent of the JScript program that you just wrote. It also prints "Hello World!" to the document window in your Web browser. Enter the highlighted code in Listing 1.2 into a standard Visual C++ HTML page, and save it as VBHello.htm.

Listing 1.2 VBHello.htm —VBScript Hello World!

```
<HTML>
<HEAD>
<META NAME="GENERATOR" Content="Microsoft Developer Studio">
<META HTTP-EQUIV="Content-Type" content="text/html; charset=iso-
8859-1">
<TITLE>VBScript Hello World!</TITLE>

<SCRIPT LANGUAGE="VBS">
<!--
     document.write "VBScript says ""Hello World!"""
// -->
</SCRIPT>

</HEAD>
<BODY>

<P>
HTML says "Hello World!"

</BODY>
</HTML>
```

Load VBHello.htm into your Web browser. Output appears as it does in Figure 1-11.

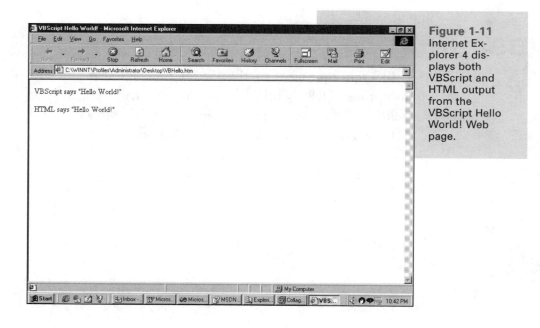

Figure 1-11 Internet Explorer 4 displays both VBScript and HTML output from the VBScript Hello World! Web page.

The code in Listing 1.2 should mostly look familiar to you because it's nearly all standard HTML. The new VBScript-specific code is shown here:

```
<SCRIPT LANGUAGE="VBS">
<!--
     document.write " VBScript says ""Hello World!"""
// -->
</SCRIPT>
```

Even this part is mostly made up of HTML tags. The `<SCRIPT LAN-GUAGE>` tag signals that the code that follows is a scripting language and, specifically, that the language is VBScript up to the `</SCRIPT>` end-tag. `VBS` is used to signify VBScript.

The `<!--` after the `<SCRIPT LANGUAGE>` tag and the `// -->` before the `</SCRIPT>` end-tag tell the browser to ignore the script between them if the browser does not recognize VBScript. Including these tags is very important; otherwise, people who have browsers that don't run VBScript will see the VBScript code on your Web page when they load it. Using the tags enables all users to view your Web page even if they don't get the added functionality provided by your scripts.

> **You can and should add comments on the same line after `<!--` and between the `//` and `-->`. For example, you can add the following:**
>
> ```
>         <!-- Begin hiding VBScript
>         // End hiding VBScript -->
> ```
>
> **These lines are included in the rest of the listings in this section.**

The key line in Listing 1.2 is

```
document.write "VBScript says ""Hello World!"""
```

This line invokes the document object's `write()` method. The document object's `write()` method includes a single parameter: the string `"VBScript says ""Hello World!"""`. The `write()` method displays the expression in a document window. This string includes two `""` sequences in it, one set before `Hello` and one set after `World!`. Doubling up the double quotes allows you to include quotations inside the string. The string itself is delimited by quotation marks. The final result is that VBScript displays the string `VBScript says "Hello World"` in your browser's document window.

Event-Driven Programming with VBScript

VBScript is an event-driven scripting language. Your first VBScript program doesn't do anything that plain old HTML can't do. It simply prints a message to the browser's document window. No user interaction is required. No events trigger the script to do something. Usually, when you add script to your Web page, you do so because you want the users to be able to do something. You want them to interact with your Web page.

Type in the highlighted code in Listing 1.3 into a standard Visual C++ HTML page, then save it as Ouch.htm.

Listing 1.3 Ouch.htm —Click Me!

```
<HTML>
<HEAD>
<META NAME="GENERATOR" Content="Microsoft Developer Studio">
<META HTTP-EQUIV="Content-Type" content="text/html; charset=iso-
8859-1">
<TITLE>Click Me!</TITLE>

<SCRIPT LANGUAGE="VBS">
<!-- Begin hiding VBScript
Sub ClickMe_OnClick
     MsgBox "Ouch!", 0, "Click Me!"
End Sub
// End hiding VBScript -->
</SCRIPT>

</HEAD>
<BODY>

<FORM>
     <INPUT TYPE="button" VALUE="Click Me" NAME="ClickMe">
</FORM>

</BODY>
</HTML>
```

Load Ouch.htm into your browser. The browser's document window should have a button with the words "Click Me" on it, as in Figure 1-12.

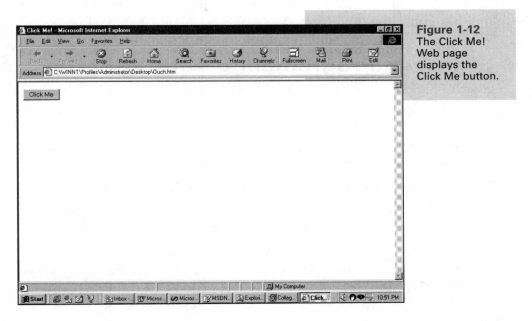

Figure 1-12
The Click Me!
Web page
displays the
Click Me button.

Click on the button, and the Click Me! dialog box appears, as in Figure 1-13.

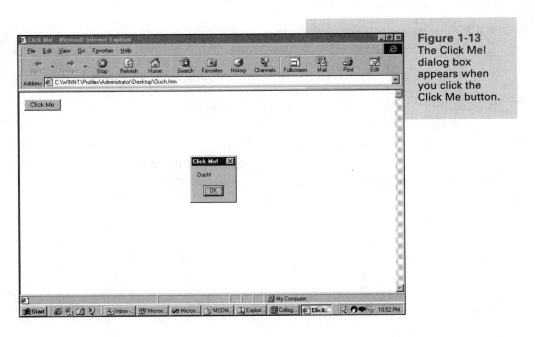

Figure 1-13
The Click Me!
dialog box
appears when
you click the
Click Me button.

There are two components to the code in Listing 1.3. A procedure is defined in the listing's header and a button is defined in the listing's body. The two components are connected through the OnClick event handler.

First, consider the lines of HTML code in the body that define the button:

```
<FORM>
    <INPUT TYPE="button" VALUE="Click Me" NAME="ClickMe">
</FORM>
```

Each item on a Web page—buttons, text fields, and the like—is considered an object to VBScript. In the preceding code, <FORM> and <INPUT> are standard HTML tags. The object type is defined by the value supplied to the TYPE attribute. You must use the NAME attribute to give the object a name. Here the button's name is ClickMe. Now VBScript treats the ClickMe button object like any other object.

To connect the button object to events, an event handler is appended to the object's name and defined as a function or procedure. Notice how the ClickMe button name is appended with the OnClick event handler in the VBScript shown again here:

```
<SCRIPT LANGUAGE="VBS">
<!-- Begin hiding VBScript
Sub ClickMe_OnClick
    MsgBox "Ouch!", 0, "Click Me!"
End Sub
// End hiding VBScript -->
</SCRIPT>
```

An underscore connects the button object's name to the event handler, and the Sub statement precedes the whole thing, ClickMe_OnClick, which is used to define a procedure. The End Sub statement marks the end of the procedure. Now, whenever a user clicks on the ClickMe button, the ClickMe_OnClick procedure is called and run.

In VBScript, and Visual Basic in general, you can define either a procedure using the `Sub` and `End Sub` statements or a function using the `Function` and `End Function` statements. The `Sub` statement is derived from the idea of a subroutine, which is now generally known as a type of procedure. The only difference between a procedure and a function is that a function can return a value to the calling code whereas a procedure cannot.

When the `ClickMe_OnClick` procedure is called, the VBScript `MsgBox` function is run. The `MsgBox` function is one of many built-in VBScript functions. As you might expect, the `MsgBox` function displays a message in a dialog box. `MsgBox` can do quite a bit more since, like many VBScript functions, it has a lot of flexibility built into it.

`MsgBox` has five arguments, one that you must pass a value to and four that you have the option to pass values to. You used three arguments in Listing 1.3. The first, and required, argument takes the message that will be shown in the dialog box. You included the message "Ouch!" The second argument tells the function the number of buttons to add to the dialog box, the type of buttons to display, the icon style to use, the identity of the default button, and the modality of the dialog box. You used the default `0` that results in a single OK button on the dialog box. The third argument takes a string that is displayed on the dialog box's Title Bar. You used the title of your Web page, `"Click Me!"` Two more arguments can be passed values to add help to the dialog box.

You've learned how to manipulate objects using VBScript, and how to connect events associated with an object a procedures or functions. By using these two new pieces of programming knowledge, you can build Web pages that connect user events to sophisticated procedures.

Summary

You covered a lot of computing space in this chapter: the Internet, the Web, and other parts of the computing enterprise. In fact, you saw how the distinctions between desktop computers, the Internet, the Web, and other networks are breaking down and are melding into a single seamless computing enterprise. That vast computing space consists of a wide range of connections and different computing machines running a variety of software, including different operating systems and protocols. One of the most important protocols is the Hypertext Transport Protocol, or HTTP, which, along with HTML documents, is the foundation on which the World Wide Web is built.

Scripts fill a niche between the markup and compiled languages used on the Web. Markup languages, most notably the Hypertext Markup Language or HTML, define Web page layout or format. In contrast, objects such as ActiveX controls, JavaBeans components, and Java applets, are programmed using compiled languages and can carry out complex procedures such as moving three-dimensional graphics or showing multimedia presentations. (Chapter 2 introduces you to software components used on the enterprise.) A *script* is the thread that connects page layout with complex procedural objects. Scripts are also useful for creating simpler procedures within an HTML document, and they provide a means for user interaction. When used properly, scripts can transform a dull and inert Web page into something stunning and useful.

2

CHAPTER

Visual C++ and the Internet

The Internet is now a central focus for computer users, and therefore it's of great importance to the software designer. More and more, users want applications that take advantage of the Internet or are entirely focused on the enterprise, that computing space that extends well beyond the individual's computer and into the Internet and other networking environments. Microsoft Visual C++, along with Visual Studio, provides a development environment tightly integrated with the Internet, particularly the World Wide Web. Visual C++ also provides programming tools that enable you to create Internet-savvy applications with ease.

Visual C++ Internet Features

Internet features are provided by the Visual C++ integrated development environment and by the language itself, in the form of classes provided by the Microsoft Foundation Classes library. These two levels of

Internet support interact in a seamless manner to enable you to develop exceptional applications for the Internet and the enterprise.

The Integrated Development Environment (IDE)

The Visual C++ integrated development environment treats the Internet as part of a seamless computing environment available to you from your desktop to around the globe. Visual C++ provides a unified environment where you create applications without concern for where critical information resides and what format or context it resides in. Visual C++ brings the information to you locally or from the Internet, and it automatically reconfigures itself to support the particular information format or context.

Don't take my word for it, you can get a sense of this integration and have fun at the same time by opening an Internet-aware Active Document in Visual C++.

You learn about Active Documents, and the Component Object Model (COM) on which they are based, later in this chapter. For now, simply be aware that Active Documents are software components that can be used like documents but that can do something, as you will soon see.

Comic Chat Room Documents

Test out the level of integration between Visual C++ and the Internet by opening up the Comic Chat Room document in the Visual C++ integrated development environment. Start Visual C++ by selecting the Microsoft Visual C++ 6.0 command from the Microsoft Visual Studio 6.0 folder on the Programs menu available from the Windows Start menu. Microsoft Visual C++ appears, as in Figure 2-1.

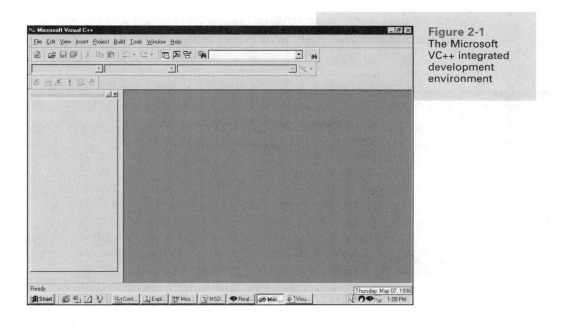

Figure 2-1
The Microsoft
VC++ integrated
development
environment

Select the New command from the File menu found on the Visual C++ menu bar. The New dialog box appears, as in Figure 2-2.

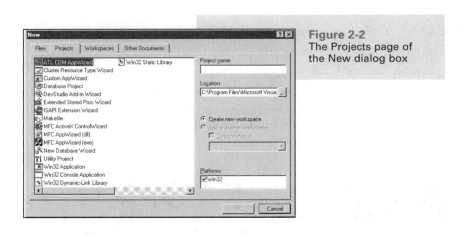

Figure 2-2
The Projects page of
the New dialog box

Click on the Other Documents tab in the New dialog box to switch to the Other Documents page, as in Figure 2-3.

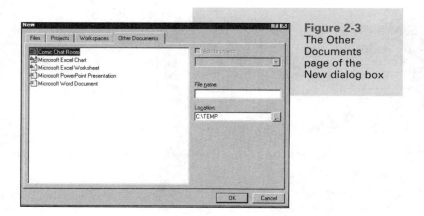

Figure 2-3
The Other Documents page of the New dialog box

Note

Be sure that you're connected to the Internet before carrying out the next steps.

The Other Documents page of the New dialog box displays a list of Active Documents, including the Comic Chat Room document. Double-click on Comic Chat Room or select Comic Chat Room and click on the OK button. The Comic Chat Room document opens and displays the Enter New Nickname dialog box, as in Figure 2-4.

Note

The list of Active Documents on the Other Documents page of the New dialog box depends on the applications that you have installed on your computer. The Comic Chat Room document is listed if you installed Microsoft Chat. You install Microsoft Chat by carrying out the Full Installation of Internet Explorer or by going to the Microsoft Web site at http://www.microsoft.com/msdownload/ieplatform/chat/chat. htm and downloading Microsoft Chat.

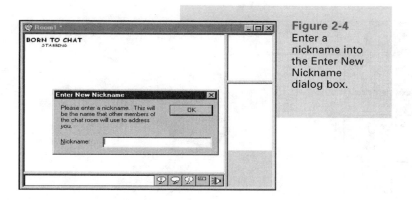

Figure 2-4
Enter a nickname into the Enter New Nickname dialog box.

Enter a nickname, your first name for instance, into the Nickname text box in the Enter New Nickname dialog box. Click on the OK button. The Connect dialog box appears, as in Figure 2-5.

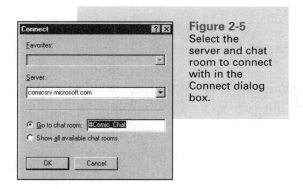

Figure 2-5
Select the server and chat room to connect with in the Connect dialog box.

You can select from a variety of servers and chat rooms to connect with from the Connect dialog box. For now, use the default settings by leaving everything as it is and clicking on the OK button. You should connect with an ongoing chat, as in Figure 2-6.

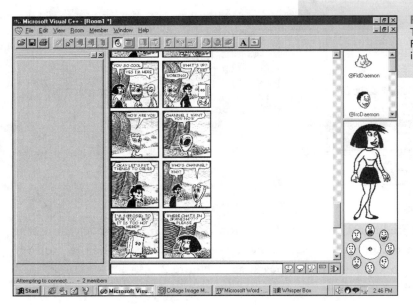

Figure 2-6
The Comic Chat Room document in action

The Visual C++ menu bar incorporates Comic Chat Room document items. For instance, notice that the View menu now includes the Comic Strip and Plain Text commands. Use these commands to switch between the comic strip view that you've seen and a plain text view. These commands are also incorporated into the Visual C++ toolbar.

Talk by typing what you want to say into the text box at the bottom of the Active Document and then clicking on the Talk button to the right of the text box. You can also think or whisper, among other actions. It's beyond the scope of this book to go into details on using the Comic Chat Room document, but you can get more information through the Help menu provided on the Visual C++ menu bar, which includes Microsoft Chat Help when the Comic Chat Room document is selected. For example, select the Product News command from the Microsoft on the Web submenu under the Help menu. A new Internet Explorer window appears displaying current information on Microsoft Chat provided by the Microsoft Web, as in Figure 2-7.

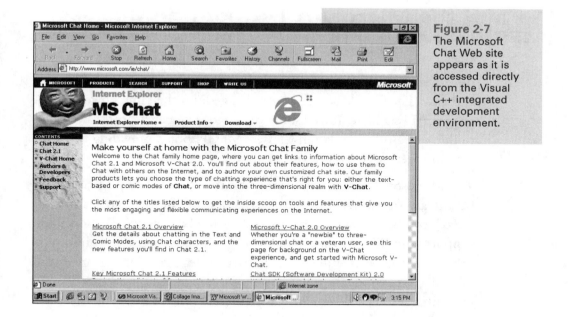

Figure 2-7
The Microsoft Chat Web site appears as it is accessed directly from the Visual C++ integrated development environment.

Disconnect from a chat server by selecting the Disconnect command from the Room menu or by clicking on the Disconnect button on the Visual C++ toolbar.

Clearly, Visual C++ is well integrated with the Internet. But it also integrates well with what are known as software components. The software components, often referred to as ActiveX controls or Active Documents, allow a high degree of integration between Visual C++ and a wide array of information contexts. You just saw the Comic Room Chat Active Document in action. As software components become ubiquitous, you will find this level of integration provided across the whole enterprise extending from your desktop to the furthest reaches of the Internet. That is, menus, toolbars, and other local tools provided to you change automatically to accommodate the data that you're currently working on. Visual C++ provides tools that change automatically to the appropriate tools for the current task at hand in building applications.

C++ and the Microsoft Foundation Classes (MFC) Library

Visual C++ provides new features at the language level to make creating full-featured applications for the Web, and for the whole enterprise, fast and easy. The C++ language hasn't changed; it's the same powerful language that was standardized some years ago. The new features are added to the Microsoft Foundation Classes (MFC) library, providing you with new Internet-aware classes and methods.

The Microsoft Foundation Classes library was created by Microsoft to be an easy-to-use yet powerful abstraction of complicated features of today's computing environments such as toolbars, status bars, database support, and Web browsing support. Each class in the class library is created as an abstraction of a particular feature. For instance, the CWnd class represents a window in your operating system's graphic user interface. The CToolBar class represents the toolbar you often see in applications, like the toolbar available in the Visual C++ integrated development environment. And finally, the CDatabase class represents a database that may be accessed through ODBC, the open database connectivity protocol.

Through most of this book, you will focus on creating Web-savvy applications based on key classes from the Microsoft Foundation Classes library. These classes often provide simple ways for you to include software components, generally ActiveX controls or other Component Object Model (COM)–based components, as part of your applications. For instance, you will create a Web browsing application that inherits most of its Web browser features from the WebBrowser control, an ActiveX control known as an Internet Explorer common control. You include the WebBrowser control in your application by using the CHtmlView class provided by the Microsoft Foundation Classes library. You learn more about how to use the Microsoft Foundation Classes library in the chapters dealing with Project 1, QuickBrowse, beginning with Chapter 3. Right now, take a closer look at software components and software component architectures.

Software Components

Most, if not all, future software will be built from components. This isn't as far-fetched as it might seem at first. Nearly all manufactured items that you use, including computers, bicycles, and automobiles, are built from components. In fact, if you use the Microsoft Windows operating system, your computer has been increasingly populated with components for some time. Software components are the future of software for a long list of reasons, including these:

1. Environments populated with components are intuitive for users.

2. Developers can focus on developing small independent software objects that do a well-defined task. This is a relief for small companies and independent software developers, since monolithic programs take vast resources to produce.

3. Components are ideal for distributed computing environments, since they're small, independent, and interactive.

4. Components make rapid application development possible. Application developers and even users can simply wire together existing software components to create applications.

Objects

Object-oriented programming revolutionized software design by breaking up software projects into self-contained chunks, or tasks, each of which was a software object holding data and the necessary methods for manipulating those data. Once an object was constructed to do a particular task, you simply plugged it into new program code. The resulting programs, however, remained large, complex, and immutable. They didn't bring the object-oriented model to the desktop. That is, a program was one indivisible thing, in contrast to, for instance, a bicycle.

A bicycle is a functional whole composed of objects: wheels, gears, frame, and so on. Each mechanical object, or bicycle component, carries out its own specialized function just as a software object does. Like the object-oriented programmer using software objects, the bicycle manufacturer simplifies the job by using bicycle components to build each bicycle. Unlike someone working with the software objects used in object-oriented programming, however, that manufacturer can manipulate each bicycle component as an independent object during both the manufacture and use of the bicycle. This last point is a subtle but crucial point.

It's true that software objects work with other software objects within the program. There are standard language specifications for software objects. However, those objects have no apparent existence outside the realm of the programming language, and they aren't apparent to the user. As already mentioned, the program that you buy is one indivisible thing. In contrast, the bicycle that you buy is made up of components that you're able to take apart and put back together. The difference is that object-oriented programming is just what it says it is—it's only object-oriented during the programming process. For software to be composed of objects as a bicycle is composed of objects, the software objects must act as discrete components while running.

Components

Actually, programmers don't even work directly with objects during object-oriented programming. They write and work with classes that represent objects, like the classes in the Microsoft Foundation Classes library. Objects are only created during run time, when both the programmer and the users no longer have direct access to them as discrete components that can be manipulated. This is where software components enter the picture.

A *software component* is a distinct object built to standard specifications so that it can fit together with other objects into functional groups. The components can carry out their functions using any of a wide variety of internal methods and properties, but they must conform to standards that specify how the components interface and interact with one another. For instance, a bicycle frame can be made of steel, aluminum, titanium, or carbon fiber, but whatever it's made of, the frame is always made so that wheels, a crankshaft, a seat, and handlebars can be added.

The software developer can build applications by assembling components that, unlike object-oriented programming objects, are working, running software objects during application development. You saw this quality earlier in the working Comic Chat Room document, which is a kind of software component. Each software component can be programmed by the software developer or bought from third-party developers in the same way that each bicycle component can be made by the manufacturer or bought from third-party manufacturers. Also, the software developer can build applications for different uses by simply assembling different software components in the same way that the bicycle manufacturer can create bicycles for different uses by assembling different bicycle components. For example, the bicycle manufacturer might add wheels with long crossed-over spokes and sturdy steel rims to a road-racing bicycle, but wheels with short, straight, rigid spokes and lightweight aluminum rims to a track-racing bicycle.

The software user benefits from using software components and applications built using software components. Software components make it easy for users to update and customize applications in the same way that bicycle users can update and customize their bicycles. For instance, a bicycle user may buy a bicycle for road racing and later decide to race on tracks. The user can simply replace the bicycle's road-racing components by buying new track-racing components, including rigid wheels. Likewise, a user of a software application that, for instance, isn't Internet-aware could add an Internet component.

Component Architectures

To make the idea of software components a reality, there must be a standard way for each piece of software to interact with other software. Generally, this means that programmers can implement the internal methods and properties of the software object in any way that they want, but they must adhere to strict interface rules.

All software components have two things in common: First, they are made up of a set of data and the methods to manipulate the data. Also, all of a software component's data are private and are only accessible through public methods. Notice that these are the features of properly written software objects in any object-oriented programming language. Component models force you to use good object-oriented programming methods.

A variety of software component architectures are available, but only a few are commonly used. ActiveX, Active Document, and JavaBeans components are the most common component architectures in use, with ActiveX components currently in the lead. Visual C++ supports ActiveX, Active Document, and other COM-based components, but it does not support JavaBeans components, an architecture designed by Microsoft's competitor Sun Microsystems.

Note   JavaBeans is the Java language component architecture specification. All JavaBeans components must be written in the Java language. This is unusual. Usually component architectures are language independent. However, the JavaBeans specification is relatively simple for a component architecture. This is mostly due to the fact that the specification depends on the Java language and, therefore, the Java Virtual Machine. You can use JavaBeans as ActiveX components by using a software bridge available from JavaSoft, a subsidiary of Sun Microsystems. For more information check the JavaSoft Web site at http://www.javasoft.com.

ActiveX Controls

ActiveX controls are currently the most commonly used software components. ActiveX controls are language independent. You can program ActiveX controls in any computer language, including C++. ActiveX controls are also platform independent. However, the components do need some special support. The extent of ActiveX's cross-platform compatibility depends on the installation of support software on client machines, which is standard on Windows machines. The ActiveX component model is a subset of the more general Component Object Model, or COM, protocol.

Active Documents

Active Documents are a type of software component that is document based and, therefore, has a close affiliation with data. That is, they are components, similar to objects in object-oriented programming, which encapsulate data specific to the component type. There are Active Documents for word processors, spreadsheets, Internet chat (as you saw earlier this chapter), and many other applications that deal with data. Active Documents have all the advantages of other software components with the special benefit of encapsulating data along with all other support information necessary to render the Active Document a complete and independent repository of those data. No matter where the Active Document is found, you are able to take advantage of the information in it as long as you have an Active Document container and Active Document server available.

Active Document containers allow you to display and manipulate documents from different application types all within the same document window. Visual C++ is an Active Document container, which is why you could use Comic Chat Room from within its environment. However, Visual C++ knows nothing about the Microsoft Chat code that underlies Comic Chat Room functionality. The Active document itself contains all of the information needed to invoke the Microsoft Chat code that the Comic Chat Room document relies on to run. This is possible because the Microsoft Chat application is an Active Document server that can be accessed and run by Active Documents. So, when you opened Comic Chat Room in Visual C++ you opened an Active document in an Active Document container. Behind the scenes and invisible to the user, the Active document invoked the Microsoft Chat application, an Active Document server, to support the chat mechanisms it used. The result was the in-place activation and use of a Microsoft Chat- based document inside Visual C++.

Active documents can, of course, be run directly by their associated Active Document server. That is, Comic Chat Room can be directly run in the Microsoft Chat application. An Active Document server is the parent application of an Active document.

Active documents, Active Document containers, and Active Document servers are all part of the Active Document model. This model is an extension of OLE compound document technology, which is a protocol built on COM.

Component Object Model

The Microsoft component models, ActiveX and Active Document in particular, are based on COM. COM is a broad set of object-oriented technology standards. COM is a language-independent, cross-platform component model. The COM specification is full of details. Nevertheless, the complex technical standards are set in place with only two main objectives: to present rigorous definitions of COM objects and of COM object interfaces.

A COM object is instantiated from a class that is the combination of an interface and the interface's methods and properties. In fact, a COM object is the same as any object defined by an object-oriented design specification except that the means of interacting with COM objects is rigidly specified so that independent software objects are able to communicate with one anther. COM objects encapsulate data and methods in the way that a locked library encapsulates its books. Accessing those data must be done through public methods. To access the library you enter through unlocked doors during the library's open hours. You gain access to a COM object's data and public methods through its interfaces. Interfaces are like the doors to the library. They are the only means of gaining access to COM objects and they're never locked.

The COM specification is concerned with defining interfaces and the way that they must be implemented so that any COM object knows how to access another COM object. The most basic interface defined is known as the IUnknown interface, which has three methods: the Query-Interface(), AddRef(), and Release() methods. It isn't important to know the details of these methods right now except that a call to the IUnknown interface QueryInterface() method returns a list of all of the interfaces supported by the object being queried. Since all COM objects have the IUnknown interface, any COM object can find out what interfaces are supported by other COM objects and access them. The list returned by the QueryInterface() method consists of a list of pointers to the interfaces themselves.

Once an object is able to access one or more of another COM object's interfaces, it's a simple thing to access the interface's methods. Further details are left until you actually start working with COM objects and their interfaces in the projects.

Internet Explorer

You've now seen the tight integration between Visual C++, the Internet, and software components. You've delved into descriptions of software component models that you can use while creating applications with Visual C++. What does all this have to do with Internet Explorer? Everything! Internet Explorer is composed of a collection of software components based on COM, especially the ActiveX and Active Document models. You can use the same components that Internet Explorer uses in your own applications, and you will do so throughout this book.

Note   You must install Internet Explorer version 4 or greater to have access to all the features discussed in this book.

Internet Explorer Architecture

When you launch Internet Explorer, a shell application is started that hosts a COM control called the WebBrowser control. This is the very same software component you can access through the CHtmlView class provided by the MFC library. The WebBrowser control is an Active Document Container used to host any Active Document Server. The WebBrowser control is responsible for giving the user an interface with which to navigate, manage subscriptions, and move around the Web.

The WebBrowser control hosts the MSHTML component, which is not a browser on its own. The MSHTML component processes HTML

Note   Since Internet Explorer may act as host to any Active Document server, it may host other active documents such as Word, Excel, or Chat documents.

documents and leaves user interface and document retrieval matters to other software components. In other words, it doesn't retrieve HTML documents from the Internet. Instead, it manages the parsing and display of HTML, COM controls, Java applets, and other objects that form Web pages.

Internet Explorer Common Controls

The software components making up Internet Explorer are available for anyone to use as long as Internet Explorer is installed on the client computer or the client computer is running Windows 98 or Windows NT 5.0 or later. Internet Explorer uses common controls that are provided by the Windows operating system to any application or user that wants to use them. These same common controls aren't available on machines running Windows 95 or Windows NT 4, since these operating systems were released before Internet Explorer 4. Install Internet Explorer version 4 or later on machines running Windows 95 or Windows NT 4 to update their common control files. Later versions of the Windows operating system include the updated common control files.

The Microsoft Foundation Classes library provides classes to make it easy for you to include many of the common controls in the applications that you create. Table 2.1 lists the MFC library classes that provide access to common controls along with the name of each common control and a description of what the control provides. The control names listed in italics are provided on the Controls toolbar that appears when you are editing certain resources such as dialog boxes, as in Figure 2-8.

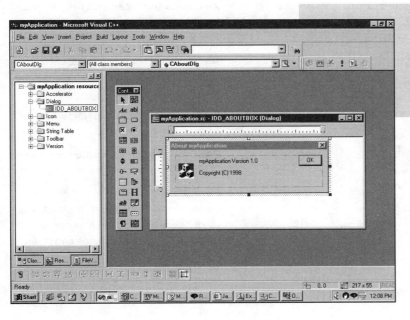

Figure 2-8
The Controls toolbar provides visual access to several of the common controls.

Table 2.1 MFC Library Access to Common Controls

Class	Control	Description
CAnimateCtrl	Animate	A rectangular window that displays AVI (Audio Video Interleaved) clips.
CDateTimeCtrl	Date Time Picker	Provides a simple interface to exchange date and time information with a user.
CHeaderCtrl	Header	A window typically positioned above columns of text or numbers that can contain a title for each column.
CHotKeyCtrl	Hot Key	Displays the user's hot key choices and ensures that the user selects a valid key combination.
CImageList	List	A collection of same-sized images, each of which may be referred to by its zero-based index.
CIPAddressCtrl	IP Address	An edit control for entering and manipulating a numerical address in the Internet Protocol (IP) format.
CListCtrl	List control	Displays a collection of items, each consisting of an icon from an image list and a label.
CMonthCalCtrl	Month Calendar	Provides a simple calendar interface from which a user can select a date.
CProgressCtrl	Progress	A window that an application can use to indicate the progress of a lengthy operation.
CReBar	Rebar	Used to create menu bars, toolbars, and other bands of message handling controls with layout persistence and state information.
CReBarCtrl	Rebar	Used to create menu bars, toolbars, and other bands of message handling controls.

Table 2.1 (continued)

Class	Control	Description
CRichEditCtrl	Rich Edit	A window where users may enter and edit text.
CSliderCtrl	Slider	A window containing a slider and optional tick marks.
CSpinButtonCtrl	Spin	A pair of arrow buttons that a user can click to increment or decrement a value, such as a scroll position or a number displayed in a companion control.
CStatusBarCtrl	Status Bar	A horizontal window, usually displayed at the bottom of a parent window, in which an application can display various kinds of status information.
CTabCtrl	Tab control	Adds tabs to multiple pages in a dialog box or window.
CToolBarCtrl	Toolbar	A rectangular child window that contains one or more buttons.
CToolTipCtrl	Tool Tip	A small pop-up window that displays a single line of text describing the purpose of a tool in an application.
CTreeCtrl	Tree control	Displays a hierarchical list of items.

You might have noticed that the CHttpView class, the class that provides access to the WebBrowser control, isn't listed in Table 2.1. The CHttpView class is one of a special set of classes that place common components into views, the client areas of frame windows that display data and accept input for documents. Table 2.2 lists these special classes along with the names of the controls that they place in a view and a description of each control.

Table 2.2 Common Controls Placed in a View Window Through MFC Library Access		
Class	**Control**	**Description**
CHttpView	WebBrowser	A window in which a user can browse the Web as well as the local file system and other networks.
CListView	List control	Displays a collection of items, each consisting of an icon from an image list and a label.
CRichEditView	Rich Edit	A window where users may enter and edit text.
CTreeView	Tree control	Displays a hierarchical list of items.

Summary

Visual C++ is tightly integrated with the Internet and the whole computing enterprise, at the integrated development environment level and at the language level. In fact, the two levels are blurred by software components—ActiveX controls and other COM components—which are little independent applications that can be glued together into any kind of application that you want to create. The Visual C++ integrated development environment and Internet Explorer are two examples of applications composed of software components. Enterprise-aware software components provide the foundation for creating distributed applications that go anywhere data and users are to be found. Application development using Visual C++ is no longer confined to your desktop computer. The global computing environment—the enterprise—is a source for information, software components, and other data for your application development efforts, and it's likewise a vast domain ready for the deployment of your new applications.

HANDS ON
PROJECT 1

QUICKBROWSE

- Develop software in the Visual C++ integrated development environment
- Modify application source code in Visual C++
- Create an application using the MFC AppWizard
- Use Internet Explorer 4 common controls
- Use the CHtmlView class from the MFC library
- Use the CTreeView class from the MFC library
- Modify menus
- Create message map functions
- Modify the toolbar

Project Overview

Learn to get the full power from the Visual C++ integrated development environment. Begin a project with many years worth of coding done for you by the MFC AppWizard and then dive into the development environment and code to learn how they are structured and how they work together.

Experience programming using the CHtmlView and CTreeView classes, which are MFC library wrapper classes to the HTML and tree controls. You also work with some other controls, such as the toolbar and rebar controls.

Modify various resources using the Visual C++ resource editor, including the string table and menus. Then add message mapping functions to connect user interactions with the resources and graphic interface with actions produced by the QuickBrowse application.

The QuickBrowse application provides topic-specific information to a set of users. Many individuals lack the time, the desire, or the understanding of how to surf the Web for information. In many instances, however, such information is required to optimize a person's time. By providing a simple application that contains a list of the sites that are specific to the user's job, you assure that the user does not have to know how to locate the desired information, but instead must merely know how to run this application.

3 CHAPTER

What Is QuickBrowse?

QuickBrowse is a custom Web browser optimized for specific information requirements. Often, feature-packed applications, including Internet Explorer, overwhelm or confuse users who simply want to get a job done. Microsoft's commitment to transform the Windows environment into a collection of software components, together with the power of the Visual C++ integrated development environment and the Microsoft Foundation Classes (MFC) library, makes it easy for you to create customized applications for your own or your client's specific use. QuickBrowse uses some of the same software components used by Internet Explorer, but its interface includes a tree of destinations, customized to meet the information needs of a specialist, that the user can easily see and click on to load into the browser.

Goals of the QuickBrowse Project

The QuickBrowse project introduces you to creating applications for the Web and the Enterprise using the Visual C++ integrated development environment. Not only is using the QuickBrowse application, shown in Figure 3-1, quick and simple to use, but also creating it is a snap with the tools at your fingertips. Here are your specific goals:

1. Develop software in the Visual C++ integrated development environment.

   The Developer Studio which comes with Visual C++ is an integrated development environment that is so powerful and full of features that a programmer can still be learning new tricks after using it for years. This project gives you a jump-start on taking full advantage of Visual C++ and teaches you the tricks of power users now.

2. Create an application using the MFC AppWizard.

   The MFC AppWizard is one of several wizards that Visual C++ provides to help you rapidly create your project's framework. The MFC AppWizard uses your answers to a number of queries to create the source code for a complete application built using the Microsoft Foundation Classes library.

3. Modify application source code in Visual C++.

   Once the MFC AppWizard is finished, you will modify the source application code to create your own custom QuickBrowse application.

4. Use Internet Explorer common controls.

   Internet Explorer is created by tying together of software components, known as ActiveX components. These components, known in this context as Internet Explorer common controls, are available for you to use in your own software projects. You use two Internet Explorer common controls in the QuickBrowse application: the HTML and Tree controls.

5. Use the CHtmlView class from the MFC library.

   You will learn how to use the MFC AppWizard to include the

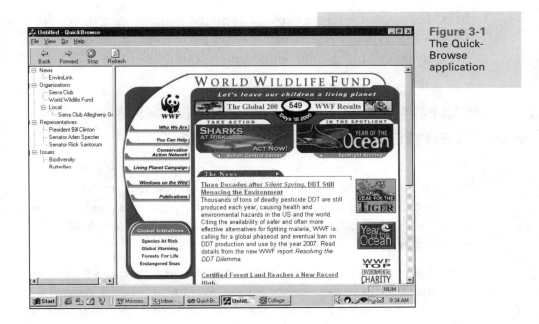

Figure 3-1
The Quick-
Browse
application

CHtml-View class in your application. Then you will learn how to use the CHtmlView class itself, a wrapper for the HTML Control, in your applications.

6. Use the CTreeView class from the MFC library.

You will learn how to use the MFC AppWizard to include the CTreeView class in your application. Then you will learn how to use the CTreeView class itself, a wrapper for the Tree Control, in your applications.

QuickBrowse System Requirements

Whether you're writing a program for yourself or for a client, you should make sure that the computer system it's destined for has the required software, hardware, and networking components. Your clients will be upset if that awesome application you created for their dozens of offices sprinkled around the world will only work if they upgrade all their computers (unless this was stipulated up front). Applications built using the

MFC library and Internet Explorer common controls, like the Quick-Browse application, demand that the computer running them have the MFC dynamic link libraries and Internet Explorer installed.

QuickBrowse Customization Requirements

A major feature of the QuickBrowse application is that it can be customized for the individual person, company, or business. It takes some planning to create a custom application. In this case, you need to know exactly what type of person, company, or business will use the Quick-Browse application.

The QuickBrowse application in this example project creates a browser customized for an environmental activist working in western Pennsylvania. If the application is for your own use, you need to decide the kinds of Web sites that you need and then gather up the Web site addresses. If you're creating the application for a client, get the client to supply this information for you. The environmental activist wants Web sites categorized into the following headings:

News

Organizations

Representatives

Issues

A deployment version of the QuickBrowse application, as opposed to the example version you're building, might include several more categories. However, four categories are enough to learn how to implement the tree view.

Each category has links to Web sites. Your example QuickBrowse application contains the links listed in Table 3.1 for each category.

Table 3.1 QuickBrowse Links for an Environmentalist		
Category	**Item Name**	**Web Address**
News	EnviroLink	http://www.envirolink.org
Organizations	World Wildlife Fund	http://www.wwf.org
Organizations	Sierra Club	http://www.sierraclub.org
Organizations\Local	Sierra Club Allegheny Group	http://host.envirolink.org/ allegheny-sc/
Representatives	President Bill Clinton	http://www.whitehouse.gov
Representatives	Senator Rick Santorum	http://www.senate.gov /~santorum/
Representatives	Senator Arlen Specter	http://www.senate.gov/ ~specter/
Issues	Biodiversity	http://www.biodiversity.org
Issues	Butterflies	http://www.butterflies.com

Table 3.1 includes the Category listing Organizations\Local. This means that there is a Local subcategory within the Organizations category. Thus the Sierra Club Allegheny Group is a local organization (to your fictional western Pennsylvania client).

Just as you would include more categories, you would probably include more links in a QuickBrowse application created for an actual client, rather than the limited number of links in this example. However, don't defeat the purpose of QuickBrowse. Simplicity! Restrict the number of categories and links to those needed by the user and no more.

Summary

In this chapter, you set your goals and requirements for the Quick-Browse project. You're ready to use a Visual C++ wizard to create a major part of the QuickBrowse project source code.

CHAPTER 4

Creating QuickBrowse

Visual C++ provides powerful tools that make it painless for you to embark on ambitious programming projects. In this chapter, you create the basic QuickBrowse application. You use the MFC AppWizard, which creates a complete application for you based on your answers to a set of queries. After you create QuickBrowse using the MFC App-Wizard, it's a matter of adding or modifying code to transform Quick-Browse into your own powerful custom application.

Creating QuickBrowse Using the MFC AppWizard

Start Microsoft Visual C++ if you haven't already, and then select the New command from its File menu. The New dialog box appears, as in Figure 4-1.

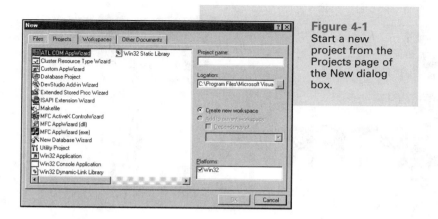

Figure 4-1
Start a new project from the Projects page of the New dialog box.

Click on the Projects tab to switch to the Projects page of the New dialog box, if it isn't displayed already.

You are presented with a wide range of options for starting a new project. QuickBrowse uses the CHtmlView class, which is part of the Microsoft Foundation Classes (MFC) library. It's also a stand-alone application. Therefore, you want a wizard that will help you create a MFC stand-alone application, which means that the application is an executable file with the .exe extension. MFC AppWizard (exe) in the Projects page listing is what you want.

Select MFC AppWizard (exe), and then type the project name, **QuickBrowse**, into the Project name text box. The Projects page of the New dialog box should look as it does in Figure 4-2.

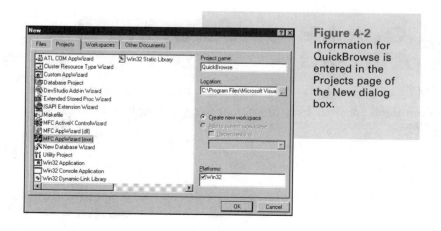

Figure 4-2
Information for QuickBrowse is entered in the Projects page of the New dialog box.

Click on the OK button. The Step 1 page of the MFC AppWizard appears, as in Figure 4-3.

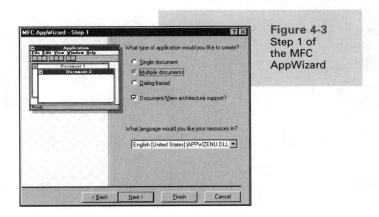

Figure 4-3
Step 1 of
the MFC
AppWizard

This is where you tell the wizard the type of application that you want. You can tell the wizard that you want your application to show only one document at a time or multiple documents at one time. You can create entirely dialog box–based applications. You can also tell the wizard if you want to use the MFC standard document/view architecture. Finally, you can select the language that you want your application to present to users.

Note

You can learn more about each option available on a Visual C++ dialog box by clicking on the question mark (?) at its upper-right corner and then pointing and clicking on the option that you want to learn more about.

QuickBrowse displays one document, a Web page, at a time. Select the Single Document radio button. QuickBrowse uses the document/view architecture, so make sure that the Document/View Architecture Support? check box is checked. Use the default language set on your computer. Step 1 of the MFC AppWizard should look similar to Figure 4-4.

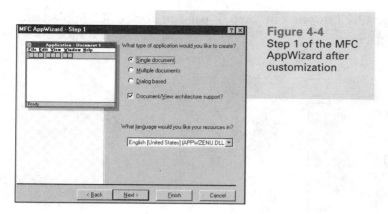

Figure 4-4
Step 1 of the MFC
AppWizard after
customization

Click on the Next button, and Step 2 of the MFC AppWizard appears
as in Figure 4-5.

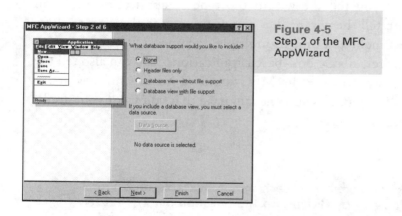

Figure 4-5
Step 2 of the MFC
AppWizard

Step 2 of the MFC AppWizard provides options for database support.
QuickBrowse doesn't provide database support, so keep the default
option, None, selected and click on the Next button. Step 3 of the MFC
AppWizard appears, as in Figure 4-6.

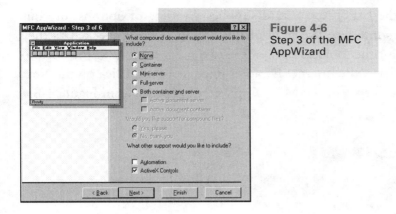

Figure 4-6
Step 3 of the MFC
AppWizard

You are provided options that enable your application to support embedded objects and compound documents in Step 3 of the MFC AppWizard. You can also specify if your application will simply act as a container or will act as a server of compound document objects. Finally, you can tell the wizard to create an application that supports automation and ActiveX controls.

QuickBrowser doesn't support embedded objects or compound documents, so select None, the default. It does support ActiveX controls, so keep the default check mark in the ActiveX Controls check box. Click on the Next button and Step 4 of the MFC AppWizard appears, as in Figure 4-7.

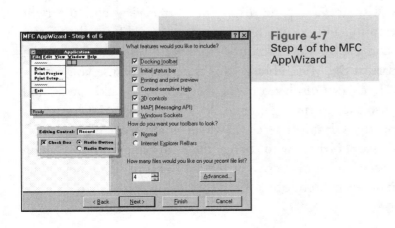

Figure 4-7
Step 4 of the MFC
AppWizard

Step 4 of the MFC AppWizard supplies a variety of options for your application's interface. Keep all of the default options checked as they are except for the toolbars option, the two radio buttons at the bottom of the list. Select the Internet Explorer ReBars option. Click on the Next Button, and Step 5 of the MFC AppWizard appears, as in Figure 4-8.

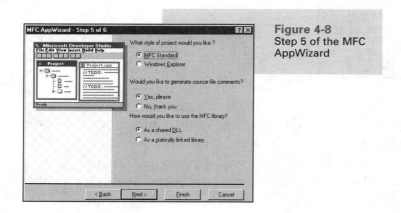

Figure 4-8
Step 5 of the MFC AppWizard

In Step 5 of the MFC AppWizard, you select the graphic user interface style, whether or not comments are added to your code, and the way you want MFC library classes to be used by your application.

The MFC Standard style is close to the style presented by Microsoft Word. For instance, whereas the Windows Explorer style is the style presented by, well, Windows Explorer. Windows Explorer presents a splitter window with the left pane displaying a tree view and the right window presenting a list view. The tree view is created from the CTreeView class, and the list view is created from the CListView class. Both classes are part of the MFC library. This is perfect because you want a tree view (CTreeView) displayed in the left pane of QuickBrowser and Web pages displayed in the right pane. A view displaying Web pages is created using the CHtmlView class, which is also part of the MFC library. You'll see shortly how to change the right pane from displaying a list (CListView) to displaying a Web page (CHtmlView). Select the Windows Explorer radio button.

It's always a good idea to include as many comments in your source code as possible. That way, when you go back through the code the comments help you to remember what it does. Let Visual C++ add helpful comments to your code by keeping the default Yes, Please radio button selected.

Finally, there are two ways to include code from the MFC library in your application. One is as a shared Dynamic Link Library, or DLL. The MFC library is provided in a DLL, which any application created using the MFC library can use. Applications that dynamically link with code in a DLL file can be smaller because they don't need to include that code in their own file space. However, the DLL file must be present on the user's machine. This isn't generally a problem because so many applications use the MFC libraries that nearly every Windows user has the appropriate DLLs installed. The other option is to statically link all of the necessary code into your application. This can result in a much larger application file size, but the code can also be quicker. A shared DLL is loaded into memory only when your application calls a function implemented in the DLL. In contrast, a statically linked library is loaded when the application is started so that when the application calls a function implemented in the library it's already in memory and ready to execute. Nevertheless, usually the time difference is small if noticeable at all, and the advantages of using shared DLLs outweigh the disadvantages. Keep the default selection, As a Shared DLL, selected.

Click on the Next button and Step 6 of the MFC AppWizard appears, as in Figure 4-9.

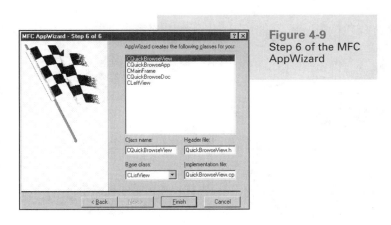

Figure 4-9
Step 6 of the MFC
AppWizard

Step 6 of the MFC AppWizard displays the names of the various classes that you are creating for the QuickBrowse project. Click on a class in the list at the top, and the class name, header, and implementation file for the class, along with the base class from which it's derived, if any, are all shown at bottom.

As mentioned, you need to make a change in the QuickBrowse view so that the right pane displays Web pages rather than lists. Click on CQuickBrowseView in the list at top. It's an instance of the CQuick-BrowseView class that displays the main view in the QuickBrowse application window. CListView should appear in the Base Class drop-down list at the bottom. If you kept the current settings, the QuickBrowse application would display a list instantiated from the CListView class in its main view. However, you want to display Web pages in the main view, so open the drop-down list by clicking on the down arrow and selecting CHtmlView. Now the QuickBrowse application will display Web pages in its main view!

Click on the Finish button, and the New Project Information dialog box appears, as in Figure 4-10.

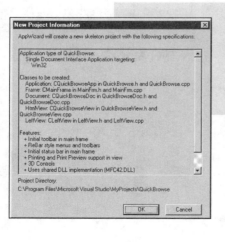

Figure 4-10
The New Project Information dialog box displays the project's application type, classes, and features.

You can review the project's application type, classes used, and features in the New Project Information dialog box. If there is something that you don't like, you can click on the Cancel button and be taken back to Step 6 of the MFC AppWizard. You can go back as many steps as you need by clicking on the Back button. After everything looks good in the New Project Information dialog box, click on the OK button.

The AppWizard creates your project and displays it in the Visual C++ integrated development environment (IDE), as in Figure 4-11.

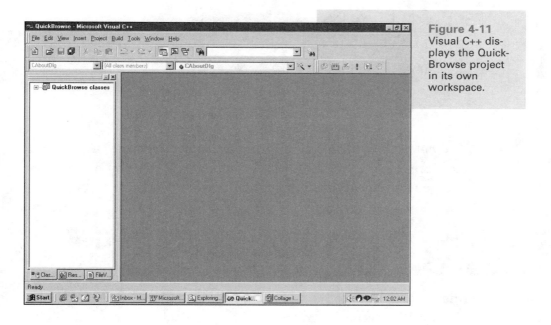

Figure 4-11
Visual C++ displays the Quick-Browse project in its own workspace.

You can't see much in this default display. Click on the plus sign (+) to the left of QuickBrowse classes in the ClassView page of the Workspace window at left. A list of the various classes that make up the project appears, as in Figure 4-12.

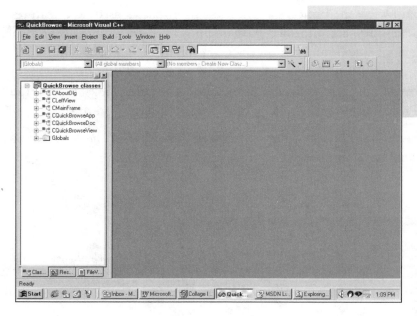

Figure 4-12
QuickBrowse
classes are
shown in the
ClassView page
of the Work-
space window.

You will explore the Visual C++ integrated development environment more as you complete the QuickBrowse project. However, you can try out the new QuickBrowse application now!

Running QuickBrowse from the Visual C++ IDE

Run QuickBrowse to see what the MFC AppWizard created for you. Click on the Execute Program button (an exclamation mark) in the Build MiniBar toolbar or select Execute QuickBrowse.exe from the Build menu. A Microsoft Visual C++ dialog box appears, as in Figure 4-13.

Note   Add and remove toolbars from the Visual C++ integrated development environment through the shortcut menu that you open by pointing to any toolbar or the toolbar area and pressing your right mouse button.

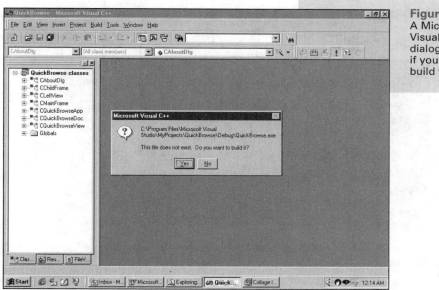

Figure 4-13
A Microsoft
Visual C++
dialog box asks
if you want to
build the file.

The project hasn't been compiled and linked yet, so Visual C++ is asking if you want the QuickBrowser executable file to be built. Click on the Yes button. The Build page of the Output window appears below and keeps you informed about what is happening during the build process, as in Figure 4-14.

Your computer should be connected with the Internet when you launch the QuickBrowser application.

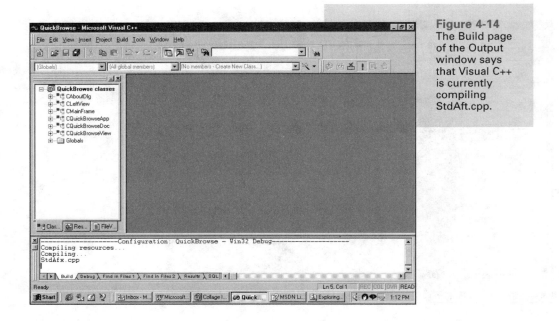

Figure 4-14
The Build page
of the Output
window says
that Visual C++
is currently
compiling
StdAft.cpp.

After the application is built, it's launched as in Figure 4-15.

QuickBrowse loads a document containing the Microsoft Visual C++ Web site Start Page by default. You can't do much else with Quick-Browse at the moment. However, QuickBrowse documents are fully functional Web pages. You can click on hyperlinks to load other pages or download files.

QuickBrowse doesn't provide the navigation tools that you are accustomed to in Internet Explorer. There is no way to jump back a page if the Web page you've loaded doesn't provide a hyperlink to do it. Quick-Browse also doesn't provide bookmark capabilities. You could add these in, but the idea of QuickBrowse is to provide a simple, easy-to-use, dedicated browser interface.

Notice that the QuickBrowse document has a right pane and a left pane. The right pane displays the Web page. It was created using the CHtmlView class from the MFC library. The left pane is blank. It was created using the CTreeView class from the MFC library. One of your

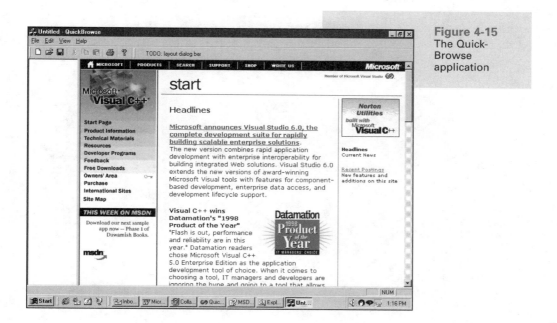

Figure 4-15
The Quick-
Browse
application

jobs in Chapter 7 is to customize the code provided by the MFC App-Wizard so that the left pane displays a tree view of Web sites that are of particular interest and usefulness to the application's target user.

Summary

You created the QuickBrowse application using the MFC AppWizard. You learned about the MFC AppWizard queries and how to customize your application based on your answers. Customization, however, only goes so far in the MFC AppWizard itself. You must add or modify code in the QuickBrowse project to fully customize the program and to make it a powerful stand-alone application. In Chapter 7 you'll learn how Visual C++ sets up an entire application framework for you when you created QuickBrowse. It's this application framework, combined with the tools provided by the Visual C++ integrated development environment that makes modifying the code to further customize the application as simple as creating the code using the MFC AppWizard.

CHAPTER 5

QuickBrowse Architecture

The objects composing QuickBrowse interact within a fixed structure enforced by Visual C++ and the MFC library. Understanding this structure, or program architecture, makes modifying the code created by the MFC AppWizard a lot simpler. In this section you learn about the software architecture used most of the time by Visual C++ when creating MFC applications.

The QuickBrowse Class Hierarchy

The six classes listed in the ClassView page of the Project Workspace window, shown in Figure 5-1, interact to form the basic architecture of the QuickBrowse application.

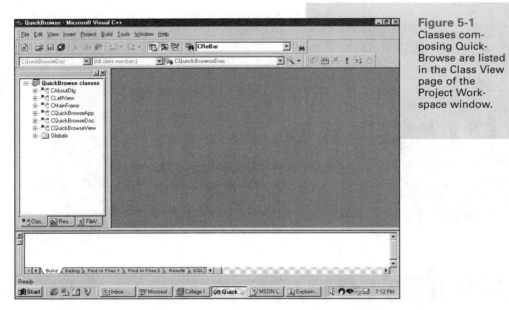

Figure 5-1
Classes composing Quick-Browse are listed in the Class View page of the Project Workspace window.

CQuickBrowseApp is the top-level class. Click on the plus sign (+) to the left of the CQuickBrowseApp listing in the ClassView page of the Project Workspace window. The CQuickBrowseApp class member functions are listed below the class name, as in Figure 5-2.

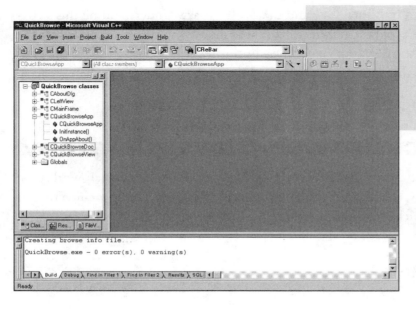

Figure 5-2
The CQuick-BrowseApp class member functions are listed under the class name when the tree is expanded.

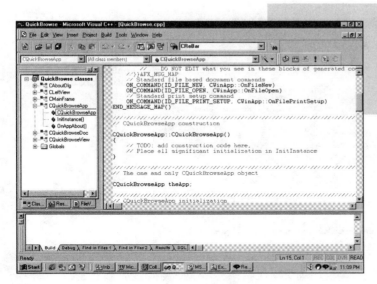

Figure 5-3
The CQuick-
BrowseApp class
definition source
file is displayed in
the Visual C++
Document window.

Note Visual C++ provides you with ample comments to help you understand the code and make modifications. The Visual C++ editor highlights comments in green by default.

Double-click on the CQuickBrowseApp class constructor, `CQuick-BrowseApp()`. The CQuickBrowseApp class definition source file appears in the Document window, QuickBrowse.cpp, opened to the class constructor definition as shown in Figure 5-3.

Notice the global variable declaration, reproduced here, under the class constructor:

```
CQuickBrowseApp theApp;
```

A CQuickBrowseApp object is assigned to the global variable, `theApp`, so that this top-level object exists for the life of the application and is available to all of the application's lower-level objects. There is a Globals folder listed in the ClassView page of the Workspace window. Click on the plus sign next to the Globals folder, and you see the `theApp` variable listed, as in Figure 5-4.

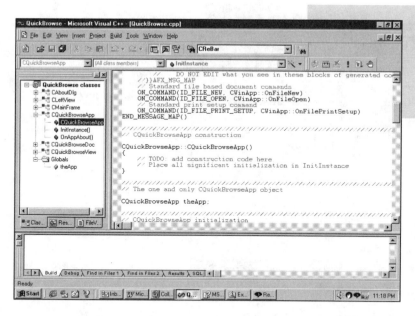

Figure 5-4
The theApp variable is QuickBrowse application's one global variable.

Besides the class constructor, there are definitions for two other CQuickBrowseApp class functions. These are the `InitInstance()` and `OnAppAbout()` functions.

Double-click on the `InitInstance()` function listed in the ClassView page of the Workspace window. The Document window displays the `InitInstance()` function definition.

Tip

Most of the time the Output window, typically displayed as a docked window at the bottom of the Visual C++ workspace, only takes up room. You can hide it while you don't need it. Point to the Output window and click your right mouse button. A shortcut menu appears. Select the Hide command from the shortcut menu, and the Output window is hidden. The window will reappear automatically as soon as Visual C++ sends output to one of the pages in the Output window.

Document/View Architecture

The InitInstance() function is where the application architecture is registered. MFC applications have what are called document templates that serve as the connection between documents, frame windows, and views. Documents hold your application's data, frame windows form its general windowing infrastructure, and views display the application's data within the frame windows. This is the basis of the document/view architecture used by most applications created with the MFC libraries.

If you look through the code in the InitInstance() function definition, you can see that the QuickBrowse application uses the single document template, represented by MFC library's CSingleDocTemplate class. Three run-time classes are registered with the single document template: the CQuickBrowseDoc, CMainFrame, and CLeftView.

QuickBrowse application's document objects are created from the CQuickBrowseDoc class, its frame window objects are created from the CMainFrame class, and one of its two types of view objects is created from the CLeftView class. The CLeftView class, derived from the CTreeView class, is the top view class used by QuickBrowse.

Excluding the CQuickBrowseApp class itself, only two of the six classes listed in the ClassView page of the Workspace window are not registered in the InitInstance() function definition: the CAboutDlg and CQuickBrowseView.

Double-click on the third and final CQuickBrowseApp class function, OnAppAbout(), and you see the following declaration:

```
CAboutDlg aboutDlg;
```

The CAboutDlg class defines the application's About dialog box. When the dialog box is asked for, the OnAppAbout() function is called, and the CAboutDlg class is instantiated.

The CQuickBrowseView class is the only one of the six main classes not referenced in the CQuickBrowseApp class. Where is this class used? Visual C++ provides a powerful tool for finding where a class is referenced within your project's program files.

The Browse Info File

Visual C++ can track where classes are referenced in your project files by creating a browse info file. In fact, it can do much more, including tell you each class's base and derived classes and show you where variables are referenced. Find what file or files in the QuickBrowse project reference the CQuickBrowseView class by telling Visual C++ to create a browse info file for the project. Select the Settings command from the Project menu. The Project Settings dialog box appears. Click on the C/C++ tab to open the C/C++ page of the Project Settings dialog box, as in Figure 5-5.

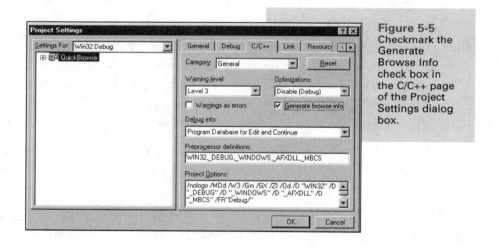

Figure 5-5
Checkmark the Generate Browse Info check box in the C/C++ page of the Project Settings dialog box.

Make sure there is a check mark in the Generate Browse Info check box at right under the Optimizations drop-down list. Next, click on the Browse Info tab to open the Browse Info page of the Project Settings dialog box, as in Figure 5-6.

Tip

You might need to click on the little arrow buttons to move the tabs in the Project Settings dialog box so that you can see the one you need to click on.

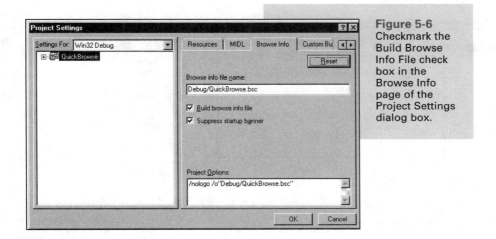

Figure 5-6
Checkmark the
Build Browse
Info File check
box in the
Browse Info
page of the
Project Settings
dialog box.

Make sure there is a check mark in the Build Browse Info File check box under the Browse Info File Name text box. Click on the OK button to close the Project Settings dialog box.

Create a browse info file for the QuickBrowse project by rebuilding the project. Click on the Build toolbar button or select the Build All command from the Build menu.

When the build is finished, you can look for references to the CQuickBrowseView class. Press your right mouse button while pointing to the CQuickBrowseView class in the ClassView page of the Workspace window. A shortcut menu appears displaying a number of commands, which include the References, Derived Classes, and Base Classes commands. All three of these commands depend on a browse info file for your project. Select the References command from the shortcut menu, because you're looking for references to the CQuickBrowseView class. The CQuickBrowseView–Definitions and References window appears, as in Figure 5-7.

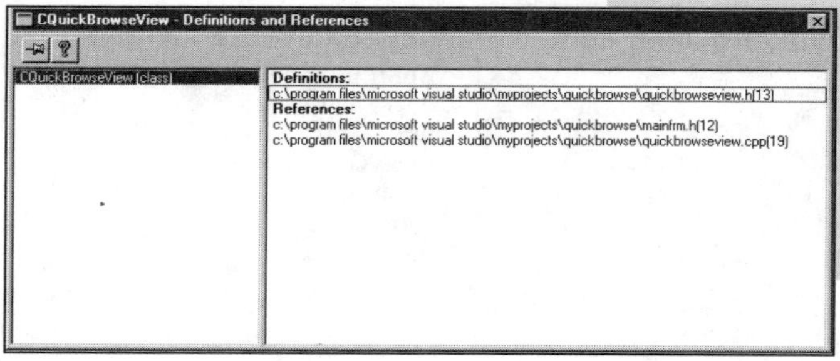

CQuickBrowseView - Definitions and References

CQuickBrowseView (class)

Definitions:
c:\program files\microsoft visual studio\myprojects\quickbrowse\quickbrowseview.h(13)
References:
c:\program files\microsoft visual studio\myprojects\quickbrowse\mainfrm.h(12)
c:\program files\microsoft visual studio\myprojects\quickbrowse\quickbrowseview.cpp(19)

Figure 5-7
Find where the CQuickBrowseView class is referenced in the CQuick-BrowseView - Definitions and References window.

At the top in the right pane of the CQuickBrowseView-Definitions and References window is the Definitions heading. Underneath the heading is the complete path to QuickBrowse project's quickbrowseview.h file. Double-click on this path listing in the CQuickBrowseView-Definitions and References window. Visual C++ loads the file in its Document window and highlights the CQuickBrowseView class declaration that is in it. You can see that the CQuickBrowseView class is derived from the CHtmlView class.

The Definitions heading is a misnomer, since what is meant is the class declaration. Anything listed under the Definitions header in the CQuickBrowseView-Definitions and References window is a class declaration.

Reopen the CQuickBrowseView-Definitions and References window by pressing your right mouse button while pointing to the CQuickBrowse-View class in the ClassView page of the Workspace window. Select the References command from the shortcut menu, and the CQuickBrowse-View-Definitions and References window reappears.

The files listed under the References heading in the CQuickBrowseView -Definitions and References include the file containing the CQuick-BrowseView class declaration and the files that reference the class declaration file. The file containing the CQuickBrowseView class definition is one of the files that reference the class declaration file. You can usually spot the class definition file, because the file is typically

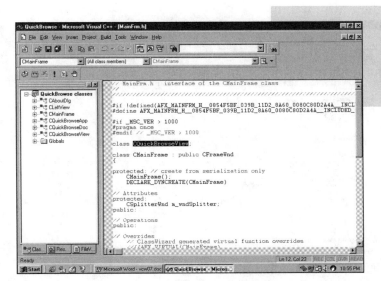

Figure 5-8
The CQuickBrowse-View class forward definition is high-lighted in the mainFrm.h file.

Tip

A forward declaration allows you to compile a reference to a class without having the entire class definition available. Nevertheless, the class must be defined somewhere in the project.

named for the class. For instance, the CQuickBrowseView class definition is found in the quickbrowseview.cpp file.

One other file, mainfrm.h, references the CQuickBrowseView class declaration. Double-click on the mainfrm.h file name and path in the CQuickBrowseView-Definitions and References window. The Visual C++ Document window displays the mainFrm.h file opened to the forward declaration of the CQuickBrowseView class, as in Figure 5-8.

The CMainFrame class uses the CQuickBrowseView class when it creates a splitter window.

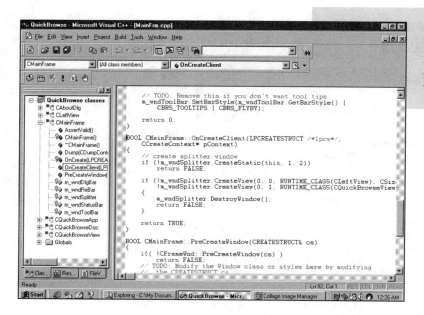

Figure 5-9
The OnCreate-Client() function creates the splitter window.

Creating a Splitter Window

MFC applications use splitter windows when they present more than one view. The window is split, in this case in two. QuickBrowse presents two views, a tree view and an HTML view.

Expand the tree under the CMainFrame class listing in the ClassView page of the Project Workspace window. Then double-click on the OnCreateClient() function. The Visual C++ Document window highlights the OnCreateClient() function in the CMainFrame class, as in Figure 5-9.

The first if statement in the OnCreateClient() function, reproduced here, includes the call to create a splitter window.

```
if (!m_wndSplitter.CreateStatic(this, 1, 2))
  return FALSE;
```

The splitter window object is assigned to the m_wndSplitter variable. Press your right mouse button while pointing to the wndSplitter variable in the ClassView page of the Workspace window, and a short-cut menu appears. Select the Go to Definition command, and you're taken straight to the variable's declaration. You can see that its data type is the CSplitterWnd class from the MFC library.

The CreateStatic() function is a member of the CSplitterWnd class that creates a static splitter window. The first argument takes the parent object of the splitter window, which is the CFrameWindow object. The second argument takes the number of rows that the window is split into. There is no horizontal split in the window, so a 1 is passed to the second argument. The third and final argument takes the number of columns into which the window is split. The window is vertically split once into two panes, so a 2 is passed to the third argument.

Note
The CreateStatic() **function returns a nonzero integer if it's successful and a 0 if it isn't. The** if **statement is a convenient way to test whether the function succeeded or not.**

Go back to the OnCreateClient() function definition by double-clicking on the function name in the ClassView page of the Workspace window. The second if statement in the OnCreateClient() function creates the two views that are displayed in the right and left panes of the splitter window. The first call to the CreateView() function creates the left view with the CLeftView class (derived from the CTreeView class) and that the second call to the CreateView() function creates the right view with the CQuickBrowseView class (derived from the CHtmlView class).

You now are acquainted with the main architectural elements of the QuickBrowse application. Figure 5-10 shows the QuickBrowse class hierarchy that you just explored. In Chapter 6, "Customizing Quick-Browse," you immerse yourself in the QuickBrowse application source code and modify it, creating your own customized application.

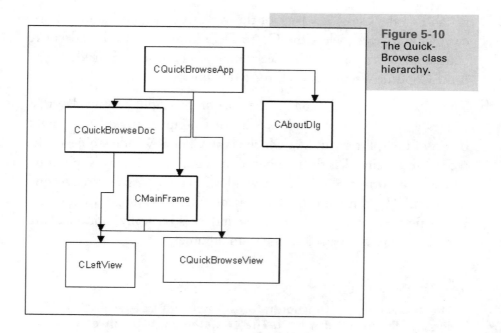

Figure 5-10
The Quick-
Browse class
hierarchy.

Summary

In this chapter you learned about document/view architecture and the relationship between the major classes of an MFC application. Along the way you learned several useful skills for effectively using the Visual C++ integrated development environment. You are now ready to modify the MFC AppWizard–generated QuickBrowse code to create a customized application.

CHAPTER 6

Customizing QuickBrowse

Visual C++ does a lot of the work of creating an application for you but not everything. You customize the code provided by the MFC App-Wizard so that you end up with a unique application designed just for you or a client. In this chapter, you modify the QuickBrowse application's left pane so that it displays hyperlink items in a tree that you can expand or collapse. You also add user interaction that allows users to double-click on these items and load Web pages in the right pane. Finally, you modify the QuickBrowse menus and toolbars to be simple to use and useful for a Web browsing application.

Modifying the Left Pane

The left pane is where the QuickBrowse Web site links tree will be located. You begin customizing the QuickBrowse application code by creating this tree.

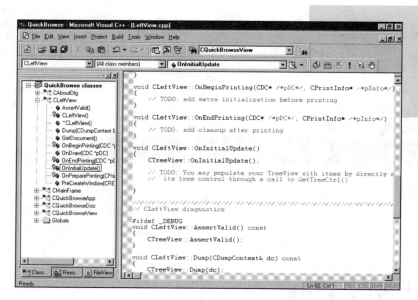

Figure 6-1
Set the style of the tree view in the OnInitial Update() CLeftView class function.

Setting the Tree View Style

The first thing is to set the tree view style, the way that the tree view is presented to the user. Set the tree view display options once, on initial update of the QuickBrowser application's left pane. Expand the member list under the CLeftView class in the Visual C++ ClassView page of the Project Workspace window and double-click on the OnInitialUpdate() function. The Visual C++ Document window opens the LeftView.cpp file to the OnInitialUpdate() CLeftView class function, as in Figure 6-1.

There are three steps to setting a new style for the tree view. First you must get the view's old style, then you modify the old style to the new style, and finally you set the new style.

Get the old style of the left pane by using the GetWindowLong() function, reproduced here:

```
LONG GetWindowLong( HWND hWnd, int nIndex )
```

This window class function gets a 32-bit value representing information about a window specified by the window handle passed to the function's first parameter, hWnd. The type of information depends on the integer constant passed to the GetWindowLong() function's second parameter nIndex. Table 6.1 lists the constants that you can use to tell the function the type of information you want returned.

Table 6.1 Get Window Long ()

Integer Constant	Description
GWL_EXSTYLE	Get the extended window styles.
GWL_STYLE	Get the window styles.
GWL_WNDPROC	Get the address of the window procedure or a handle representing the address of the window procedure.
GWL_HINSTANCE	Get the handle of the application instance.
GWL_HWNDPARENT	Get the handle of the parent window, if any.
GWL_ID	Get the identifier of the window.
GWL_USERDATA	Get the 32-bit value associated with the window.

Add your first line of code right under the comment that reads

```
// TODO: You may populate your TreeView with items by directly accessing
//  its tree control through a call to GetTreeCtrl().
```

in the OnInitialUpdate() function. In this line of code, pass the m_hWnd variable to the hWnd parameter of the GetWindowLong() function and, since you want to get the window style, pass the GWL_STYLE integer constant to the nIndex parameter of the GetWindowLong() function. The first line of code you add to the OnInitialUpdate() function should look like this statement:

```
long lStyleOld = GetWindowLong(m_hWnd, GWL_STYLE);
```

Next, modify the current window style assigned to the lStyleOld variable to the style that you want. You have a wide range of options for defining the look of a tree view, as indicated by the long list of integer constants in Table 6.2.

Table 6.2 Tree View Styles

Integer Constant	Description
TVS_CHECKBOXES	Enables check boxes for tree control items.
TVS_DISABLEDRAGDROP	Disables drag-and-drop feature.
TVS_EDITLABELS	Lets user edit labels of tree control items.
TVS_FULLROWSELECT	Enables full row selections.
TVS_HASBUTTONS	Displays plus (+) and minus (–) buttons to the left of parent tree control items.
TVS_HASLINES	Displays lines to show tree control item hierarchy.
TVS_INFOTIP	Enables tool tips for tree control items.
TVS_LINESATROOT	Displays lines to link items at the root of the tree control.
TVS_NONEVENHEIGHT	Enables you to set odd height values for item listings.
TVS_NOSCROLL	Disables horizontal and vertical scrolling.
TVS_NOTOOLTIPS	Disables tool tips for tree control items.
TVS_RTLREADING	Displays text for right-to-left reading (for Hebrew, Arabic, Chinese, etc).
TVS_SHOWSELALWAYS	Selected item remains selected when tree control view loses focus.
TVS_SINGLEEXPAND	Enables single-click expansion and collapse of tree.
TVS_TRACKSELECT	Enables hot tracking.

The QuickBrowser tree view will display lines to show tree control item hierarchy (TVS_HASLINES), lines to link items at the root of the tree control (TVS_LINESATROOT), and plus (+) and minus (–) buttons to the left of parent tree control items (TVS_HASBUTTONS). Add this statement just below the previous statement you added in the OnInitialUpdate() function:

```
lStyleOld = lStyleOld | TVS_HASLINES | TVS_HASBUTTONS | TVS_LINESATROOT;
```

You modify the value of the old window style by applying a bitwise OR

(¦) with each of the styles that you want added. Once this is done, you're ready to set the window's style using the `SetWindowLong()` function. The `SetWindowLong()` function signature is reproduced here:

```
LONG SetWindowLong(  HWND hWnd, int nIndex, LONG dwNewLong )
```

This window class function changes a 32-bit window attribute for the window specified by the window handle passed to the function's first parameter, `hWnd`. The type of attribute changed depends on the integer constant passed to the `SetWindowLong()` function's second parameter, `nIndex`. Table 6.1 lists the constants that you can use to tell the function the type of information you want changed. Finally, the new value of the changed attribute is passed to the `SetWindowLong()` function's third parameter, `dwNewLong`.

Add a third line of code, right below the previous two lines, that sets the window's style using the `SetWindowLong()` function. The new statement is listed here:

```
SetWindowLong(m_hWnd, GWL_STYLE, lStyleOld);
```

The statement is nearly identical to when you used the `GetWindowLong()` function, except that you're now passing the modified style value, assigned to the `lStyleOld` variable, back to the window.

Adding Items to the Tree

Once you've set the style of the tree view window, you're ready to add items to the tree. The items are the text or images that you see appear in a tree view, like the classes, functions, and variables listed in the ClassView page of the Project Workspace window.

Each tree item is associated with a handle of the `HTREEITEM` type. A tree item's handle is returned when you use the CTreeCtrl class `InsertItem()` function to add an item to a tree.

A view derived from the CTreeView class has special access to the CTreeCtrl class. In the CLeftView class, which is derived from the CTreeView class, you use the `GetTreeCtrl()` function to get the reference to the tree control associated with the view.

Adding the News Category

Add a simple text item to the tree control by adding this line of code in the CLeftView class `OnInitialUpdate()` function, right below the code you just added to change the view's style:

```
HTREEITEM hItem = GetTreeCtrl().InsertItem("News");
```

To the right in the equality expression, the `GetTreeCtrl()` function is called, which returns a reference to the view's tree control. Then the tree control's (a CTreeCtrl object) `InsertItem()` function is called. The text composing the item—in this case `"News"`—is passed to the `InsertItem()` function, which adds the text and returns a handle to the tree item. The handle, which is of the `HTREEITEM` data type, is assigned to the `hItem` variable. You will use this same statement with different text to create each of the remaining three root category tree items you plan to add to the tree view. All four root categories are listed here:

```
News

Organizations

Representatives

Issues
```

Chapter 3—"What is QuickBrowse?"—describes the categories and links that you are using in the tree view.

Recall that you are adding items—links to Web sites—under each of the four root categories. You use the same `InsertItem()` function from the CTreeCtrl class to add these items to the tree. However, these items are a bit more complicated to create. They are children of parent items. That is, an item such as the EnviroLink item is a child to a parent root item such as the News item. You use the standard tree view data structure `TVINSERTSTRUCT` to keep track of these relationships.

Adding a Private Member Variable

Create a private member variable, named m_treeItems, in the CLeftView class to assign an array of TVINSERTSTRUCT data. Point to the CLeftView class listed in the ClassView page of the Project Workspace window and press your right mouse button. A shortcut menu appears. Select the Add Member Variable command from the shortcut menu. The Add Member Variable dialog box appears, as in Figure 6-2.

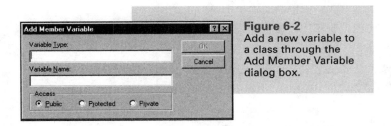

Figure 6-2
Add a new variable to a class through the Add Member Variable dialog box.

Type the variable's data type, **TVINSERTSTRUCT**, in the Variable Type text box. Next, type the variable's name, **m_treeItems**, into the Variable Name text box. Each of the nine items within categories plus the one subcategory will have its own TVINSERTSTRUCT data; therefore, the variable is an array with ten members. Add a pair of braces ([]) with the number 10 between to the end of the variable name. Finally, this is a private variable; therefore select the Private radio button in the Access area of the Add Member Variable dialog box. Your Add Member Variable dialog box should look like Figure 6-3.

Figure 6-3
Add the m_treeItems variable through the Add Member Variable dialog box.

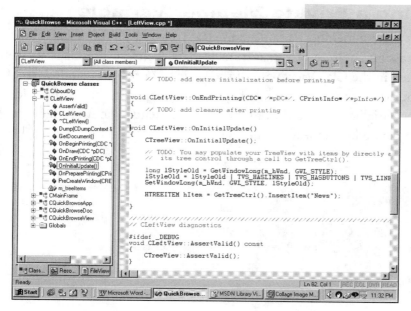

Figure 6-4
The current state
of the CLeftView
class and its
`OnInitial
Update()`
function

Click on the OK button. The `m_treeItems` variable should be listed under the CLeftView class in the ClassView page of the Project Workspace window, as in Figure 6-4.

You can look at the `m_treeItems` variable declaration added to the Left-View.h file by double-clicking on `m_treeItems` in the ClassView page of the Workspace window.

The TVINSERTSTRUCT Data Structure

Each item in the `m_treeItems` array is a TVINSERTSTRUCT data structure. The declaration of TVINSERTSTRUCT is listed here:

```
typedef struct tagTVINSERTSTRUCT {
    HTREEITEM hParent;
    HTREEITEM hInsertAfter;
```

```
#if (_WIN32_IE >= 0x0400)
    union
    {
        TVITEMEX itemex;
        TVITEM item;
    } DUMMYUNIONNAME;
#else
    TVITEM item;
#endif
} TVINSERTSTRUCT, FAR *LPTVINSERTSTRUCT;
```

Three members of the TVINSERTSTRUCT data structure are of particular importance to the tree view in QuickBrowse. They are the hParent, hInsertAfter, and item variables.

Adding the EnviroLink Item

Assign the item handle, a HTREEITEM data type, of the current item's parent item to the hParent variable. For instance, the first item in the m_treeItems array is EnviroLink, which is under the News category. Therefore, add this line after the statement inserting the News item into the tree view in the OnInitialUpdate() function of the CLeftView class:

```
m_treeItems[0].hParent = hItem;
```

At this point in the function, the handle to the News item is assigned to the hItem variable. This is the item that you want as the parent to the EnviroLink item. The handle to the News item is assigned to the hParent variable, which is a member of the first data structure assigned to the m_treeItems array.

Next, assign a handle or one of three integer constants to the hInsertAfter variable, part of the TVINSERTSTRUCT data structure, to determine the place the new item is added under the News item category. The current item is added after the item that the item handle you assign to the hInsertAfter variable belongs to. Otherwise, assign one of these three integer constants:

TVI_FIRST

Inserts the tree item at the beginning of the list.

TVI_LAST

Inserts the tree item at the end of the list.

TVI_SORT

Inserts the tree item into the list in alphabetical order.

Add the EnviroLink item in alphabetical order by using the TVI_SORT integer constant. Insert this line after the previous statement you added to the OnInitialUpdate() function of the CLeftView class:

```
m_treeItems[0].hInsertAfter = TVI_SORT;
```

You complete filling out the TVINSERTSTRUCT data structure for the EnviroLink tree item with the next three statements you add to the OnInitialUpdate() function. All three statements assign data to the item member variable of the TVINSERTSTRUCT data structure, which is itself a data structure.

The item variable data structure contains information about the tree item itself rather than the location of the tree item. It's a TVITEM data type, declared as listed here:

```
typedef struct tagTVITEM{
    UINT      mask;
    HTREEITEM hItem;
    UINT      state;
    UINT      stateMask;
    LPTSTR    pszText;
    int       cchTextMax;
    int       iImage;
    int       iSelectedImage;
    int       cChildren;
    LPARAM    lParam;
} TVITEM, FAR *LPTVITEM;
```

You can see that the TVITEM data structure has several members. You use two of them in the QuickBrowse application's tree control: the mask and pszText variables.

The value assigned to the mask variable, an unsigned integer (UINT) data type, indicates which of the other TVITEM structure members contain valid data. You can assign one or more of the integer constants in Table 6.3 to the mask variable.

Table 6.3 TVITEM Structure Mask Values

Integer Constant	Description
TVIF_CHILDREN	Validates the cChildren member.
TVIF_HANDLE	Validates the hItem member.
TVIF_IMAGE	Validates the iImage member.
TVIF_PARAM	Validates the lParam member.
TVIF_SELECTEDIMAGE	Validates the iSelectedImage member.
TVIF_STATE	Validates the state and stateMask members.
TVIF_TEXT	Validates the pszText and cchTextMax members.

Validate the pszText member variable by assigning the TVIF_TEXT integer constant to the mask variable with the statement listed here:

```
m_treeItems[0].item.mask = TVIF_TEXT;
```

Assign the pszText variable in the TVITEM data structure to the tree item's text. This is the text that appears to the user in the tree view. Assign the "EnviroLink" text to the pszText variable with the line of code here:

```
m_treeItems[0].item.pszText = "EnviroLink";
```

"EnviroLink" is the name of the item under the News category that will be displayed in the tree view as it was discussed in Chapter 3 "What is QuickBrowse?" Table 3.1 from Chapter 3 is reproduced here as Table 6.4 for your easy reference.

Table 6.4 QuickBrowse Links for an Environmentalist		
Category	**Item Name**	**Web Address**
News	EnviroLink	http://www.envirolink.org
Organizations	World Wildlife Fund	http://www.wwf.org
Organizations	Sierra Club	http://www.sierraclub.org
Organizations\Local	Sierra Club Allegheny Group	http://host.envirolink.org/ allegheny-sc/
Representatives	President Bill Clinton	http://www.whitehouse.gov
Representatives	Senator Rick Santorum	http://www.senate.gov/ ~santorum/
Representatives	Senator Arlen Specter	http://www.senate.gov/ ~specter/
Issues	Biodiversity	http://www.biodiversity.org
Issues	Butterflies	http://www.butterflies.com

The last thing you need to do to create the EnviroLink item data structure is to add the item to the tree control and assign the item handle to the hItem member of the TVITEM data structure. Add this line of code to the OnInitialUpdate() function of the CLeftView class:

```
m_treeItems[0].item.hItem = GetTreeCtrl().InsertItem( &m_treeItems[0] );
```

Pass a reference to the tree item data structure, &m_treeItems[0], to the tree control's InsertItem() function. The InsertItem() function returns the handle to the item, which you then assign to the item data structure's hItem member variable. That completes the first item in the m_treeItems array. If you compile and run the QuickBrowse application now, you will see one category listed in the left view, the News category, with a plus sign (+) to its left. Click on the plus sign (+), and the tree opens to display the EnviroLink item, as in Figure 6-5.

Figure 6-5
The QuickBrowse application with the first category and link item added

You create each of the other nine items in the same way, except use the handle for the particular category that the item is listed in and assign the correct text for the item. The way you add each of the remaining items, in order, is briefly described in the following sections.

Adding the Organizations Category

The Organizations category is the second category to add to the Quick-Browse application tree view. Add this line of code to the CLeftView class `OnInitialUpdate()` function after the code you added previously:

```
hItem = GetTreeCtrl().InsertItem("Organizations");
```

Adding the World Wildlife Fund Item

Add the World Wildlife Fund item to the Organizations category. There is nothing new in the code used to fill this item's data structure, shown next, except that this is the second member of the `m_treeItems` array and you assign `"World Wildlife Fund"` to the `pszText` variable:

```
m_treeItems[1].hParent = hItem;
m_treeItems[1].hInsertAfter = TVI_SORT;
m_treeItems[1].item.mask = TVIF_TEXT;
m_treeItems[1].item.pszText = "World Wildlife Fund";
m_treeItems[1].item.hItem = GetTreeCtrl().InsertItem( &m_treeItems[1] );
```

The tree item handle assigned to the hItem **variable is to the Organizations item, since you place the code creating the World Wildlife Fund item data structure after the code that inserts the Organizations item into the tree control.**

Adding the Sierra Club Item

Add the Sierra Club item to the Organizations category. There is nothing new in the code used to fill this item's data structure, shown next, except that this is the third member of the m_treeItems array and you assign "Sierra Club" to the pszText variable:

```
m_treeItems[2].hParent = hItem;
m_treeItems[2].hInsertAfter = TVI_SORT;
m_treeItems[2].item.mask = TVIF_TEXT;
m_treeItems[2].item.pszText = "Sierra Club";
m_treeItems[2].item.hItem = GetTreeCtrl().InsertItem( &m_treeItems[2] );
```

The "Sierra Club" item ends up listed before the "World Wildlife Fund" item since TVI_SORT **was assigned to the** hInsertAfter **variable and 'S' goes before 'W'.**

Adding the Local Subcategory

Creating a subcategory is similar to creating hyperlink items under a category. In fact, the difference is only in the implementation of user interaction that you work on later in this chapter. The code you use to add the Local subcategory to the Organizations category, listed here, is similar to the code you used to add the previous items:

```
m_treeItems[3].hParent = hItem;
m_treeItems[3].hInsertAfter = TVI_LAST;
m_treeItems[3].item.mask = TVIF_TEXT;
m_treeItems[3].item.pszText = "Local";
m_treeItems[3].item.hItem = GetTreeCtrl().InsertItem( &m_treeItems[3] );
```

The main difference is that the TVI_LAST integer constant is assigned to the data structure's hInsertAfter member variable. That's simply because we want to keep the subcategories somewhat separate from the hyperlink items. Rather than mixing in the Local subcategory alphabetically with the hyperlink items, it's put last in the list under the Organizations category.

Adding the Sierra Club Allegheny Group Item

Adding an item to a subcategory is somewhat different than adding an item to the root items. However, the difference is trivial. A quick glance at the code for creating the Sierra Club Allegheny Group item data structure, listed here, confirms that the code isn't much different than the code you wrote earlier to add hyperlink items to a category:

```
m_treeItems[4].hParent = m_treeItems[3].item.hItem;
m_treeItems[4].hInsertAfter = TVI_SORT;
m_treeItems[4].item.mask = TVIF_TEXT;
m_treeItems[4].item.pszText = "Sierra Club Allegheny Group";
m_treeItems[4].item.hItem = GetTreeCtrl().InsertItem( &m_treeItems[4] );
```

On closer examination, you see that the first line of code is a bit different. The previous data structure's hItem member variable is assigned to the current data structure's hParent member variable.

The handle to the Organizations item remains assigned to the hItem variable. However, you want the Sierra Club Allegheny Group item to be a child of the Local subcategory item. The Local item is the fourth data structure in the m_treeItems array. That's why you assign the item handle in the fourth item in the array to the hParent variable in the data structure of the new, fifth, array item. That makes the Local item the parent of the Sierra Club Allegheny Group item.

Recall that C++ arrays are zero-indexed. That is, the fourth item in an array is accessed with an index of 3, and the fifth item in an array is accessed with an index of 4.

Adding the Representatives Category

Adding the Representatives category is just like adding the other root items to the tree control. Type the statement shown in the CLeftView class OnInitialUpdate() function after the other code you added:

```
hItem = GetTreeCtrl().InsertItem("Representatives");
```

Adding the President Bill Clinton Item

Type in this code to add the President Bill Clinton hyperlink item to the Representatives category:

```
m_treeItems[5].hParent = hItem;
m_treeItems[5].hInsertAfter = TVI_SORT;
m_treeItems[5].item.mask = TVIF_TEXT;
m_treeItems[5].item.pszText = "President Bill Clinton";
m_treeItems[5].item.hItem = GetTreeCtrl().InsertItem( &m_treeItems[5] );
```

Adding the Senator Rick Santorum Item

Type in this code to add the Senator Rick Santorum hyperlink item to the Representatives category:

```
m_treeItems[6].hParent = hItem;
m_treeItems[6].hInsertAfter = TVI_SORT;
m_treeItems[6].item.mask = TVIF_TEXT;
m_treeItems[6].item.pszText = "Senator Rick Santorum";
m_treeItems[6].item.hItem = GetTreeCtrl().InsertItem( &m_treeItems[6] );
```

Adding the Senator Arlen Specter Item

Type in this code to add the Senator Arlen Specter hyperlink item to the Representatives category:

```
m_treeItems[7].hParent = hItem;
m_treeItems[7].hInsertAfter = TVI_SORT;
m_treeItems[7].item.mask = TVIF_TEXT;
m_treeItems[7].item.pszText = "Senator Arlen Specter";
m_treeItems[7].item.hItem = GetTreeCtrl().InsertItem( &m_treeItems[7] );
```

Adding the Issues Category

Add the last category, the Issues category, by typing this statement into the CLeftView class OnInitialUpdate() function:

```
hItem = GetTreeCtrl().InsertItem("Issues");
```

Adding the Biodiversity Item

Type in this code to add the Biodiversity hyperlink item to the Issues category:

```
m_treeItems[8].hParent = hItem;
m_treeItems[8].hInsertAfter = TVI_SORT;
m_treeItems[8].item.mask = TVIF_TEXT;
m_treeItems[8].item.pszText = "Biodiversity";
m_treeItems[8].item.hItem = GetTreeCtrl().InsertItem( &m_treeItems[8] );
```

Adding the Butterflies Item

Type in this code to add the Butterflies hyperlink item to the Issues category:

```
m_treeItems[9].hParent = hItem;
m_treeItems[9].hInsertAfter = TVI_SORT;
m_treeItems[9].item.mask = TVIF_TEXT;
m_treeItems[9].item.pszText = "Butterflies";
m_treeItems[9].item.hItem = GetTreeCtrl().InsertItem( &m_treeItems[9] );
```

Viewing the Tree View

The QuickBrowser tree view structure is complete. You added the private m_treeItems member variable, declared as a ten-member array, to the CLeftView class. This declaration should be part of the CLeftView class declaration file, LeftView.h, under the private keyword:

```
TVINSERTSTRUCT m_treeItems[10];
```

You also added many lines of code to the CLeftView class OnInitialUp-date() function. These are highlighted in bold type in Listing 6.1.

Listing 6.1 The CLeftView class OnInitialUpdate()
function in LeftView.cpp

```
void CLeftView::OnInitialUpdate()
{
    CTreeView::OnInitialUpdate();

    // TODO: You may populate your TreeView with items by directly accessing
    //   its tree control through a call to GetTreeCtrl().

    long lStyleOld = GetWindowLong(m_hWnd, GWL_STYLE);
    lStyleOld = lStyleOld | TVS_HASLINES | TVS_HASBUTTONS | TVS_LINESATROOT;
    SetWindowLong(m_hWnd, GWL_STYLE, lStyleOld);

    HTREEITEM hItem = GetTreeCtrl().InsertItem("News");

    m_treeItems[0].hParent = hItem;
    m_treeItems[0].hInsertAfter = TVI_SORT;
    m_treeItems[0].item.mask = TVIF_TEXT;
    m_treeItems[0].item.pszText = "EnviroLink";
    m_treeItems[0].item.hItem = GetTreeCtrl().InsertItem( &m_treeItems[0] );

    hItem = GetTreeCtrl().InsertItem("Organizations");

    m_treeItems[1].hParent = hItem;
    m_treeItems[1].hInsertAfter = TVI_SORT;
    m_treeItems[1].item.mask = TVIF_TEXT;
    m_treeItems[1].item.pszText = "World Wildlife Fund";
    m_treeItems[1].item.hItem = GetTreeCtrl().InsertItem( &m_treeItems[1] );

    m_treeItems[2].hParent = hItem;
    m_treeItems[2].hInsertAfter = TVI_SORT;
    m_treeItems[2].item.mask = TVIF_TEXT;
    m_treeItems[2].item.pszText = "Sierra Club";
    m_treeItems[2].item.hItem = GetTreeCtrl().InsertItem( &m_treeItems[2] );

    m_treeItems[3].hParent = hItem;
    m_treeItems[3].hInsertAfter = TVI_LAST;
    m_treeItems[3].item.mask = TVIF_TEXT;
    m_treeItems[3].item.pszText = "Local";
    m_treeItems[3].item.hItem = GetTreeCtrl().InsertItem( &m_treeItems[3] );
```

```
  m_treeItems[4].hParent = m_treeItems[3].item.hItem;
  m_treeItems[4].hInsertAfter = TVI_SORT;
  m_treeItems[4].item.mask = TVIF_TEXT;
  m_treeItems[4].item.pszText = "Sierra Club Allegheny Group";
  m_treeItems[4].item.hItem = GetTreeCtrl().InsertItem( &m_treeItems[4] );

  hItem = GetTreeCtrl().InsertItem("Representatives");

  m_treeItems[5].hParent = hItem;
  m_treeItems[5].hInsertAfter = TVI_SORT;
  m_treeItems[5].item.mask = TVIF_TEXT;
  m_treeItems[5].item.pszText = "President Bill Clinton";
  m_treeItems[5].item.hItem = GetTreeCtrl().InsertItem( &m_treeItems[5] );

  m_treeItems[6].hParent = hItem;
  m_treeItems[6].hInsertAfter = TVI_SORT;
  m_treeItems[6].item.mask = TVIF_TEXT;
  m_treeItems[6].item.pszText = "Senator Rick Santorum";
  m_treeItems[6].item.hItem = GetTreeCtrl().InsertItem( &m_treeItems[6] );

  m_treeItems[7].hParent = hItem;
  m_treeItems[7].hInsertAfter = TVI_SORT;
  m_treeItems[7].item.mask = TVIF_TEXT;
  m_treeItems[7].item.pszText = "Senator Arlen Specter";
  m_treeItems[7].item.hItem = GetTreeCtrl().InsertItem( &m_treeItems[7] );

  hItem = GetTreeCtrl().InsertItem("Issues");

  m_treeItems[8].hParent = hItem;
  m_treeItems[8].hInsertAfter = TVI_SORT;
  m_treeItems[8].item.mask = TVIF_TEXT;
  m_treeItems[8].item.pszText = "Biodiversity";
  m_treeItems[8].item.hItem = GetTreeCtrl().InsertItem( &m_treeItems[8] );

  m_treeItems[9].hParent = hItem;
  m_treeItems[9].hInsertAfter = TVI_SORT;
  m_treeItems[9].item.mask = TVIF_TEXT;
  m_treeItems[9].item.pszText = "Butterflies";
  m_treeItems[9].item.hItem = GetTreeCtrl().InsertItem( &m_treeItems[9] );
}
```

Once you're satisfied that the code is entered correctly, build the
QuickBrowse project by clicking on the Build button on the Visual
C++ toolbar or select the Build QuickBrowse.exe command from the
Build menu. Once Visual C++ is finished building the application, click

Your computer should be connected to the Internet when you launch the QuickBrowser application.

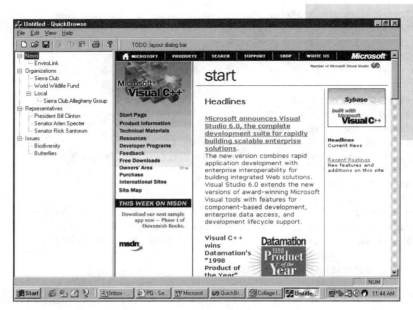

Figure 6-6
QuickBrowse displays the complete tree control structure in the left view after you click on all of the plus signs (+).

on the Execute Program button on the toolbar or select the Execute QuickBrowse.exe command from the Build menu. The QuickBrowse application should appear and display your new tree control structure in the left view, as in Figure 6-6.

You implemented the complete tree control structure, but when the QuickBrowse application is launched it still automatically loads a page from the Visual C++ Web site; you can click on the tree view items as much as you want but nothing happens. Your next task is to connect the action of a user clicking on a tree control item displayed in the left view with the loading of the item's associated Web page into the HTML control displayed in the right pane.

Connecting User Interaction and Web Page Display

Users click on tree link items in the QuickBrowse left view to load Web pages in right view. Now that you've created the tree, you need to add the code that listens for a double mouse click on a hyperlink item in the tree control and then loads the appropriate Web page in the HTML control displayed in the right view. Accomplish this task by performing these four steps:

1. Add the Uniform Resource Locator (URL) resources to the project.

2. Add a public member variable, m_strURL, which holds the current URL resource to the QuickBrowse document class, CQuickBrowseDoc.

3. Add a message map to the CLeftView class that intercepts the WM_LBUTTONDBLCLK message (window message, double-click of the left mouse button) produced when a user double-clicks the left mouse button in the QuickBrowse left view.

4. Add program logic to the CLeftView class OnLButtonDblClk() function that checks which tree item was clicked on, assigns the proper URL to the CQuickBrowseDoc class member variable m_strURL, and causes the right pane to update.

Adding the URL Resources

QuickBrowse uses a list of nine Web addresses, known as URLs, to load the nine Web pages corresponding to the nine hyperlink items listed in its tree view. The URLs are strings of individual characters, known simply as strings, that are best stored as string resources.

Visual C++ makes creating and using resources simple with its integrated resource tools, including the string table. Open the Project window to the ResourceView page by clicking on the ResourceView tab. Once the tree of the QuickBrowse resources is displayed, open the QuickBrowse resources tree by clicking on the plus sign (+) next to the

QuickBrowse resources item and then open the listings under String Table by clicking on the plus sign (+) to the left of the String Table folder. Double-click on the String Table item under the String Table folder to load the string table resources, as in Figure 6-7.

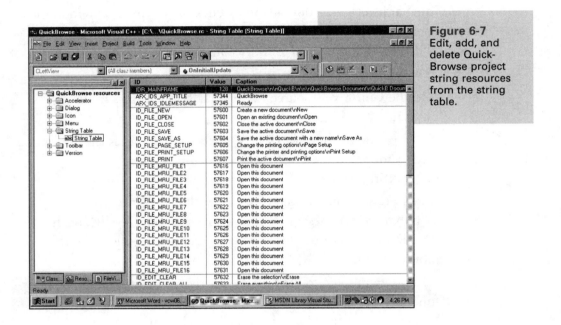

Figure 6-7
Edit, add, and delete Quick-Browse project string resources from the string table.

You went over the nine Web addresses accessed by the nine hyperlink items in the tree view in Chapter 3. Table 6.4, shown earlier, reproduces the list from that chapter. Table 6.5 lists the nine string resource identifiers and corresponding Web addresses.

Table 6.5 QuickBrowse String Resource Identifiers and Web Addresses	
String Resource ID	**Web Address**
IDS_ENVIROLINK	http://www.envirolink.org
IDS_WORLD_WILDLIFE_FUND	http://www.wwf.org
IDS_SIERRA_CLUB	http://www.sierraclub.org
IDS_SIERRA_CLUB_ALLEGHENY_GROUP	http://host.envirolink.org/allegheny-sc/
IDS_PRESIDENT_BILL_CLINTON	http://www.whitehouse.gov
IDS_SENATOR_RICK_SANTORUM	http://www.senate.gov/~santorum/
IDS_SENATOR_ARLEN_SPECTER	http://www.senate.gov/~specter/
IDS_BIODIVERSITY	http://www.biodiversity.org
IDS_BUTTERFLIES	http://www.butterflies.com

Begin by adding the EnviroLink Web address to the string table. Point anywhere in the String Table resources window and press your right mouse button. A shortcut menu appears. Select the New String command from the shortcut menu; the String Properties dialog box appears, as in Figure 6-8.

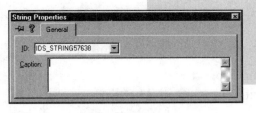

Figure 6-8
Add and edit strings in a string table through the String Properties dialog box.

Figure 6-9
The String Properties
dialog box filled in
with the EnviroLink
string identifier and
Web address

The identifier displayed in the String Properties dialog box ID text box
and drop-down list depends on where you were pointing. It always
begins with IDS_STRING but ends with the particular ID number automatically assigned to the string identifier. Supply a meaningful string
identifier and your own different and unique number. Type this into the
ID text box:

```
IDS_ENVIROLINK=10000
```

This sets the string identifier to IDS_ENVIROLINK, which is meaningful,
since it's used to identify the EnviroLink URL. An equals sign after a
string identifier followed by a number sets the identifier to a number of
your own choice. It's handy to have your string identifiers together in
their own group in the string table. Giving them numbers that are continuous but not continuous with other numbers in the table does the
job. Finally, type the actual EnviroLink Web address shown into the
String Properties dialog box Caption text area:

```
http://www.envirolink.org
```

The String Properties dialog box should look like that in Figure 6-9.

Click anywhere outside the String Properties dialog box or click the little button at the upper right with the x on it. The dialog box should
close and the EnviroLink string identifier and Web address is added to
the string table, as in Figure 6-10.

Add the rest of the URLs to the string table in the same way except let
Visual C++ automatically assign contiguous integers to the string identifiers, rather than setting them manually. For example, add the World
Wildlife Fund URL to the string table by pointing to the EnviroLink
entry and pressing your right mouse button. A shortcut menu appears.

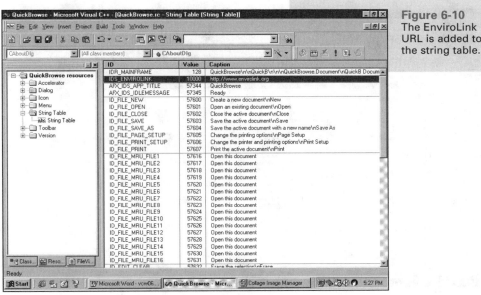

Figure 6-10
The EnviroLink
URL is added to
the string table.

Select the New String command and the String Properties dialog box appears with this string identifier in the ID text box and drop-down list:

```
IDS_STRING10001
```

The number at the end of the identifier is one larger than the number you assigned to the EnviroLink identifier. That's just what you want. Modify the string to IDS_WORLD_WILDLIFE_FUND, type http://www.wwf.org into the Caption text area, and close the dialog box.

Notice that Visual C++ adds the new string identifier and URL to the string table and then automatically adds a new blank line under it, which is then highlighted. Simply start typing the URL for your next entry, this time the Sierra Club URL http://www.sierraclub.org, and the String Properties dialog box automatically appears. Modify the string identifier to IDS_SIERRA_CLUB, close the dialog box, and you've added the Sierra Club string identifier and URL to the string table. Repeat this action for each of the remaining URLs listed in Table 6.5. When you're finished you should have nine new string IDs, values, and URLs listed in the QuickBrowse string table, as in Figure 6-11.

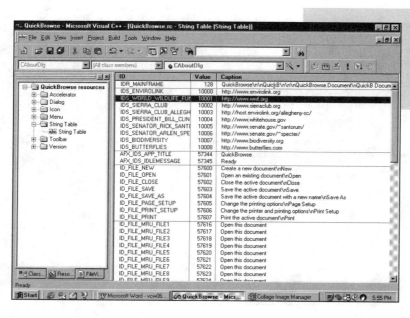

Figure 6-11
The Quick-
Browse string
table is
displaying all
nine new entries.

Note Start your string identifiers with "IDS," standing for ID String, followed by an underscore and the title all in capital letters. Separate each word in the title with an underscore.

Save the new string resources by clicking on the Save button in the Visual C++ toolbar or by selecting the Save command from the File menu. Then close the string table by clicking on the button with the x at the level of the Visual C++ menu bar.

You just added the nine Web addresses to the QuickBrowse project that correspond to the nine hyperlink items listed in the tree view of the QuickBrowse application. The QuickBrowse application uses the Web addresses to load and display Web pages from the nine Web sites. It does this by assigning the address of the currently selected Web site to a variable and then accessing that variable when a Web page is to be displayed.

Adding a URL Resource Variable to the Document Class

The MFC document/view architecture stipulates that program data are associated with the application's document class and are displayed in some way by the application's view class. In the QuickBrowser application, users select the current data displayed in the main (right) view by clicking on tree items in the left view. User interaction with the tree in the left view sets the data, the URL, assigned to a public variable, m_strURL, in the QuickBrowse document class, CQuickBrowseDoc. The string assigned to the m_strURL variable, in turn, defines the Web page that is loaded in the right pane or the CQuickBrowseView object.

To add the variable, point to CQuickBrowseDoc in the ClassView page of the Project window and press your right mouse button. A shortcut menu appears. Select the Add Member Variable command from the shortcut menu; the Add Member Variable dialog box appears, as in Figure 6-12.

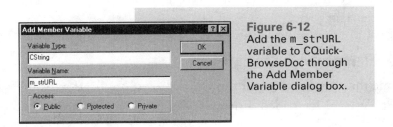

Figure 6-12
Add the m_strURL variable to CQuick-BrowseDoc through the Add Member Variable dialog box.

Type the variable data type, CString, into the Add Member Variable dialog box Variable Type text box. The CString class is a powerful MFC class used for storing and manipulating character strings. Type the variable name, m_strURL, into the Variable Name text box and make sure that the Public radio button is selected in the Access area. Click on the OK button and the m_strURL variable is added to the CQuickBrowseDoc class. The variable should appear in the ClassView page tree under the CQuickBrowseDoc listing.

You never want an unknown value assigned to the m_strURL variable. Initialize the variable in the CQuickBrowseDoc class constructor. Double-click on the CQuickBrowseDoc() listing under the CQuickBrowseDoc class in the ClassView page of the Project window. The Visual C++ document window should be opened to the CQuickBrowseDoc class constructor definition. Under the "TODO" remark in the class constructor add this line of code:

```
m_strURL.LoadString(IDS_ENVIROLINK); // Default Web site
```

The CString class LoadString() function is called. The LoadString() function loads a string from the string resource determined by the string resource identifier you pass. In this case, the IDS_ENVIROLINK identifier is passed to the LoadString() function, making the EnviroLink Web site the default.

You added a public member variable, m_strURL, which holds the current URL to the document class of the QuickBrowse application. Next you need to modify code in the CQuickBrowseView class so that Web pages pointed to by the string assigned to the m_strURL variable are loaded and displayed by the right pane.

Loading Web Pages

From the time that you first created the QuickBrowse application using the MFC AppWizard, it loaded a default Web page, a page from the Visual C++ Web site. The code that loads the Web page, shown here, was added to the CQuickBrowseView class OnInitialUpdate() function by the wizard:

```
Navigate2(_T("http://www.microsoft.com/visualc/"),NULL,NULL);
```

The statement is inserted below the "TODO" remark in the function, as shown in Figure 6-13.

The Navigate2() function is a member of the CHtmlView class, which is the base class from which CQuickBrowseView is derived. A string representing the address of the Web page that is loaded and displayed in the view is passed to the function's first parameter. The other two parameters are passed NULL values. You need to modify this statement so that

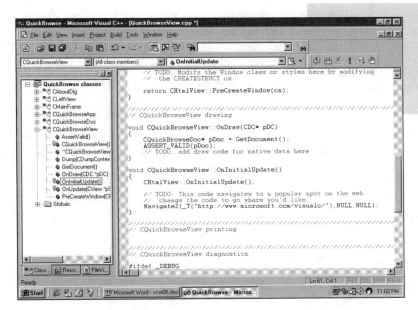

Figure 6-13
The MFC
AppWizard
provides a
default call to the
Navigate2()
function.

the string assigned to the m_strURL variable in the CQuickBrowseDoc class is passed to Navigate2() function.

Public members of document classes are available to view classes through GetDocument() functions, implemented by every view class. These functions return a pointer to the particular document class implemented by the application; in this case, it's a pointer to CQuickBrowseDoc objects.

Tip

You can examine the GetDocument() **implementation by double-clicking on the function listing in the ClassView page of the Project window. You will find an inline function that returns a pointer to the value assigned to the** m_pDocument **variable. You can use the Visual C++ browse tools, accessible through the Goto Definition command from the shortcut menu, to explore the parent class where the variable is defined and initialized.**

Add these two lines of code in the CQuickBrowseView class OnInitialUpdate() function before the statement containing the Navigate2() function:

```
CQuickBrowseDoc* pDoc = GetDocument();
ASSERT_VALID(pDoc);
```

The first statement calls the CQuickBrowseView class GetDocument() function and assigns the returned pointer to the CQuickBrowseDoc object to the pDoc variable. The second statement uses a macro for error checking. You learn more about error checking in Chapter 7.

Once you have a pointer to the document object, it's a simple thing to access the public m_strURL variable. Replace the default statement containing the Navigate2() function with this statement:

```
Navigate2(_T(pDoc->m_strURL),NULL,NULL);
```

The statement now accesses the m_strURL variable in the document object and passes the string to the Navigate2() function's first parameter.

With these modifications, QuickBrowse application's right view is properly loaded with a Web page and displayed on initial start up. However, there is one more thing you must do so that further updates to the view are carried out correctly, for instance, when you load a new Web page by clicking on a tree item in the left view. You need to add the same code that you added to the OnInitialUpdate() function to the CQuickBrowseView class OnUpdate() function.

Double-click on the OnUpdate() listing under CQuickBrowseView in the ClassView page of the Project window and type these three lines of code under the "TODO" remarks in the function:

```
CQuickBrowseDoc* pDoc = GetDocument();
ASSERT_VALID(pDoc);
Navigate2(_T(pDoc->m_strURL),NULL,NULL);
```

QuickBrowse now loads and displays the Web page pointed to by the URL assigned to the m_strURL variable, as in Figure 6-14. The m_strURL variable is a member of the application's document object. Your final task is to make the application responsive to user interaction with the tree items in the left view.

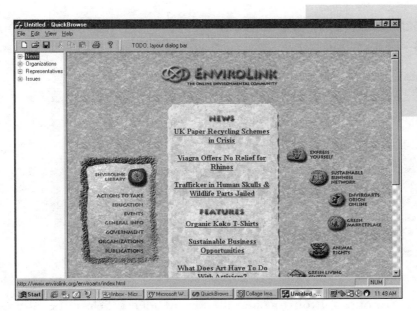

Figure 6-14
The EnviroLink address is assigned to the m_strURL variable by default.

User Interaction

QuickBrowse users double-click on hyperlink items in the left pane's tree to load Web pages in the HTML control and display them in the right pane. Message mapping functions provide the key to connecting user actions to program activity.

Each time a user carries out an action in an application's graphic interface, such as pointing the mouse cursor and pressing a mouse button, a message specific to the action is generated. Message-mapping functions sift through the generated messages looking for specific messages, a message indicating the double-click of the left mouse button, for instance. When the message is found, the function carries out an action that often depends on information carried by the message itself.

Add a message map function to the CLeftView class that looks for messages created by double-clicking the left mouse button (the WM_LBUTTONDBLCLK message) in the left-view user interface. Point to CLeftView in the ClassView page of the Workspace window and press

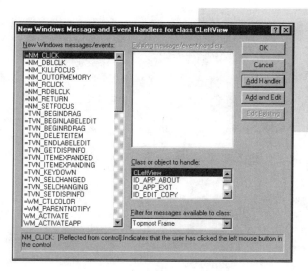

Figure 6-15
Create a message
map function
through the New
Windows Message
and Event Handlers
for Class CLeftView
dialog box.

your right mouse button to open a shortcut menu. Select the Add
Windows Message Handler command from the shortcut menu; the
New Windows Message and Event Handlers for Class CLeftView dialog
box appears, as in Figure 6-15.

Find and select WM_LBUTTONDBLCLK windows message (indicates double-
click of left mouse button), in the New Windows Messages/Events list
on the left side of the dialog box. Make sure that the CLeftView class
is selected in the Class or Object to Handle list. Finally, leave the
default Topmost Frame selected in the Filter for Messages Available to
Class drop-down list. Click on the Add Handler button and the
WM_LBUTTONDBLCLK event handler is added to the CLeftView class. The
New Windows Message and Event Handlers for Class CLeftView dialog
box should look like in Figure 6-16.

Go to the new event handler function by clicking on the Edit Existing
button in the New Windows Message and Event Handlers for Class
CLeftView dialog box. The Visual C++ document window displays the
LeftView.cpp file opened to the new OnLButtonDblClk() message handling function, as in Figure 6-17.

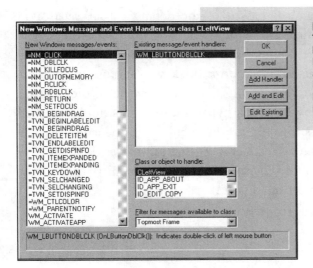

Figure 6-16
The WM_LBUTTON
DBLCLK event
handler has been
added as indicated
in the dialog box's
Existing Message/
Event Handlers list.

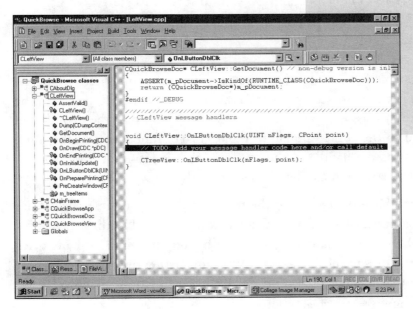

Figure 6-17
Pressing the Edit
Exiting button
takes you
directly to the
definition of the
new message
handling
function.

Notice that a CPoint value is passed to the default OnLButtonDblClk() function's second parameter, providing the function with the screen coordinates of the mouse pointer when the left mouse button was double-clicked. Access to this information is the key to setting up an effective key mapping function. The main thing the QuickBrowse application needs to know is which hyperlink item was double-clicked in the left view. You pass the CPoint value assigned to the point variable to the CTreeCtrl class HitTest() member function to get the handle to the tree item that was double-clicked. Add this statement right after the "TODO" remark in the OnLButtonDblClk() function:

```
HTREEITEM hItem = GetTreeCtrl().HitTest(point);
```

> **Note** The one default statement in the CLeftView class
> OnLButtonDblClk() **function is a call to the CTreeView class**
> OnLButtonDblClk() **function. Be sure to leave this statement as
> it is and at the end of any code that you add.**

The statement uses the GetTreeCtrl() function inherited from the CTreeView class to get a pointer to the tree control object, and then the CTreeCtrl() class HitTest() function is called. You pass the coordinates assigned to the point variable to the HitTest() function, and the function returns the handle of the tree item that is found at those coordinates. The tree item handle is assigned to the hItem variable.

Once you have the handle to the tree item that was double-clicked, it's simply a matter of identifying the hyperlink item and loading the appropriate Web page. You identify the item by looping through the ten tree item structures in the m_treeItems array and testing their handles against the one that was returned from the HitTest() function, as shown here:

```
for (int iCount = 0; iCount < 10; iCount++) {
  if ( m_treeItems[iCount].item.hItem == hItem ) {
    ...
  }
  ...
}
```

> **Note**
>
> The **...** in the body of the `if` statement and part of the `for` loop indicates that you will add code there shortly. Focus on the first two lines of code for now.

When the conditional in the `if` statement is true, the number assigned to the `iCount` variable indicates the tree item structure in the `m_treeItems` array that corresponds to the item that the user double-clicked on. Create a local CString variable named `strTemp` in the body of the `if` statement and then add a `switch` statement using the `iCount` variable. The `switch` statement contains a lot of code, so it's best to follow this programming logic by looking at the completed `OnLButtonDblClk()` function code in Listing 6.2. The code you add, including the statements you just added, is highlighted in bold type.

Listing 6.2 The CLeftView Class OnLButtonDblClk() Function in LeftView.cpp

```cpp
void CLeftView::OnLButtonDblClk(UINT nFlags, CPoint point)
{
    // TODO: Add your message handler code here and/or call default
    HTREEITEM hItem = GetTreeCtrl().HitTest(point);
    for (int iCount = 0; iCount < 10; iCount++) {
        if ( m_treeItems[iCount].item.hItem == hItem ) {
            CString strTemp = "";
            switch (iCount) {
                case 0:
                    strTemp.LoadString(IDS_ENVIROLINK);
                    break;
                case 1:
                    strTemp.LoadString(IDS_WORLD_WILDLIFE_FUND);
                    break;
                case 2:
                    strTemp.LoadString(IDS_SIERRA_CLUB);
                    break;
                case 4:
                    strTemp.LoadString(IDS_SIERRA_CLUB_ALLEGHENY_GROUP);
                    break;
                case 5:
                    strTemp.LoadString(IDS_PRESIDENT_BILL_CLINTON);
                    break;
```

```
          case 6:
            strTemp.LoadString(IDS_SENATOR_RICK_SANTORUM);
            break;
          case 7:
            strTemp.LoadString(IDS_SENATOR_ARLEN_SPECTOR);
            break;
          case 8:
            strTemp.LoadString(IDS_BIODIVERSITY);
            break;
          case 9:
            strTemp.LoadString(IDS_BUTTERFLIES);
            break;
        }
      if( strTemp != "" ) {
        GetDocument()->m_strURL = strTemp;
        GetDocument()->UpdateAllViews(NULL);

      }
    }
  }
  CTreeView::OnLButtonDblClk(nFlags, point);
}
```

Each case in the switch statement tests the iCount variable to see if it is one of the nine hyperlink items stored as tree item structures between members 0 and 9 of the m_treeItems array. Since C++ uses zero-based array indexing, the fourth member, number 3, is assigned the Local tree item structure, which isn't a hyperlink item. The number assigned to iCount must be one of these nine numbers, or nothing happens. When it is one of the nine numbers, the LoadString() function is called from the temporary CString variable named strTemp. The string resource appropriate to the hyperlink item that was double-clicked on is assigned to the strTemp variable. Recall that these string resources are the actual Web addresses that are used to load the Web pages.

The two statements reproduced here are executed after the switch statement as long as a string was assigned to the strTemp variable:

```
GetDocument()->m_strURL = strTemp;
GetDocument()->UpdateAllViews(NULL);
```

The first statement assigns the string, a Web address, from the strTemp variable to the application's document object m_strURL variable. Then the document object's UpdateAllViews() function is called, which forces an update of the application views resulting in the display of the newly requested Web page.

You've now completed the code that enables user interaction in the QuickBrowse application! Build the project and try it out. The rest of your work on QuickBrowse will be to polish off the interface by making the menus and toolbar slicker and more useful.

Modifying the Menus and Toolbar

QuickBrowse provides a tree of hyperlink items that you can double-click on to load Web pages into the right view, but its current menus and toolbar are less than helpful in the Web environment. Modify the menus and toolbar so that you can easily move forward and backward and stop downloading a Web page or refresh your Web page display.

Modifying the Menus

Modify the QuickBrowse menus so that they better reflect useful commands for the Web browser user. For instance, the editing commands currently available under the Edit menu are not useful for the Web browser, and the absence of menu commands for stopping or refreshing Web page downloads is a handicap for the Web browsing individual. Click on the ResourceView tab to switch to the Resource-View page of the Project Workplace window. Click on the plus sign (+) to the left of the QuickBrowse resources folder and then click on the plus sign (+) to the left of the Menu subfolder. Finally, double-click on the IDR_MAINFRAME item to open the QuickBrowse menu resource, as in Figure 6-18.

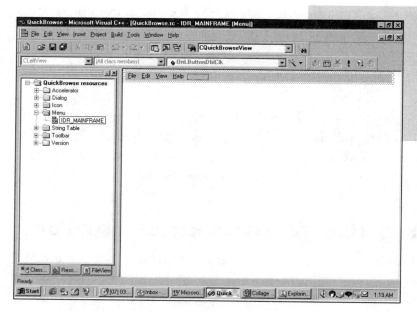

Figure 6-18
Edit menu resources visually in the Visual C++ menu editor displayed in the document window.

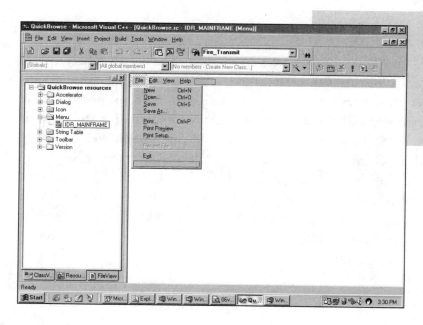

Figure 6-19
The default File menu created using the MFC AppWizard has commands inappropriate for a Web browser.

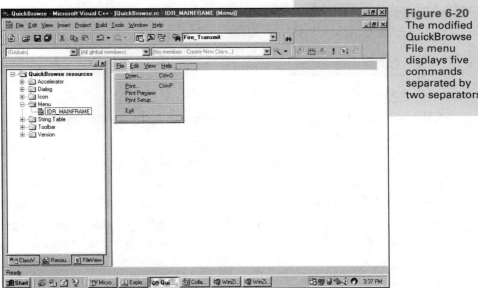

Figure 6-20
The modified QuickBrowse File menu displays five commands separated by two separators.

Click on File in the resource editor to display the File menu, as in Figure 6-19.

Only the Open, Print, Print Preview, Print Setup and Exit commands in the File menu are appropriate for a Web browser. Delete the other commands by selecting each command on the menu and then, while a highlight box surrounds the command, selecting Delete from the Visual C++ Edit menu or pressing the Delete key on your keyboard. Use the same procedure to delete extra separators in the menu. When you're finished, the File menu should look like in Figure 6-20.

Delete the entire Edit menu. Highlight the Edit menu and select Delete from the Visual C++ Edit menu or press the Delete key on your keyboard. The Microsoft Visual C++ dialog box appears, as in Figure 6-21.

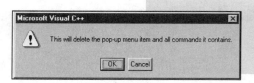

Figure 6-21
The Microsoft Visual C++ dialog box queries to make sure that you want to delete the Edit menu.

Click on the OK button in the Microsoft Visual C++ dialog box, since you do want to delete the entire Edit menu.

Next, add two new commands to the View menu: the Stop and Refresh commands. Open the View menu in the resource editor and double-click your left mouse button while pointing to the blank line at the end of the menu. The Menu Item Properties dialog box appears. Insert a separator here by checking the Separator check box, as in Figure 6-22.

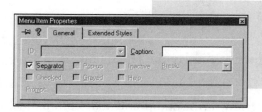

Figure 6-22
Add a separator to a menu by checking the Separator check box on the Menu Item Properties dialog box.

Close the Menu Item Properties dialog box by clicking outside the dialog box or by clicking on the button displaying the x at the upper-right corner of the dialog box.

Next, add the Stop command by highlighting the blank line after the separator you just added and typing **Sto&p\tEsc.** The Menu Item Properties dialog box appears with Sto&p\tEsc displayed in the Caption text box. Type this text into the Prompt text box:

```
Stops opening a Web page.\nStop
```

Text in the Prompt text box is displayed in the application's status bar when the command is selected, and the text after the new line character (\n) is displayed as a tool tip while you point to the command's toolbar button. The Menu Item Properties dialog box should look like that in Figure 6-23.

Note

The "&" character proceeds the menu item's accelerator key, in this case the letter "p." The accelerator key appears underlined on the menu. The "\t" is the tab character that inserts a tab between "Stop" and the alternate command key, "Esc."

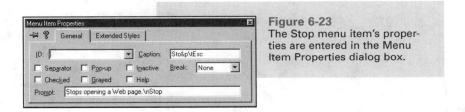

Figure 6-23
The Stop menu item's properties are entered in the Menu Item Properties dialog box.

Note

Visual C++ creates menu command identifier names that start with ID, for identifier, followed by an underscore and the menu name, VIEW for instance. Finally, another underscore is added followed by the command name, such as STOP.

You probably notice that the ID box is empty. Visual C++ creates the appropriate ID when you close the Menu Item Properties dialog box. Check this out by reopening the dialog box after you close it. You should see the new menu command identifier named ID_VIEW_STOP listed.

Add the Refresh command to the View menu in the same way. Highlight the blank line after the Stop command you just added and type `&Refresh\tF5`. The Menu Item Properties dialog box appears with &Refresh\tF5 displayed in the Caption text box. Type this text into the Prompt text box:

```
Refreshes the contents of the current page.\nRefresh
```

The completed QuickBrowse View menu should look that like in Figure 6-24.

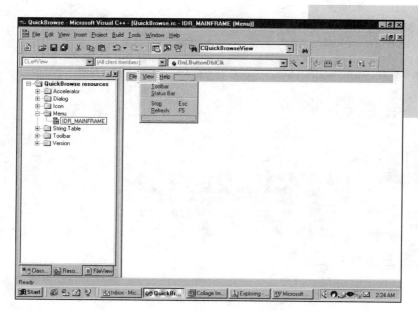

Figure 6-24
The modified
QuickBrowse
View menu
displays four
commands and
a separator.

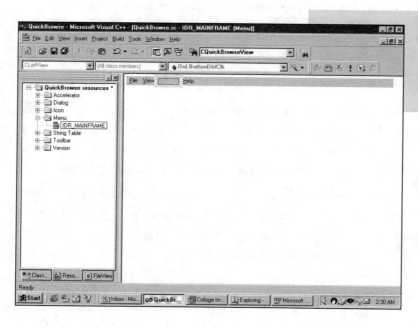

Figure 6-25
The Go menu
will be added in
the blank box
to the left of the
Help menu.

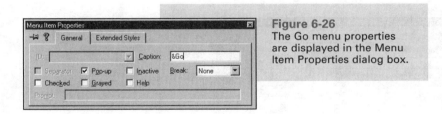

Figure 6-26
The Go menu properties
are displayed in the Menu
Item Properties dialog box.

Display the final two new commands, Back and Forward, on a new Go menu. On the menu bar in the resource editor, point to the empty box on the right side of the Help menu. Press and hold down your left mouse button while dragging the box to the left side of the Help menu, and then release the mouse button. The QuickBrowse menu bar should look like that in Figure 6-25.

With the blank box still highlighted, type in **&Go**. The Menu Item Properties dialog box appears with &Go displayed in the Caption text box and with the pop-up check box checked, as in Figure 6-26.

Close the dialog box and add the Back and Forward commands to the Go menu in the same way that you added commands to a menu before.

First add the Back command to the Go menu. Highlight the blank line and type **&Back\tAlt+Left Arrow**. The Menu Item Properties dialog box appears with &Back\tAlt+Left Arrow displayed in the Caption text box. Type this text into the Prompt text box:

```
Goes back one step.\nBack
```

Next add the Forward command to the Go menu. Highlight the blank line after the Back command and type **&Forward\tAlt+Right Arrow**. The Menu Item Properties dialog box appears with &Forward\tAlt+Right Arrow displayed in the Caption text box. Type this text into the Prompt text box:

```
Goes forward one step.\nForward
```

The completed QuickBrowse Go menu should look like that in Figure 6-27.

Figure 6-27
The new
QuickBrowse
Go menu
displays two
commands.

Adding Menu Logic

You connect user interaction with menu commands with procedures that the application carries out through mapping messages to functions. In fact, whenever you connect user interactions with program actions in Visual C++, it's through message maps and message map functions. You associate the menu identifiers assigned to each menu item by Visual C++ with a function.

Add the message map functions for the four new menu commands, Stop, Refresh, Back, and Forward, to the CQuickBrowseView through the ClassWizard. The message map function call CHtm class functions that are easily accessible from the QuickBrow class, since it is derived from the CHtmlView class. Select the Wizard command from the Visual C++ View menu. The MFC Wizard dialog box appears, as in Figure 6-28.

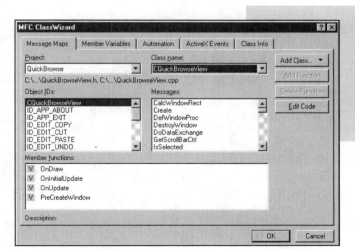

Figure 6-28
The Message Maps page of the MFC ClassWizard dialog box is displaying message map information for the CQuickBrowseView class.

Click on the Message Maps tab to display the Message Maps page of the MFC ClassWizard dialog box, if it isn't displayed already. Also, make sure that CQuickBrowseView is selected in the Class Name drop-down list.

You can see functions that are already created listed in the Member functions list toward the bottom of the MFC ClassWizard dialog box. The V you see to the left of each of these functions tells you that they are virtual functions.

Add a message map function for the View menu's Stop command. Select ID_VIEW_STOP in the Object IDs list. The contents of the Messages list should change when you select the message identifier. Select COMMAND in the Messages list. The MFC ClassWizard dialog box should look like that in Figure 6-29.

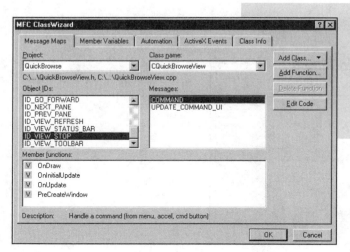

Figure 6-29
The appropriate object identifier and type of message handler are selected for the Stop command in the Message Maps page of the MFC ClassWizard dialog box.

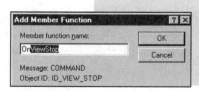

Figure 6-30
The Add Member Function dialog box provides a suggested name for the new function and displays the message map information.

Click on the Add Function button on the Message Maps page of the MFC ClassWizard dialog box. The Add Member Function dialog box appears, as in Figure 6-30.

Accept the function name suggested by Visual C++, OnViewStop(), by clicking on the OK button. The function along with the message map information is added to the Member Functions list. The W displayed to the left of the listing means that it's a window function.

The final step to adding a new message map function is to add the code that carries out the application's action in the body of the new function. With the OnViewStop() function still selected in the Member functions list of the MFC ClassWizard dialog box, click on the Edit Code button. You are taken directly to the new OnViewStop() function definition in the CQuickBrowseView class, as in Figure 6-31.

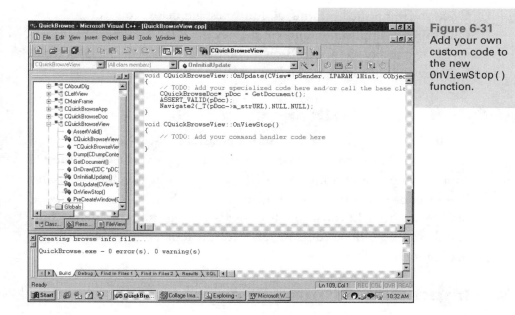

Figure 6-31
Add your own custom code to the new OnViewStop() function.

Type this line of code right after the "TODO" remark in the OnView-Stop() function definition:

```
Stop();
```

The statement is a simple call to the CHtmlView class Stop() function, which stops the downloading of a Web page. You are finished creating the Stop command's message map. Create the remaining three maps in the same way. Table 6.5 lists the information you need to create the message map functions in the MFC ClassWizard and the code you need to add to the new function created in the CQuickBrowseView class.

Table 6.5 Menu Command Message Map Information

Object IDs	Messages	Code
ID_VIEW_STOP	COMMAND	Stop();
ID_VIEW_REFRESH	COMMAND	Refresh();
ID_GO_BACK	COMMAND	GoBack();
ID_GO_FORWARD	COMMAND	GoForward();

Once you're finished creating all four message maps, you can build the QuickBrowse application and try the new menu commands. Your final task is to modify the QuickBrowse toolbar so that it only displays the four new commands that you just added.

Modifying the Toolbar

An application toolbar should provide easy access to commonly used commands. The default toolbar currently displayed by the QuickBrowse application provides commands that aren't useful in a Web browser and that just don't have that Web browser look and feel. In this section, you modify the QuickBrowse toolbar to display the four browsing commands you just added to its menus with the look and feel of the Internet Explorer toolbar.

Importing Bitmap Resources

The Back, Forward, Stop, and Refresh commands are the first four commands on the Internet Explorer toolbar. Use the same images that Internet Explorer uses for those commands to create the Quick-Browse toolbar.

The modified QuickBrowse toolbar is created from two bitmap files: coldtool.bmp and hottool.bmp. QuickBrowse displays the coldtool.bmp image almost all of the time. It's the pale version of the toolbar. When a user points to a particular button, then the hottool.bmp image for that button with its bright colors is displayed. Import these two bitmap image files and add them to the QuickBrowse resources.

 The coldtool.bmp and hottool.bmp files are available on the CD-ROM provided with this book.

Open the QuickBrowse project's Project Workspace window to the ResourceView page. Click your right mouse button while pointing to any of the resource folders and a shortcut menu appears. Select the

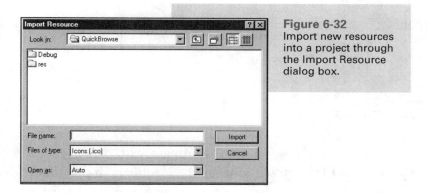

Figure 6-32
Import new resources into a project through the Import Resource dialog box.

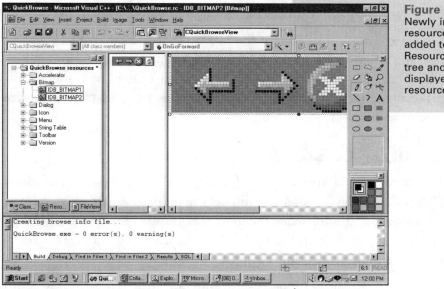

Figure 6-33
Newly imported resources are added to the ResourceView tree and are displayed in the resource editor.

Import command from the shortcut menu and the Import Resource dialog box appears, as in Figure 6-32.

Select All Files (*.*) in the Files of type drop-down list. Then change the current folder of the Import Resource dialog box to where the coldtool.bmp and hottool.bmp files reside. Select the two files and click on the Import button. The bitmaps are added to the ResourceView page under a Bitmap folder, as in Figure 6-33.

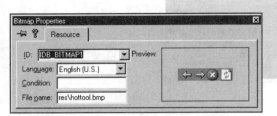

Figure 6-34
Change the identifier in the Bitmap Properties dialog box.

Visual C++ provides the newly imported bitmaps with default identifiers, IDB_BITMAP1 and IDB_BITMAP2. Change the identifiers so that they're more descriptive. Find the brightly colored bitmap, point to its listing on the ResourceView page, and press your right mouse button to open a shortcut menu. Select the Properties command from the shortcut menu; the Bitmap Properties dialog box appears, as in Figure 6-34.

Modify the name displayed in the Bitmap Properties dialog box ID text box and drop-down list so that it reads IDB_HOTTOOLBAR then close the dialog box. Do the same thing for the toolbar bitmap with muted colors, except change the identifier so that it reads IDB_COLDTOOLBAR. Be sure to save your work!

Toolbar Logic

You need to add many lines of code to QuickBrowse application's CMainFrame class to load and display the proper bitmap, set the size of the toolbar, and implement the logic that displays the hot toolbar button in full color. Open the CMainFrame class to the OnCreate() function, where the toolbar logic resides.

The first statement in the OnCreate() function created by the MFC App-Wizard should look like this:

```
if (CFrameWnd::OnCreate(lpCreateStruct) == -1)
  return -1;
```

This if statement includes a bootstrap call to the OnCreate() function. Right after this you should see this if statement:

```
if (!m_wndToolBar.CreateEx(this) ||
  !m_wndToolBar.LoadToolBar(IDR_MAINFRAME))
{
```

```
TRACE0("Failed to create toolbar\n");
return -1;        // fail to create
}
```

The first expression in the `if` statement creates a CToolBar object by calling the CToolBar class `CreateEx()` function. The second expression, ORed (¦¦) with the first expression, loads the `IDR_MAINFRAME` resource into the toolbar. You don't want this to happen anymore, since Quick-Browse will use the new bitmap resources that you just imported. Delete this expression so that the `if` statement reads like this:

```
if (!m_wndToolBar.CreateEx(this))
{
  TRACE0("Failed to create toolbar\n");
  return -1;        // fail to create
}
```

The third `if` statement provided by the MFC AppWizard is this:

```
if (!m_wndDlgBar.Create(this, IDR_MAINFRAME,
  CBRS_ALIGN_TOP, AFX_IDW_DIALOGBAR))
{
  TRACE0("Failed to create dialogbar\n");
  return -1;        // fail to create
}
```

The code in this `if` statement sets up the dialog bar. The QuickBrowse application won't use a dialog bar, however, so delete this entire `if` statement.

The fifth `if` statement provided in the `OnCreate()` function by the MFC AppWizard is reproduced here:

```
if (!m_wndReBar.Create(this) ¦¦
  !m_wndReBar.AddBar(&m_wndToolBar) ¦¦
  !m_wndReBar.AddBar(&m_wndDlgBar))
{
  TRACE0("Failed to create rebar\n");
  return -1;        // fail to create
}
```

The expressions in this statement create a CReBar object and then assign references to the CToolBar and CDialogBar objects to it. Delete the expressions that call the CReBar class `AddBar()` function and the OR operators (¦¦) so that the modified statement looks like this:

```
if (!m_wndReBar.Create(this))
{
  TRACE0("Failed to create rebar\n");
  return -1;       // fail to create
}
```

The sixth, and final, `if` statement provided in the `OnCreate()` function by the MFC AppWizard is reproduced here:

```
if (!m_wndStatusBar.Create(this) ||
  !m_wndStatusBar.SetIndicators(indicators,
  sizeof(indicators)/sizeof(UINT)))
{
  TRACE0("Failed to create status bar\n");
  return -1;       // fail to create
}
```

This statement creates the CStatusBar object and sets the indicators that it'll display. Leave this `if` statement intact as it is.

The next thing you should see in the CMainFrame class `OnCreate()` function is a "TODO" remark followed by a statement that sets the CToolBar object's style, as reproduced here:

```
// TODO: Remove this if you don't want tool tips
m_wndToolBar.SetBarStyle(m_wndToolBar.GetBarStyle() |
  CBRS_TOOLTIPS | CBRS_FLYBY);
```

Keep this statement but add another control bar style (CBRS) by doing a bitwise OR with the other two styles already used. The CBRS_TOOLTIPS style causes the toolbar to display tool tips and the CBRS_FLYBY style causes message text for the status bar to be updated at the same time as tool tips. Add the CBRS_SIZE_FIXED style to fix the size of the Quick-Browse toolbar buttons so that users can't change them. The modified statement should read like this:

```
// TODO: Remove this if you don't want tool tips
m_wndToolBar.SetBarStyle(m_wndToolBar.GetBarStyle() |
  CBRS_TOOLTIPS | CBRS_FLYBY | CBRS_SIZE_FIXED);
```

Only one statement is left that was added by the MFC AppWizard, the one reproduced here:

```
return 0;
```

Keep the `return` statement, which returns a `0` from the `OnCreate()` function when it successfully executes. Add all of the code that follows before the `return` statement.

Declare this local variable in the `OnCreate()` function before the `return` statement:

```
CImageList img;
```

The `img` variable data type is the CImageList class. The CImageList class encapsulates a collection of same-sized images, each of which can be referred to by its zero-based index. Perfect for holding toolbar button images.

Now you are ready to set up toolbar properties. Enter the following remark and statement:

```
// set up toolbar properties
m_wndToolBar.GetToolBarCtrl().SetButtonWidth(50, 150);
```

The CToolBar class is a wrapper class of the toolbar control, represented in the MFC library by the CToolBarCtrl class. You have access to the toolbar control functions, such as the `SetButtonWidth()` function, through the `GetToolBarCtrl()` function that returns a reference to a CToolBarCtrl object.

The CToolBarCtrl class `SetButtonWidth()` function sets the range of widths that the toolbar buttons can display. The first parameter, which is passed a `50`, sets the minimum button width in pixels, and the second parameter, which is passed a `150`, sets the maximum button width in pixels.

Next you create a temporary image list encapsulated by the CImageList object assigned to the `img` variable. Call the CImageList class `Create()` function with the statement shown here:

```
img.Create(IDB_HOTTOOLBAR, 22, 20, RGB(255, 0, 255));
```

The first parameter is passed the bitmap identifier to the hot toolbar, `IDB_HOTTOOLBAR`. The second parameter, passed a `22`, takes the width, in pixels, of each image in the list, and the third parameter, passed a `20`, takes the height, in pixels, of each image in the list. The fourth, and last, parameter is passed the value of the color used to generate a color mask. Each pixel of this color in the bitmap is changed to black.

Next a reference to the image list is assigned to the CToolBar object with this statement:

```
m_wndToolBar.GetToolBarCtrl().SetHotImageList(&img);
```

The CToolBarCtrl class GetToolBarCtrl() function sets the toolbar button images with the bright colors as the QuickBrowse toolbar hot button images.

Finally, detach the hot toolbar image list object from the CImageList with this statement:

```
img.Detach();
```

Add a set of statements, shown here, similar to the previous three to add the cold toolbar to the CToolBar object:

```
img.Create(IDB_COLDTOOLBAR, 22, 20, RGB(255, 0, 255));
m_wndToolBar.GetToolBarCtrl().SetImageList(&img);
img.Detach();
```

These statements are familiar except that you create the image list from the cold toolbar bitmap, IDB_COLDTOOLBAR, and you call the CToolBarCtrl class SetImageList() function to set the cold toolbar image list.

Next, modify the style of the toolbar with this statement:

```
m_wndToolBar.ModifyStyle(0, TBSTYLE_FLAT | TBSTYLE_TRANSPARENT);
```

The statement makes a call to the ModifyStyle() function inherited by the CToolBar class from the CWnd class. The 0 passed to the first parameter indicates that no window styles are to be removed. Two toolbar style integer constants are ORed together and passed to the second parameter, which takes the window styles to be added to the window. These are the TBSTYLE_FLAT and TBSTYLE_TRANSPARENT toolbar styles.

Set the number of toolbar elements to 4 in this statement:

```
m_wndToolBar.SetButtons(NULL, 4);
```

The call to the CToolBar class SetButtons command passes NULL to the first parameter, since you set the button command identifiers individually rather than passing an array of identifiers. You pass the number of buttons on the toolbar, 4, to the second parameter.

Set up each of the four toolbar buttons. Add this remark followed by a statement calling the CToolBar class SetButtonInfo() function:

```
// set up each toolbar button
m_wndToolBar.SetButtonInfo(0, ID_GO_BACK, TBSTYLE_BUTTON, 0);
```

The SetButtonInfo() function sets a button's command identifier, style, and image. Pass the first parameter the button's zero-based index, in this case 0. Pass the second parameter the command identifier of the command that is carried out when the button is selected. Selecting this button carries out the Back command, and therefore you pass the SetButtonInfo() function's second parameter ID_GO_BACK. This ties the button into the same ID_GO_BACK message-handling function that you set up for the Back command on the Go menu. Pass TBSTYLE_BUTTON to the third parameter, which sets the button's style to a standard push button. Finally, the fourth and last parameter takes the zero-based index of the button's image. In this case the button images have the same index value in the image lists as the button does in the toolbar; therefore pass a 0 to the fourth parameter.

Once you've set the button's information, you need to set the button's text with the statement shown here

```
m_wndToolBar.SetButtonText(0, "Back");
```

The call to the CToolBar class SetButtonText() function sets the text to the first button array to "Back." The first SetButtonText() function parameter takes the button's index, in this case 0, and the second parameter takes the text, "Back," that will be displayed on the button.

Use similar statements to set up each of the three remaining toolbar buttons. This code sets up the Forward, Stop, and Refresh toolbar buttons:

```
m_wndToolBar.SetButtonInfo(1, ID_GO_FORWARD, TBSTYLE_BUTTON, 1);
m_wndToolBar.SetButtonText(1, "Forward");
m_wndToolBar.SetButtonInfo(2, ID_VIEW_STOP, TBSTYLE_BUTTON, 2);
m_wndToolBar.SetButtonText(2, "Stop");
m_wndToolBar.SetButtonInfo(3, ID_VIEW_REFRESH, TBSTYLE_BUTTON, 3);
m_wndToolBar.SetButtonText(3, "Refresh");
```

Add this declaration of a variable with a CRect data type:

```
CRect rectToolBar;
```

CRect objects encapsulated rectangular coordinates. You use the rect-ToolBar local variable to help set up toolbar button sizes. Add this comment and two lines of code to the OnCreate() function:

```
// set up toolbar button sizes
m_wndToolBar.GetItemRect(0, &rectToolBar);
m_wndToolBar.SetSizes(rectToolBar.Size(), CSize(30,20));
```

The first statement makes a call to the CToolBar class GetItemRect() function. This function assigns the rectangle coordinates of the button specified by the index passed to the first parameter to the CRect object passed to the second parameter.

The second statement makes a call to the CToolBar class SetSizes() function, which sets the toolbar's buttons to the size, in pixels, specified by the value passed to its first parameter. A call to the CRect class Size() function from the rectToolBar variable is passed to the first parameter. The result is that the toolbar is set to the size of four of these buttons. The size of each toolbar button bitmap image is passed to the second parameter.

Next, add the toolbar to the rebar. Type in the following comment and statement:

```
// add the toolbar to the rebar
m_wndReBar.AddBar(&m_wndToolBar);
```

The CReBar class AddBar() function adds the toolbar band of buttons to the rebar. Pass the function a reference to the child window, the CTool-Bar object, to insert into the rebar.

Fill in a rebar band information structure for the QuickBrowse rebar. This helps to set up ideal sizes for various pieces of the rebar band. Add

Note	A rebar is a control bar that acts as a container for child windows. These child windows, such as toolbars, are assigned to a rebar control band. The Internet Explorer toolbar is a good example of a toolbar inserted in a rebar control.

the following comment and variable declaration to the code in the `OnCreate()` function:

```
// set up min/max sizes and ideal sizes for pieces of the rebar
REBARBANDINFO rbbi;
```

The `rbbi` variable is declared as a `REBARBANDINFO` data type. The REBAR-BANDINFO data structure has a long list of members as shown here:

```
typedef struct tagREBARBANDINFO{
  UINT cbSize;
  UINT fMask;
  UINT fStyle;
  COLORREF clrFore;
  COLORREF clrBack;
  LPTSTR lpText;
  UINT cch;
  int iImage;
  HWND hwndChild;
  UINT cxMinChild;
  UINT cyMinChild;
  UINT cx;
  HBITMAP hbmBack;
  UINT wID;
#if (_WIN32_IE >= 0x0400)
  UINT cyChild;
  UINT cyMaxChild;
  UINT cyIntegral;
  UINT cxIdeal;
  LPARAM lParam;
  UINT cxHeader;
#endif
} REBARBANDINFO, FAR *LPREBARBANDINFO;
```

In the QuickBrowse application you need only be concerned with six of the `REBARBANDINFO` data structure members: `cbSize`, `fMask`, `cxMinChild`, `cyMinChild`, `cx`, and `cxIdeal`.

Assign the size of the REBARBANDINFO data structure, in bytes, to its cbSize member variable. Add this statement to the CMainFrame class OnCreate() function:

```
rbbi.cbSize = sizeof(rbbi);
```

The sizeof keyword gets the amount of storage, in bytes, associated with the rbbi variable, and the returned value is assigned to the cbSize member variable.

Next, assign flags that indicate which members of the data structure are valid to the fMask member variable. Add this statement to the OnCreate() function:

```
rbbi.fMask = RBBIM_CHILDSIZE | RBBIM_IDEALSIZE | RBBIM_SIZE;
```

RBBIM_CHILDSIZE validates the cxMinChild, cyMinChild, cyChild, cyMaxChild, and cyIntegral member variables; RBBIM_IDEALSIZE validates the cxIdeal member variable; and RBBIM_SIZE validates the cx member variable.

Add these two lines of code to set the minimum width and height of the toolbar:

```
rbbi.cxMinChild = rectToolBar.Width();
rbbi.cyMinChild = rectToolBar.Height();
```

The statements simply return the width and height, in pixels, of the toolbar, as assigned to the rectToolBar variable, and assigns them to the cxMinChild and cyMinChild data structure member variables.

Add this statement to assign the length of the rebar band to the cx and cxIdeal member variables:

```
rbbi.cx = rbbi.cxIdeal = rectToolBar.Width() * 4;
```

The length of the band is 4 button widths; therefore, a button width, in pixels, is obtained through a call to the CRect class Width() function and is multiplied by four. Assign the length of the band to the cx variable and the ideal length of the band to the cxIdeal variable.

Assign the current rebar information data structure to the rebar control with this statement:

```
m_wndReBar.GetReBarCtrl().SetBandInfo(0, &rbbi);
```

The CReBar class is a wrapper for the rebar control represented by the CReBarCtrl class in the MFC library. You can make calls to rebar control functions from a CReBar object by getting a reference to the object using the GetReBarCtrl() function. The SetBandInfo() function sets the rebar object information data structure for the band with the zero-based index passed to the function's first parameter, 0 in this case, and a reference to the REBARBANDINFO structure passed to the second parameter.

You are finished adding the toolbar logic to the QuickBrowse application. Listing 6.3 shows the completed CMainFrame class OnCreate() function with new or modified lines of code highlighted in bold type. Build the project and run the application. It should look like that in Figure 6-35.

Listing 6.3 The CMainFrame Class OnCreate() Function in MainFrm.cpp

```cpp
int CMainFrame::OnCreate(LPCREATESTRUCT lpCreateStruct)
{
  if (CFrameWnd::OnCreate(lpCreateStruct) == -1)
    return -1;

  if (!m_wndToolBar.CreateEx(this))
  {
    TRACE0("Failed to create toolbar\n");
    return -1;       // fail to create
  }

  if (!m_wndReBar.Create(this))
  {
    TRACE0("Failed to create rebar\n");
    return -1;       // fail to create
  }

  if (!m_wndStatusBar.Create(this) ||
    !m_wndStatusBar.SetIndicators(indicators,
      sizeof(indicators)/sizeof(UINT)))
  {
    TRACE0("Failed to create status bar\n");
    return -1;       // fail to create
  }

  // TODO: Remove this if you don't want tool tips
  m_wndToolBar.SetBarStyle(m_wndToolBar.GetBarStyle() |
```

```
                CBRS_TOOLTIPS | CBRS_FLYBY | CBRS_SIZE_FIXED);

        CImageList img;

        // set up toolbar properties
        m_wndToolBar.GetToolBarCtrl().SetButtonWidth(50, 150);
        img.Create(IDB_HOTTOOLBAR, 22, 20, RGB(255, 0, 255));
        m_wndToolBar.GetToolBarCtrl().SetHotImageList(&img);
        img.Detach();
        img.Create(IDB_COLDTOOLBAR, 22, 20, RGB(255, 0, 255));
        m_wndToolBar.GetToolBarCtrl().SetImageList(&img);
        img.Detach();
        m_wndToolBar.ModifyStyle(0, TBSTYLE_FLAT | TBSTYLE_TRANSPARENT);
        m_wndToolBar.SetButtons(NULL, 4);

        // set up each toolbar button
        m_wndToolBar.SetButtonInfo(0, ID_GO_BACK, TBSTYLE_BUTTON, 0);
        m_wndToolBar.SetButtonText(0, "Back");
        m_wndToolBar.SetButtonInfo(1, ID_GO_FORWARD, TBSTYLE_BUTTON, 1);
        m_wndToolBar.SetButtonText(1, "Forward");
        m_wndToolBar.SetButtonInfo(2, ID_VIEW_STOP, TBSTYLE_BUTTON, 2);
        m_wndToolBar.SetButtonText(2, "Stop");
        m_wndToolBar.SetButtonInfo(3, ID_VIEW_REFRESH, TBSTYLE_BUTTON, 3);
        m_wndToolBar.SetButtonText(3, "Refresh");

        CRect rectToolBar;

        // set up toolbar button sizes
        m_wndToolBar.GetItemRect(0, &rectToolBar);
        m_wndToolBar.SetSizes(rectToolBar.Size(), CSize(30,20));

        // add the toolbar to the rebar
        m_wndReBar.AddBar(&m_wndToolBar);

        // set up min/max sizes and ideal sizes for pieces of the rebar
        REBARBANDINFO rbbi;

        rbbi.cbSize = sizeof(rbbi);
        rbbi.fMask = RBBIM_CHILDSIZE | RBBIM_IDEALSIZE | RBBIM_SIZE;
        rbbi.cxMinChild = rectToolBar.Width();
        rbbi.cyMinChild = rectToolBar.Height();
        rbbi.cx = rbbi.cxIdeal = rectToolBar.Width() * 4;
        m_wndReBar.GetReBarCtrl().SetBandInfo(0, &rbbi);

        return 0;
}
```

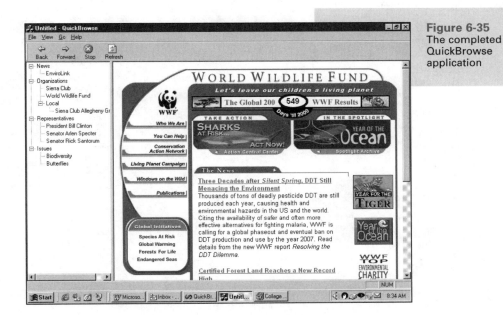

Figure 6-35
The completed
QuickBrowse
application

Summary

In this chapter, you worked with most of the important components of an MFC application by customizing the QuickBrowse application you initially created using the MFC AppWizard. You customized a tree view and worked with the tree control. You handled user interaction with a view, menus, and a toolbar. And you set up a working Web browser. Finally, you modified the toolbar and used a rebar control. You are well on your way to tapping the full power of the Visual C++ integrated development environment.

CHAPTER 7

Testing QuickBrowse

You've completed the QuickBrowse application; now you can test it and prepare it for final deployment. The Visual C++ integrated development environment provides a wide range of tools that help you test your programs and hunt down any bugs that might appear. Once you're satisfied that your application is stable, change your project settings so that Visual C++ builds a release version of your application. Visual C++ provides tools, including an install shield wizard, to assist you in deploying your applications and making it easy for users to install them.

Exploring QuickBrowse Using the Debugger

Visual C++ has built-in debugging facilities that you'll typically use when you find a bug while running your application. By default, Visual C++ builds the debug version of your application. Check the current Visual C++ build configuration by selecting the Configurations command from the Build menu. The Configurations dialog box appears, as in Figure 7-1.

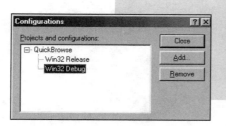

Figure 7-1
According to the Configurations dialog box, Visual C++ is set to create 32-bit Windows programs with debug information.

You build a release version of the QuickBrowse application later in this chapter in the section "Building the Release Version." For now, keep the build that contains debug information so that you can explore the internal operation of QuickBrowse using the Visual C++ debugger.

When you build a debug version of your program, information is added to the program's executable file. This file, along with other intermediate files, is placed in a Debug folder inside your project folder, named after the project. For instance, the QuickBrowse project folder is named QuickBrowse. The debug information included in the executable file helps the Visual C++ debugger to perform the duties that you are about to experience.

Launch the QuickBrowse application and start the Visual C++ debugger. Open the Start Debug submenu on the Build menu, and then select the Go command. Visual C++ switches into debug mode, as in Figure 7-2, and the QuickBrowse application appears.

Note Connect your computer to the Internet before you start the QuickBrowse application.

Put the Debug toolbar in a handy yet out-of-the-way spot. Then look at the various commands available on it. At the moment, focus on the last six buttons on the toolbar. Use these to display or remove windows that allow you to peer into the internal workings of your program and your computer.

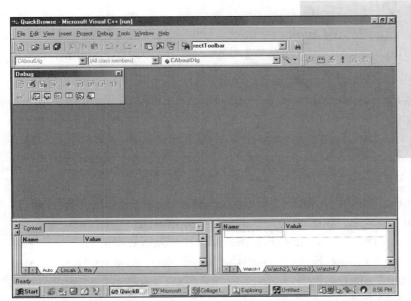

Figure 7-2
The Visual C++ integrated development environment is in debug mode and displays the Debug toolbar, the Variable window, and the Watch window.

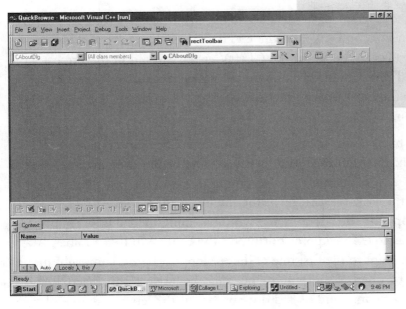

Figure 7-3
The Debug toolbar is moved to a convenient place just above the Variable window.

The Watch Window

Click on the Watch toolbar button. One of the two open windows should disappear, as in Figure 7-3. That was the Watch window.

Click on the Variables toolbar button, to the right of the Watch button, to close the Variables window. Then click on the Watch toolbar button again; the Watch window reappears. You watch the values assigned to variables in the Watch window. That is, you can see a variable's value change while a program executes. This is an extremely useful tool when you are trying to track down a subtle bug.

Try out the Watch window, but first display the Workspace window so that you can open source files easily and drop variables that you want to watch from the source files into the Watch window. You can open the Workspace window by selecting the Workspace command from the View menu. Alternatively, point to the Project window and press your right mouse button. A shortcut menu appears. Select the Workspace command from the shortcut menu, and the Workspace window appears. Your QuickBrowse workspace should currently look like that in Figure 7-4.

Watch the program logic you added to the CLeftView class `OnLButtonDbl Clk()` function in action. Expand the CLeftView class tree by clicking on the plus sign (+) to the left of the CLeftView class listed in the Project window and then double-clicking on the `OnLButtonDblClk()` function listing to open the LeftView.cpp file to the CLeftView class `OnLButton-DblClk()` function.

Add a breakpoint at the second statement in the `OnLButtonDblClk()` function. Program execution is paused just before the statement that is marked as a breakpoint. Pause program execution just before the `for` loop in the `OnLButtonDblClk()` function by clicking on the first line of the `for` loop in the document window and then clicking on the Insert/Remove Breakpoint button on the Build MiniBar toolbar. Alternatively, point to the first line of the `for` loop and press your right mouse button to open a shortcut menu and then select the Insert/Remove Breakpoint command. A red dot appears to the left of the line of code where the breakpoint is inserted, as in Figure 7-5.

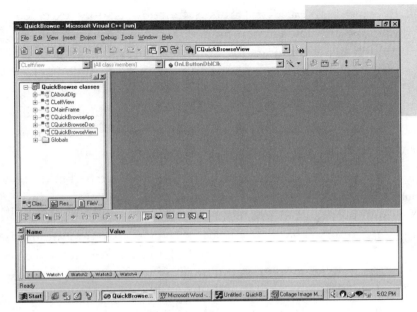

Figure 7-4
The Quick-Browse workspace in debug mode displays the Project window.

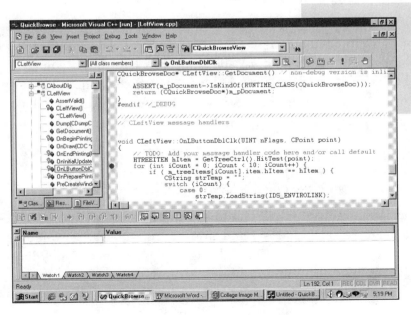

Figure 7-5
A dot appears to the left of the first line of the for loop where you inserted a breakpoint.

The CLeftView class `OnLButtonDblClk()` function is only executed when you double-click on a hyperlink item listed in the QuickBrowse left view. Switch to the running QuickBrowse application and double-click on the Sierra Club item under the Organizations category. The Visual C++ debugger automatically gains the focus and displays the `OnLButtonDblClk()` function code with a yellow arrow pointing from the left-hand side of the code to the next statement to be executed. This statement is the same one to which you added the breakpoint.

There are four variables that you might find fun to watch. These are the `iCount`, `m_treeItems[iCount].item.hItem`, `hItem`, and `strTemp` variables. The number assigned to `iCount` by the `for` loop designates the current loop count. The `m_treeItems[iCount].item.hItem` variable accesses the item handle assigned to one of the ten tree item data structures. The specific structure is defined by the value assigned to `iCount`. The item handle from the recently double-clicked tree item is assigned to the `hItem` variable. Finally, the `strTemp` variable is assigned a string designating the Web address appropriate to the item that was double-clicked on in the QuickBrowse application's left view.

Add the `iCount` variable to the Watch window by double-clicking on the `iCount` variable listed in the source code displayed by the document window. Point to the highlighted variable and press (and hold) your left mouse button while dragging the variable to the Watch window. Release your mouse button to drop the `iCount` variable into the Watch window. The Watch window displays the `iCount` variable, as in Figure 7-6.

The value assigned to the `iCount` variable at this point can be almost anything, since the variable hasn't been initialized. Don't be surprised if the value is different from the one displayed in Figure 7-6.

Carry out the same procedure to add the three other variables, `treeItems[iCount].item.hItem`, `hItem`, and `strTemp`, to the Watch window. When you're done, the Visual C++ debug workspace should look like that in Figure 7-7.

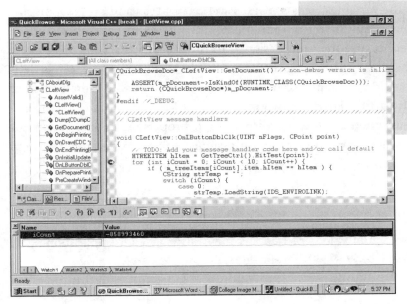

Figure 7-6
The Watch window displays a variable's name in the Name column and its current value in the Value column.

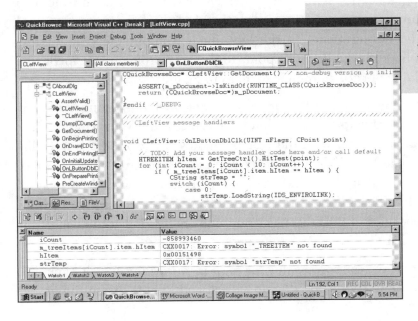

Figure 7-7
The Watch window with four variables added

Two of the variables, `treeItems[iCount].item.hItem` and `strTemp`, display error messages. The `treeItems[iCount].item.hItem` variable doesn't make sense yet because the value assigned to the `iCount` variable is most likely outside the range of the `treeItems` array. In this case -858993460 is definitely outside the range of 0 to 9. The `strTemp` variable remains out of scope. It isn't declared for two more lines. One variable, the `hItem` variable, is assigned a value and displaying it properly. The first statement in the `OnLButtonDblClk()` function assigned the `hItem` variable the item handle from the tree item you double-clicked on.

> **Note** The actual values of handles may differ in your application from the ones displayed here.

You're now in the position to watch the variable assignments change as the program's code is run one statement at a time. Click on the Step Over button on the Debug toolbar or select the Step Over command from the Debug menu. In the Document window, the yellow arrow should have moved down to point to the next program statement, the second line of code in the `for` loop, as in Figure 7-8.

The first line of code in the `for` loop was executed, initializing the `iCount` counter variable to 0. This action is reflected in the Value column next to the `iCount` variable in the Watch window where a red 0 is now displayed. The Visual C++ debugger displays just-assigned values in red. Notice also, that the `treeItems[iCount].item.hItem` variable displays a valid value. That's because the 0 assigned to the `iCount` variable is within the valid range of the `treeItems` array. You are looking at the handle for the first item in the `treeItems` array.

Recall that the purpose of this `for` loop is to find out which hyperlink item in the tree view was double-clicked and then to assign the proper

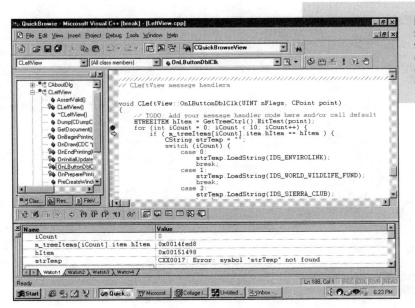

Figure 7-8
Step through the execution of your code one statement at a time.

Web address to the QuickBrowseDoc class m_strURL member variable. In other words, when the handle assigned to the treeItems [iCount].item.hItem variable matches the handle assigned to the hItems variable, then the index number assigned to the iCount variable represents the item number that was double-clicked on. You can watch the values of the treeItems[iCount].item.hItem and hItems variables displayed by the Watch window while the for loop is executed and see for yourself when they match up.

Click on the Step Over button again on the Debug toolbar or select the Step Over command from the Debug menu. Or easier yet, press the F10 key. The yellow arrow points to the for loop's closing brace, since the values of the treeItems[iCount].item.hItem and hItems variables didn't match up when they were conditionally tested in the if statement inside the for loop. Notice that the strTemp variable is in scope and is assigned an empty string.

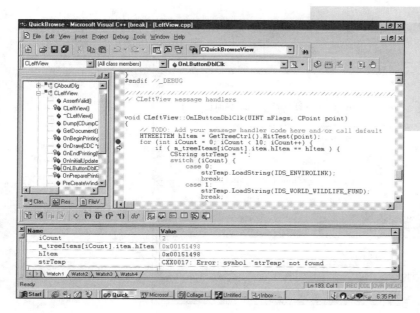

Figure 7-9
The handle of
the item clicked
on matches
the handle
assigned to
`treeItems[2]`
`.item.hItem`.

Step over again; the yellow arrow now points back to the first line of the `for` loop. The `strTemp` variable is back out of scope. Step over again; `iCount` is assigned a `1` and the `treeItems[iCount].item.hItem` variable displays the handle of its second item. Keep stepping through the `for` loop in this way until the values of the `treeItems[iCount].item.hItem` and `hItems` variables match. This should happen when a `2` is assigned to the `iCount` variable, as in Figure 7-9.

Now when you step over, you move into the body of the `if` statement inside the `for` loop, since the conditional test was true. When you execute the `switch` statement, execution should jump to statements following case 2. Watch the value assigned to the `strTemp` variable change as you execute these statements. The Sierra Club Web address should load from the string table and be assigned to the `strTemp` variable, as in Figure 7-10.

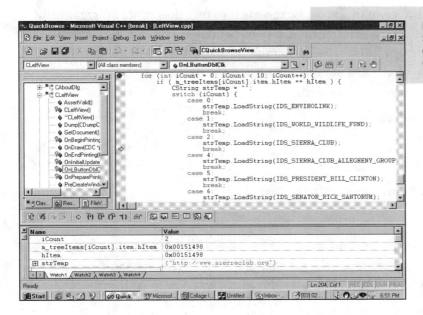

Figure 7-10
Statements in
case 2 are
executed.

Executing the `break` statement takes you out of the `switch` statement. You should be poised to execute an `if` statement that checks if a string was assigned to the `strTemp` variable. This must be done just in case there was a double-click on an item that isn't a hyperlink item, for instance, item 3, which is the Local subcategory.

Keep stepping through the code. The Web address assigned to the `strTemp` variable is assigned to the QuickBrowseDoc class `m_strURL` member variable. Then the QuickBrowse application views are updated. Step over again, and you're taken back up to the first line of the `for` loop. Step again, and 3 is assigned to the `iCount` variable.

Wait a minute! You've gotten what you needed from the `for` loop. Why continue to go through the loop seven more times for nothing? You detected inefficiency in the QuickBrowse application code. It's not a bug. The application runs properly and doesn't crash. However, it would be more efficient if it didn't waste time executing needless code.

Make the code in the OnLButtonDblClk() function more efficient using a break statement. Select the Go command from the Debug menu so that the program finishes executing the for loop. Then add the following line of code as the last statement in the if statement that tests the strTemp variable for an empty string.

```
break;
```

This if statement now should read like this:

```
if ( strTemp != "" ) {
  GetDocument()->m_strURL = strTemp;
  GetDocument()->UpdateAllViews(NULL);
  break;
}
```

Incorporate the new code and test it on the fly, without interrupting your debug session. Select the Apply Code Changes command from the Debug menu; Visual C++ applies the new code to your project.

Test the revision by double-clicking on the EnviroLink item in the QuickBrowse application. You should be taken to the breakpoint in the CLeftView class OnLButtonDblClk() function. Step through the code. It should go fast, since EnviroLink is the first item, index 0. After the Web address is assigned to the m_strURL variable and the views are updated, the program breaks out of the for loop and continues on its way without wasting any time. Select the Go command from the Debug menu so that the QuickBrowse application continues to execute.

The Variables Window

Open the Variables window by clicking on the Variables button on the Debug toolbar or by selecting the Variables command from the Debug Windows submenu on the View menu. Double-click on a hyperlink item in the QuickBrowse application so that program execution stops at the breakpoint in the CLeftView class OnLButtonDblClk() function. The Visual C++ debugger workspace should look similar to Figure 7-11.

Note The Output window is probably open from when you applied code changes. You can close the Output window by pressing your right mouse button while pointing to the window and selecting the Hide command from the shortcut menu that appears.

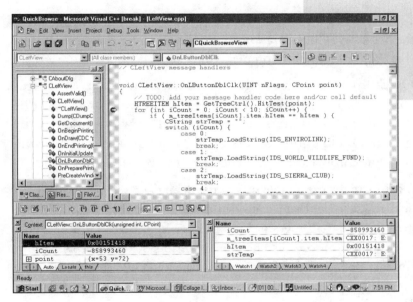

Figure 7-11
The Variables and Watch windows are displayed by Visual C++.

The Variables window is a kind of sibling to the Watch window. Notice that the Variables window displays two of the same variables that you added to the Watch window earlier. These are the two variables, iCount and hItem, that are currently in scope. The Variables window displays all variables that are currently in scope.

Click on the Stop Debugging button on the Debug toolbar or select the Stop Debugging command from the Debug menu to stop the current debug session. As you see, the Visual C++ debugger is a powerful full-featured tool. You learn about other features in future projects.

Building the Release Version

By default you've been building your project in the debug configuration. Debug builds add a lot of overhead to a program's executable file, which makes it possible to debug the application. You can deploy an application built using the debug configuration without any apparent harm done. However, the executable file is much larger and the application probably runs slower than when it's built using the release configuration.

Build a 32-bit Windows release version of the QuickBrowse application. Select the Set Active Configuration command from the Build menu. The Set Active Project Configuration dialog box appears, as in Figure 7-12.

Select QuickBrowse - Win32 Release in the Set Active Project Configuration dialog box Project configurations list and then click on the OK button. Build the release version of the QuickBrowse application by clicking on the Build button on the Build MiniBar toolbar or selecting the Build QuickBrowse.exe command from the Build menu.

You can compare the executable files of the debug and release builds. Find the QuickBrowse folder that sits inside the MyProjects folder. Usually, you find these in the C:\Program Files\Microsoft Visual Studio\MyProjects\QuickBrowse\ directory. The debug version of QuickBrowse.exe is placed in the Debug folder found inside the QuickBrowse folder. The release version is placed in the Release folder inside the QuickBrowse folder. If you check the file sizes, you'll find that the debug version is about 140 kilobytes and the release version is about 44 kilobytes.

Deploying QuickBrowse with InstallShield

Visual C++ provides InstallShield for you to use to deploy your applications. Applications distributed on floppy disk or CD-ROM are set up on computers running Windows by a setup program with a graphic user interface. InstallShield provides you with an advanced setup program so that you don't need to spend a significant amount of time creating your own.

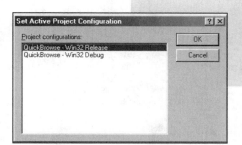

Figure 7-12
Select the project build configuration in the Set Active Project Configuration dialog box.

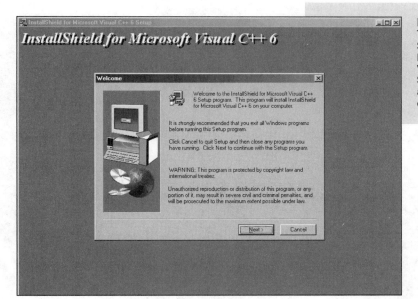

Figure 7-13
The Install-Shield for Microsoft Visual C++ 6 Setup window and Welcome dialog box

Setting Up InstallShield

Set up InstallShield on your computer if you haven't already. You should find the InstallShield setup programs in the Ishield folder on the Visual C++ setup CD-ROM. Run the Setup.exe program in the Ishield folder. The InstallShield for Microsoft Visual C++ 6 Setup window and Welcome dialog box appears, as in Figure 7-13.

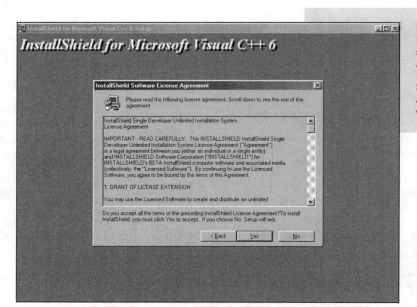

Figure 7-14
Read the software license agreement in the InstallShield Software License Agreement dialog box.

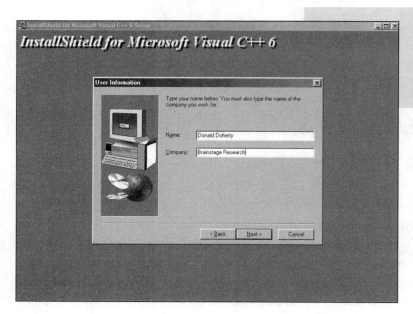

Figure 7-15
Enter your name and company into the User Information dialog box.

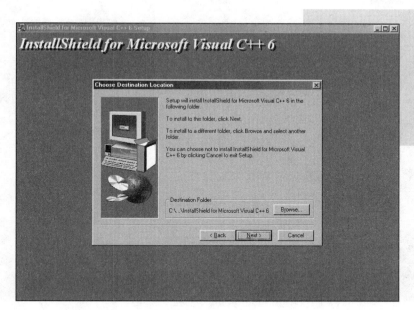

Figure 7-16
Choose where
you want
InstallShield
placed on your
computer in the
Choose Destina-
tion Location
dialog box.

Click on the Next button; the InstallShield Software License Agreement
dialog box appears, as in Figure 7-14.

Click on the Yes button if you agree to the terms of the license agreement.
Otherwise, you are not able to install the program. If you click on the Yes
button, the User Information dialog box appears, as in Figure 7-15.

Click on the Next button; the Choose Destination Location dialog box
appears, as in Figure 7-16.

Use the default destination suggested or select your own by clicking on
the Browse button and choosing your own destination in the Choose
Folder dialog box. Once you've chosen a destination, click on the Next
button. The Setup Type dialog box appears, as in Figure 7-17.

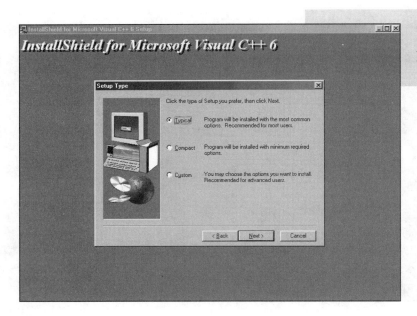

Figure 7-17
Select a setup
type in the Setup
Type dialog box.

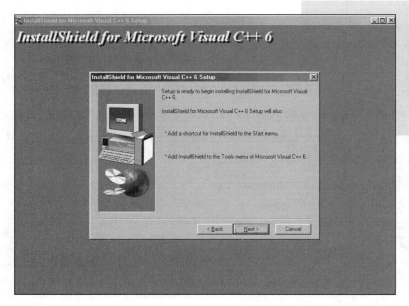

Figure 7-18
A summary of
selected installa-
tion options is
displayed in the
InstallShield for
Visual C++ 6
Setup dialog
box.

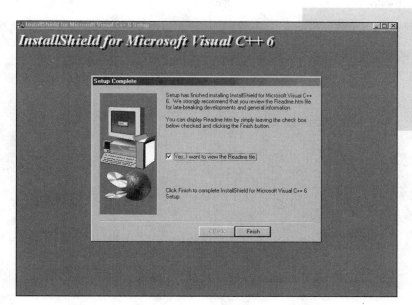

Figure 7-19
The Setup
Complete dialog
box appears at
the end and
provides an
option to display
the readme file.

It's recommended that you select Typical for your setup type. Once you select a setup type, click on the Next button. The InstallShield for Visual C++ 6 Setup dialog box appears, as in Figure 7-18, summarizing the items that will be installed.

If you're unhappy with any of the listed items that will be added to your computer, click on the Back button and change your options. Otherwise, click on the Next button to install InstallShield. The Setup Complete dialog box eventually appears, as in Figure 7-19.

Click on the Finish button. InstallShield is installed on your computer and is integrated with the Visual C++ integrated development environment. An InstallShield Wizard, which will aid you in deploying programs with InstallShield, is added to the Visual C++ Tools menu.

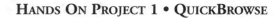
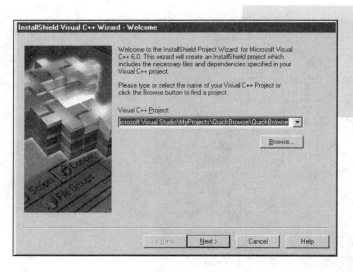

Figure 7-20
Select the QuickBrowse project in the Welcome page of the InstallShield Visual C++ Wizard dialog box.

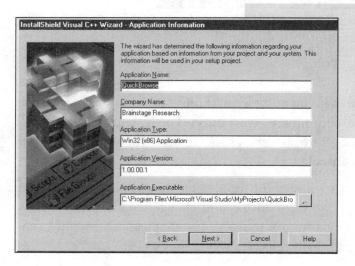

Figure 7-21
Enter information about your application in the Application Information page of the InstallShield Visual C++ Wizard dialog box.

Using the InstallShield Wizard

Deploy the QuickBrowse application with InstallShield by using the InstallShield Wizard. Start up Visual C++ and load the QuickBrowse project. Then select the InstallShield Wizard command from the Tools menu. The Welcome page of the InstallShield Visual C++ Wizard dialog box appears, as in Figure 7-20.

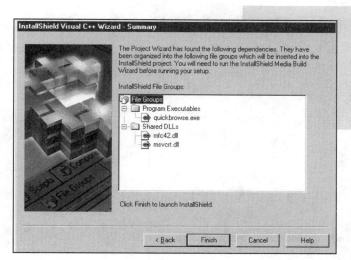

Figure 7-22
Review the files that
are included in your
project on the
Summary page of
the InstallShield
Visual C++ Wizard
dialog box.

By default, the QuickBrowse project should be selected in the Visual C++ Project textbox and drop-down list on the Welcome page of the InstallShield Visual C++ Wizard dialog box. Type in or select the Quick-Browse project if it isn't selected already. Then click on the Next button. The Application Information page appears, as in Figure 7-21.

Most of the default information displayed in the Application Information page is good. However, you probably want to make some modifications. Type those in. And be absolutely sure that the QuickBrowse.exe file referenced in the Application Executable text box is the release version of the QuickBrowse application file. The file should be in the Release folder inside the QuickBrowse folder. Typically, the file's full path is C:\Program Files\Microsoft Visual Studio\MyProjects\Quick-Browse\Release\QuickBrowse.EXE. If the file is not in the Release folder, you can select the appropriate file by clicking on the ellipsis button to the right of the Application Executable text box so that the Open dialog box appears. Find the release version of the QuickBrowse executable file, select it, and click on the Open button. Once you're satisfied with the information contained in the Application Information page, click on the Next button. The Summary page of the InstallShield Visual C++ Wizard dialog box appears, as in Figure 7-22.

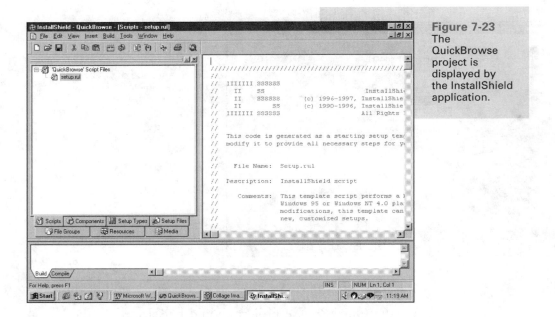

All of your application files and support files, such as MFC dynamic-link library files, are gathered by the wizard and displayed in the Summary page of the InstallShield Visual C++ Wizard dialog box. You told the InstallShield Wizard the application file (or files) that you want to deploy. The wizard is smart enough to know what support files the application file needs. If the Summary page is missing a file or files that you want deployed, go back to earlier pages by clicking on the Back button. Otherwise, click on the Finish button; the wizard launches Install-Shield as in Figure 7-23.

InstallShield is a powerful application that provides a wide range of options for you. It's beyond the scope of this book to go into full details on this program, but you can find excellent guides from the Install-Shield Help menu, including the Getting Started and Getting Results online books.

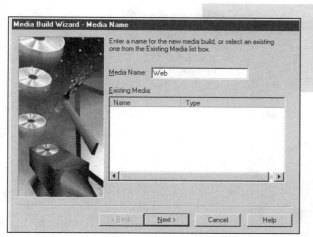

Figure 7-24
The Media Name
page of the Media
Build Wizard
dialog box

Once you are satisfied with the project's setup program you can build the QuickBrowse project setup program by clicking on the Media Build toolbar button or selecting the Media Build Wizard command from the Build menu. The Media Name page of the Media Build Wizard dialog box appears, as in Figure 7-24.

You can build the default setup program for the QuickBrowse application put together by the InstallShield Wizard.

Type in a name designating the medium you will be using to distribute your application, such as **Web**. Click on the Next button; the Disk Type page of the Media Build Wizard dialog box appears, as in Figure 7-25.

The Web is a distribution medium. You can post your application on the Web for others to download.

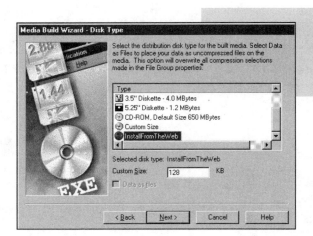

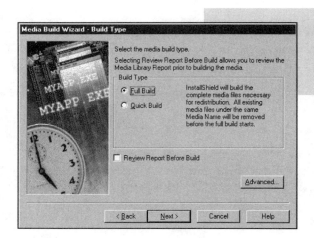

The Type list on the Disk Type page displays several types of media that you can deploy your application from including various floppy disk sizes, CD-ROMs, and the Web itself. Select Install From The Web in the Type list. The Custom Size text box displays the amount of disk space available to you for deploying the QuickBrowse application and auxiliary files. You probably have much more room than the default if you have a Web site. Click on the Next button; the Build Type page of the Media Build Wizard dialog box appears, as in Figure 7-26.

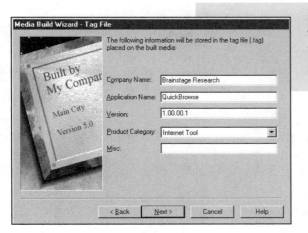

Figure 7-27
The Tag File page
of the Media
Build Wizard
dialog box

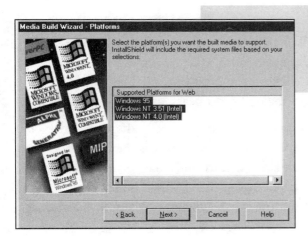

Figure 7-28
The Platforms
page of the Media
Build Wizard
dialog box

Select Full Build from the Build Type page of the Media Build Wizard dialog box. The full build gives you complete media files ready for distributing the QuickBrowse application over the Web. Click on the Next button; the Tag File page of the Media Build Wizard dialog box appears, as in Figure 7-27.

Enter information about the application in the Tag File page. Select the appropriate product category in the Product Category drop-down list. Internet Tool is appropriate for the QuickBrowse application. When you're satisfied with the information, click on the Next button. The Platforms page of the Media Build Wizard dialog box appears, as in Figure 7-28.

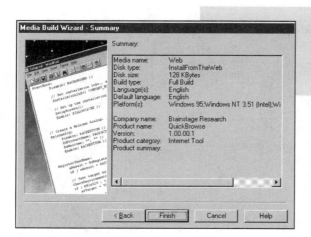

Figure 7-29
The Summary page of the Media Build Wizard dialog box

QuickBrowse supports all of the platforms listed in the Supported Platforms for Web list, since they are all 32-bit Windows platforms. Leave them all highlighted and click on the Next button. The Summary page of the Media Build Wizard dialog box appears, as in Figure 7-29.

Check over the contents of the Summary page to make sure that everything will be set up as you want it. If not, click on the Back button to go back to previous pages of the wizard and change the information. Otherwise, click on the Finish button. InstallShield builds the medium. When it's finished, the Building Media dialog box displays a message that the build was a success, as in Figure 7-30.

Click on the Finish button. The media files are ready to deploy on the Web. You can use the Send Media To command on the Build menu to deploy the media files.

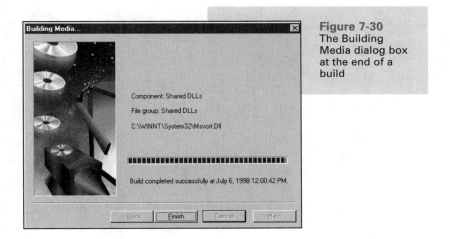

Figure 7-30
The Building
Media dialog box
at the end of a
build

Summary

Visual C++ provides a full development environment from start to finish. In this chapter you used the Visual C++ debugger to watch the QuickBrowse application in action. You were able to spot inefficient code while debugging and fix it on the fly! Once you were satisfied with the stability of the QuickBrowse application, you built a release version of the application's executable file. Finally, you used InstallShield to package the application along with necessary support files so that users can install QuickBrowse properly using a professional setup program.

Project 1 Summary

The first project introduced you to software development using the Visual C++ integrated development environment. You began creating an enterprise-savvy application with many years worth of work done for you by the MFC AppWizard and Visual C++. Then you learned about the architecture of the code generated and the Microsoft Foundation Classes library.

You gained experience using the CHtmlView and CTreeView classes that are MFC library wrapper classes to the HTML and tree controls. You also learned how to program using other controls, such as the toolbar and rebar controls.

You modified application resources, such as the string table and menus, using the Visual C++ resource editor. Then you learned about and added message mapping functions and how they connect user interactions with actions produced by the application.

The result of completing the QuickBrowse project was to learn all of these things, and more, while creating an application that provides topic-specific information to a set of users. The QuickBrowse application is a real-world application that works across the enterprise. You learned how incredibly easy Visual C++ makes it for you to produce powerful applications for the Web and the entire computing enterprise.

HANDS ON
PROJECT 2

LOGOMAGIC

- Use the MFC ActiveX ControlWizard to create an ActiveX control
- Learn about the Component Object Model (COM) specification
- Learn what makes a software component an ActiveX control
- Implement sophisticated properties in your ActiveX control
- Design the LogoMagic control property page

Project Overview

You begin by using the Microsoft Foundation Class (MFC) ActiveX ControlWizard to rapidly create your project's framework. The MFC ActiveX ControlWizard uses your answers to a number of queries to create a complete ActiveX control with MFC library support.

Next, you learn about the COM specification, which is the specification on which ActiveX controls are based. COM is a language-independent specification of software component interfaces that cares nothing for what is encapsulated by the component—only how it displays its methods and properties to other components and application software. In other words, COM is a binary specification for the interface between component software. Understand the COM specification, and you are a long way toward being able to create outstanding software components.

Next you create a bitmap property class from the CCachedDataPathProperty class in the MFC library. This class forms the basis of an enterprise-aware LogoMagic image property. You use visual design methods in the Visual C++ resource editor to create a property page where users can set the values of the LogoMagic control properties. Users with access to the control's property page set the image property to a particular bitmap image file and place the control on a Web page or other ActiveX control–enabled place. The actual bitmap image file can reside anywhere on the enterprise and, for instance, if the company logo changes, the file can be changed (keeping the same name) and the control automatically displays the new version of the logo.

LogoMagic is an ActiveX control that displays bitmap images from wherever they reside on the computing enterprise. Use the LogoMagic control to display your company logo on Web pages, Word documents, Excel spreadsheets, Active Desktops, or anywhere else that you can place an ActiveX control.

8 CHAPTER

What Is LogoMagic?

LogoMagic is an ActiveX control that displays bitmap images from whereever they reside on the computing enterprise. The enterprisewide-computing environment is being turned over to software components, autonomous pieces of software that can work with other component software. The Component Object Model (COM) is a leading specification for software components, and ActiveX controls are a leading implementation of COM. The Visual C++ integrated development environment provides everything you need to rapidly create ActiveX controls. In fact, the Microsoft Foundation Classes (MFC) library and the MFC ActiveX ControlWizard make creating a working ActiveX control a snap. You use these tools to create the LogoMagic control, but you dive far deeper than the surface to create a control with sophisticated properties that transfer bitmap files from anywhere on the enterprise—from your own computer's hard disk drive or from anywhere on the Internet. Use the LogoMagic control to display your company logo on Web pages, Word documents, Excel spreadsheets, Active Desktops, or anywhere that you can place an ActiveX control.

Goals of the LogoMagic Project

The LogoMagic project introduces you to the MFC ActiveX Control-Wizard and the creation of ActiveX controls. This project takes you inside an ActiveX control so that, after the Wizard creates the skeleton code, you are able to write custom code that makes your control go well beyond a toy application.

The LogoMagic control, shown in Figure 8-1, appears simple enough. It displays a company logo. However, looks can be deceiving. This control takes full advantage of the fact that it can exist anywhere on the computing enterprise that accepts ActiveX controls by being able to load bitmap images from anywhere on the enterprise.

Work through Project 2, the LogoMagic project, and do the following:

1. Create an ActiveX control using the MFC ActiveX ControlWizard.

   The MFC ActiveX ControlWizard is one of several wizards that Visual C++ provides to help you rapidly create your project's framework. The MFC ActiveX ControlWizard uses your answers to a number of queries to create a complete ActiveX control with Microsoft Foundation Class library support.

2. Learn about the Component Object Model (COM) specification.

   ActiveX controls are based on the COM specification. COM is a language-independent specification of software component interfaces that cares nothing for what is encapsulated by the component, only how it displays its methods and properties to other components and application software. In other words, COM is a binary specification for the interface between component software. Understanding the COM specification is crucial to being able to create outstanding software components.

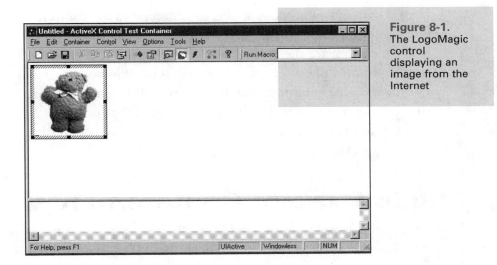

Figure 8-1.
The LogoMagic control displaying an image from the Internet

3. Learn what makes a software component an ActiveX control.

   Not all COM-based software components are ActiveX controls. ActiveX controls follow a software component specification that specifies particular interfaces and methods. These specifications conform to the COM specification that they sit on top of, but they also define a specific kind of software component, which is the ActiveX control.

4. Implement sophisticated properties in your ActiveX control.

   Create a bitmap property class from the CCachedDataPath-Property class in the MFC library. This class forms the basis of an enterprise-aware LogoMagic image property.

5. Design the LogoMagic control property page.

   Use visual design methods in the Visual C++ resource editor to create a property page where users can set the values of the

LogoMagic control properties. Users with access to the control's property page set the image property to a particular bitmap image file and place the control on a Web page or other ActiveX control–enabled place. The actual bitmap image file can reside anywhere on the enterprise and, for instance, if the company logo changes, the contents of the file can be changed (but not its name), and the control will automatically display the new version of the logo.

LogoMagic System Requirements

Like other applications built using the MFC library, computers running the LogoMagic ActiveX control must have the MFC dynamic link libraries available to them. In addition, the LogoMagic control includes Unicode features only available on Windows NT. All ActiveX controls use Unicode so that they're truly universal and ready for the enterprise. Recall that Unicode is a wide character standard that is able to display all the scripts of the world. Both Windows 95 and Windows 98 support Unicode, but they do not implement all Unicode features. The enterprisewide file-transfer mechanisms implemented by the LogoMagic control require Unicode features implemented only on the Windows NT platform.

LogoMagic Customization Requirements

The MFC ActiveX ControlWizard provides a complete and working ActiveX control. However, the LogoMagic control goes well beyond the skeleton project and takes you inside COM-based software components in general and ActiveX control architecture in particular. To begin, you need a business or company logo in the bitmap file format. In addition, you must decide where to deploy the LogoMagic control. You can deploy it in a wide range of places, which are discussed in Chapter 12.

Summary

Your goals and requirements for the LogoMagic project are set. Your COM and ActiveX control odyssey beings in Chapter 9, where you use the Visual C++ MFC ActiveX ControlWizard to create the skeleton code of the LogoMagic ActiveX control.

CHAPTER 9

Creating LogoMagic

Visual C++ simplifies the creation of ActiveX controls to such a large extent that you might never guess that ActiveX controls can be among the most difficult software elements to program. In this chapter, you use the Microsoft Foundation Class (MFC) ActiveX Control Wizard to create the skeleton of the LogoMagic software component; the Wizard creates a complete ActiveX component for you based on your answers to a set of queries. Then you can add or modify code to transform the Wizard's LogoMagic into your own custom ActiveX component that can be deployed anywhere on the computing enterprise.

Using the MFC AppWizard (exe) to Create LogoMagic

Start Microsoft Visual C++ if you haven't already; then select the New command from the File menu to open the New dialog box, shown in Figure 9.1.

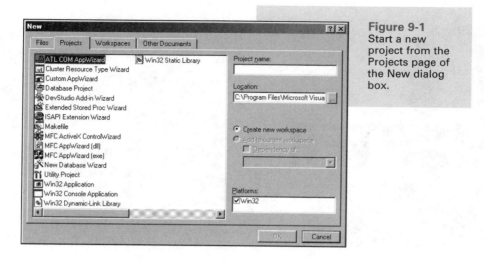

Figure 9-1
Start a new
project from the
Projects page of
the New dialog
box.

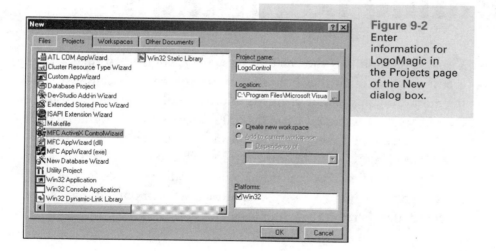

Figure 9-2
Enter
information for
LogoMagic in
the Projects page
of the New
dialog box.

Click on the Projects tab to switch to the Projects page of the New dialog box if it isn't displayed already and then select MFC ActiveX ControlWizard. Type the project name, LogoMagic, into the Project Name text box. Figure 9-2 shows the Projects page of the New dialog box.

Click on the OK button to open the Step 1 page of the MFC ActiveX ControlWizard dialog box, shown in Figure 9-3.

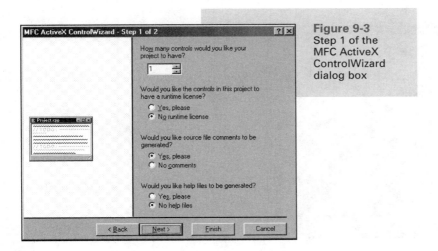

Figure 9-3
Step 1 of the
MFC ActiveX
ControlWizard
dialog box

You need to provide four pieces of information on the Step 1 page of the MFC ActiveX ControlWizard dialog box.

1. The number of ActiveX controls to include in your new project.

   The LogoMagic project includes only one ActiveX control, so keep the default number, 1, in the How many controls would you like your project to have? field.

2. Whether you want the controls to have a runtime license.

   You do want to include a runtime license for the control. Users must be licensed to run your software. Click on the Yes, please radio button under the Would you like the controls in this project to have a runtime license? query.

3. Whether the wizard should add comments to the C++ source code.

   Try to include as many comments as possible in your program source code. Click on the Yes, please radio button under the Would you like source file comments to be generated? query.

4. Whether the wizard should generate help files for the controls.

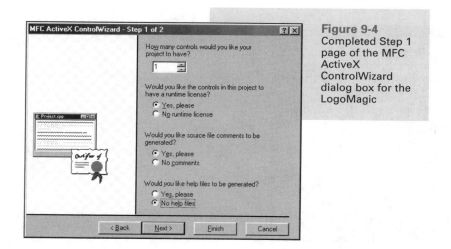

Figure 9-4
Completed Step 1
page of the MFC
ActiveX
ControlWizard
dialog box for the
LogoMagic

The LogoMagic ActiveX control doesn't have an overly sophisticated user interface, so there is no need for context sensitive help. Click on the No help files radio button under the Would you like help files to be generated? query.

Figure 9-4 shows the completed Step 1 page of the MFC ActiveX ControlWizard dialog box.

Click on the Next button to open the Step 2 of the MFC ActiveX ControlWizard dialog box, shown in Figure 9-5.

Step 2 of the MFC ActiveX ControlWizard provides a long list of options. First, you can select the particular control for which you want to modify options in the drop-down list box at the top of the page. Because the LogoMagic project includes only one ActiveX control, only one control is listed.

The Edit Names button is to the right of the drop-down list box. You can click on this button to display the Edit Names dialog box where you can edit the names of the control's classes, files, types, and identifiers. Keep the default names for the LogoMagic component.

Step 2 of the MFC ActiveX ControlWizard dialog box displays five feature-related check boxes.

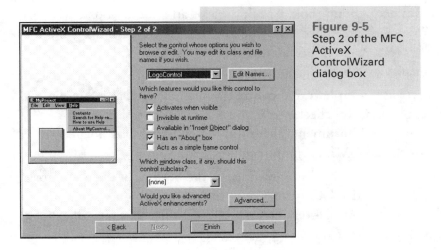

Figure 9-5
Step 2 of the MFC
ActiveX
ControlWizard
dialog box

1. **Activates when visible.** Check the Activates When Visible check box if you want the control to automatically be activated when it becomes visible to the user on a computer screen. Check this check box for the LogoMagic.

2. **Invisible at runtime.** Check the Invisible at Runtime check box if you want the control to be invisible to users. Software that runs behind the scenes, a timer for instance, can be invisible. The LogoMagic component is a visible control that displays graphics and animation, so leave this check box unchecked.

3. **Available in "Insert Object" dialog.** Check the Available in "Insert Object" Dialog check box if you want the control to be available through the Insert Object dialog box provided by applications that can contain ActiveX controls. Word, Excel, and FrontPage are only a few of the wide range of applications with documents that can contain ActiveX controls. Users will want to insert the LogoMagic into many of these documents to display their company logo in documents and Web pages. Check this feature check box.

4. Has an "About" box. Check the Has an "About" Box check box to include an About dialog box in your ActiveX control. Check this feature check box so that the LogoMagic component can display an About dialog box.

5. Acts as a simple frame control. Check the Acts as a Simple Frame Control check box if you want the control to act as a compound document. Leave this feature check box unchecked for the LogoMagic component.

Select a class from the drop-down list at the bottom of the Step 2 page of the MFC ActiveX ControlWizard dialog box if you want to derive your ActiveX control from a previously existing class. For the Logo-Magic, keep the default None.

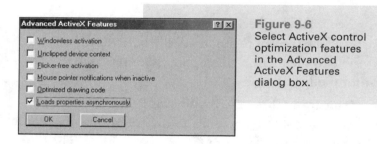

Figure 9-6
Select ActiveX control optimization features in the Advanced ActiveX Features dialog box.

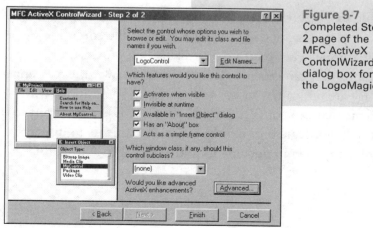

Figure 9-7
Completed Step 2 page of the MFC ActiveX ControlWizard dialog box for the LogoMagic

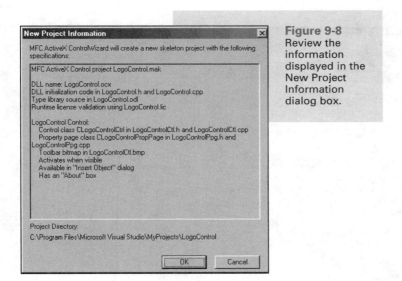

Figure 9-8
Review the
information
displayed in the
New Project
Information
dialog box.

Finally, click on the Advanced button to open the Advanced ActiveX Features dialog box, shown in Figure 9-6.

The features in this dialog box optimize various aspects of the performance of your ActiveX control. Check the Loads properties asynchronously check box. The LogoMagic control will be able to load bitmaps asynchronously from anywhere on the enterprise. Click on the OK button to close the Advanced ActiveX Features dialog box.

Figure 9-7 shows the completed Step 2 page of the MFC ActiveX ControlWizard dialog box.

Click on the Finish button. The New Project Information dialog box, shown in Figure 9-8, opens.

The New Project Information dialog box displays the specifications for the control that the MFC ActiveX ControlWizard is about to create. To change any of the options that you selected, click on the Cancel button. To accept all the options, click on the OK button. The MFC ActiveX ControlWizard finishes creating the skeleton LogoMagic software component and displays it in the Visual C++ integrated development environment (IDE), as shown in Figure 9-9.

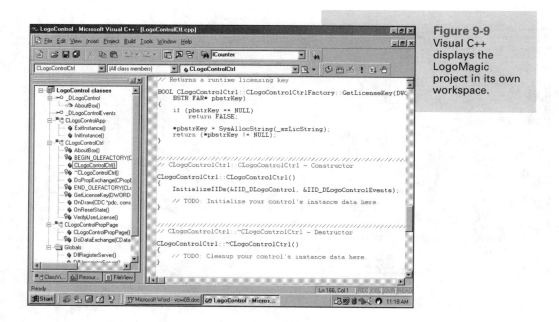

Figure 9-9
Visual C++
displays the
LogoMagic
project in its own
workspace.

Running LogoMagic from the Visual C++ IDE

Run the LogoMagic software component to see what the MFC ActiveX ControlWizard created for you. Click on the Execute Program button (displays an exclamation mark) on the Build MiniBar toolbar or select Execute from the Build menu. The Microsoft Visual C++ dialog box shown in Figure 9-10 opens.

The project hasn't been compiled and linked yet, so Visual C++ asks whether you want to build the LogoMagic software component. Click on the Yes button. The Build page of the Output Window appears

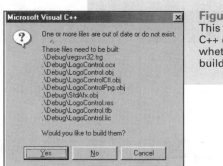

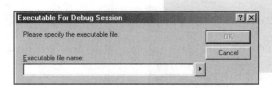

Figure 9-10
This Microsoft Visual
C++ dialog box asks
whether you want to
build the program.

Figure 9-11
Select the ActiveX Control Test
Container from the Executable
for Debug Session dialog box.

below and keeps you informed about the progress of the build process. After the ActiveX control is built, Visual C++ displays the Executable for Debug Session dialog box shown in Figure 9-11.

Click on the right-pointing arrowhead at the right of the text box in the Executable for Debug Session dialog box. From the menu, select the ActiveX Control Test Container command; then click on the OK button. Figure 9-12 shows the ActiveX Control Test Container.

Test the LogoMagic software component by inserting it into the ActiveX Control Test Container application. Select the Insert New Control command from the Edit menu to open the Insert Control dialog box, shown in Figure 9-13.

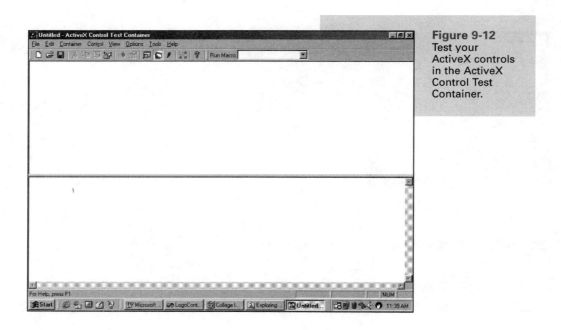

Figure 9-12
Test your
ActiveX controls
in the ActiveX
Control Test
Container.

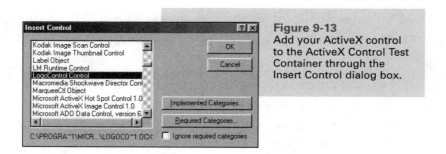

Figure 9-13
Add your ActiveX control
to the ActiveX Control Test
Container through the
Insert Control dialog box.

Select LogoMagic Control from the Insert Control dialog box list and click on the OK button. The LogoMagic appears in the upper-left corner of the upper pane of the ActiveX Control Test Container window, as shown in Figure 9-14.

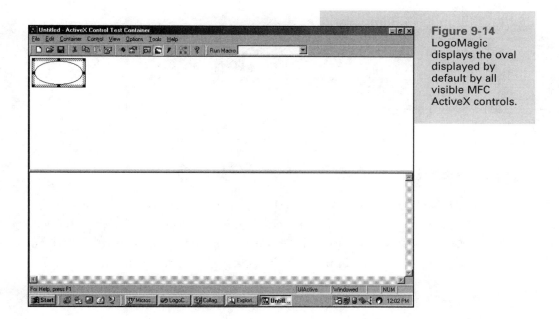

Figure 9-14
LogoMagic
displays the oval
displayed by
default by all
visible MFC
ActiveX controls.

Note **You can use drag-and-drop mouse techniques to move the LogoMagic software component around or change its size.**

Creating ActiveX controls involves a lot of programming overhead. But thanks to Visual C++ and the ActiveX ControlWizard, much of the work is done for you. In Chapter 10 you learn about some of the ActiveX component mechanics going on behind the scenes.

To close the ActiveX Control Test Container running the LogoMagic, select the Exit command from the File menu. An ActiveX Control Test Container dialog box, shown in Figure 9-15, asks whether you want to save the current session. Click on the No button so that the session isn't saved.

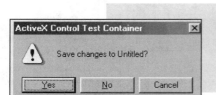

Figure 9-15
You can save the current state of a test session through the ActiveX Control Test Container dialog box.

Summary

In this chapter, you used the MFC ActiveX ControlWizard to create the LogoMagic ActiveX component. You learned about the MFC ActiveX ControlWizard queries and how to customize your control based on your answers. Customization, however, goes only so far in the MFC ActiveX ControlWizard itself. You must add or modify code in the LogoMagic project to fully customize the control. In Chapter 10, you learn details about ActiveX controls and the Component Object Model (COM) on which they are based. You also see how Visual C++ has taken care of the significant overhead to make a COM-compatible ActiveX component for you. The integrated tools in the Visual C++ IDE enhance ActiveX control development by making it relatively easy to modify the MFC ActiveX ControlWizard–created code.

CHAPTER 10

LogoMagic Architecture

LogoMagic is a Microsoft Foundation Class (MFC) library ActiveX control with an architecture determined by both MFC and Component Object Model (COM) specifications. You learned about MFC and the document/view architecture in Project 1. You focus in this chapter on understanding ActiveX controls and the COM specification on which they rely. You also see how Visual C++ uses the MFC library to create ActiveX controls. When you're finished, you will be ready to modify the code created by the MFC ActiveX ControlWizard so that you can build a custom LogoMagic software component.

The Component Object Model (COM)

COM is a specification for software components, and ActiveX controls are software components based on the COM specification. As long as the specification is followed, you can use any language to program the components. COM enables independently engineered software components to exist in common computational space just as independent objects exist in your own space.

> **Note**
>
> **Several software component models are available. Probably the most popular is the JavaBeans component model. Its strength is that it's a relatively simple specification. However, part of the reason JavaBeans software components are easy to implement is that the model is language specific. You must use the Java language. COM is language independent. You can use Java to program software components based on the COM specification. You may also create them using a number of other languages, so long as the program adheres to the specification.**

Each object that follows the COM specification encapsulates functions and data, often known as methods and attributes, just like an object in an object-oriented programming language. However, COM objects, unlike objects used by programmers in traditional object-oriented programming, must be able to exist as independent entities after they're deployed. In addition, COM objects must be able to interact with other software components.

Even though we talk of independent objects, we know that everything must interact somehow. A rock within your field of vision seems independent enough. Nevertheless, if the sun didn't emit light to reflect off the rock and into your eyes, you wouldn't see it. It takes interaction between the sun, light, the rock, and you for all of this to happen. The simple act of seeing a rock involves a lot of communicating.

Without communication, independent software components become virtual blobs, encapsulating methods and attributes that can't do anything. As soon as ActiveX controls can recognize other ActiveX controls, or other software objects based on the COM specification, the possibilities become nearly limitless. Each software component can have its own specialty, such as security or video display. The video display component can recognize the security component and query that component to secure its video feed. The security component recognizes the query and provides security without knowing anything about video. The two software components work together, applying their expertise in a cooperative manner.

Note

Software components based on the COM specification are often referred to as coclasses.

One of the most important standards that the COM specification brings to software components is the interface, which is the aspect of COM-based components that enables them to communicate with other components.

A COM interface is a set of related functions encapsulated by a software component. An interface does not include an implementation of the function. The component does that. Technically, the interface is a publicly accessible array of pointers to each of the functions listed. Software component functions can be accessed only through one of the component's interfaces.

Without an interface, an ActiveX control would be invisible. In fact, part of the definition of an ActiveX control, and a COM object, is that it has at least one interface, known as the IUnknown interface.

The IUnknown Interface

All objects based on the COM specification, including ActiveX controls, implement the IUnknown interface. That way a COM object can always query other surrounding objects without knowing anything about them. A COM object simply queries the IUnknown interfaces of other COM objects, and the components return information about their functions.

> **Note** By convention, most COM interface names begin with a capital I for Interface.

The IUnknown interface must include three methods: the `QueryInterface()`, `AddRef()`, and `Release()` methods. The `QueryInterface()` method returns a pointer to any interface supported by a software component. The `AddRef()` and `Release()` methods work together to manage the lifetime of software components based on the COM specification. ActiveX controls encapsulate a counter that holds the number of other objects that are currently referencing them. When this counter reaches zero, the object is free to be disposed of and the resources that it's using can be made available to other processes. A call to the `AddRef()` method adds one to this internal counter, and a call to the `Release()` method subtracts one from it.

Much more can be said about the COM specification and ActiveX controls, but actually seeing these ideas at work in software that you've created is far more fun. Start up Visual C++ and display the LogoMagic project if it isn't displayed already.

LogoMagic Class Hierarchy

The listing in the LogoMagic project Workspace window, shown in Figure 10-1, includes three classes and two new kinds of entries, _DLogoMagic and _DLogoMagicEvents, which are interfaces.

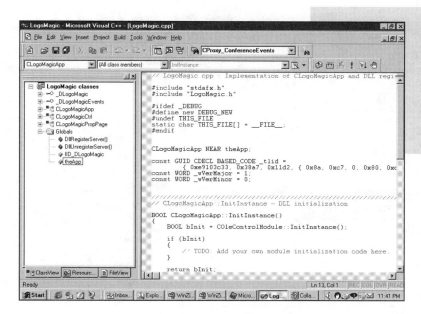

Figure 10-1
Classes and interfaces composing the LogoMagic project are listed in the ClassView page of the Workspace window.

Note The IUnknown interface isn't listed in the ClassView page of the Workspace window. The reason is that every ActiveX control has an IUnknown interface, and it always includes pointers to the same three methods you learned about in the previous section. Nevertheless, you can find the definition of the IUnknown interface in the Unknwn.h file, which you can find in the Visual C++ Include folder. This folder is usually found in the C:\Program Files\Microsoft Visual\ Studio\Vc98\Include\ path.

The COleControlModule Class

The CLogoMagicApp class is the top class in the LogoMagic ActiveX control class hierarchy. Expand the Globals folder in the Workspace window and double-click on the theApp variable listing. Visual C++ should display the LogoMagic.cpp file in its Document window, opened to the declaration of the theApp variable, which is declared as a CLogoMagicApp data type. This global declaration assures that the object is always accessible to the entire software component.

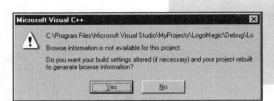

Figure 10-2
Tell Visual C++ to create browse information for this project through the Microsoft Visual C++ dialog box.

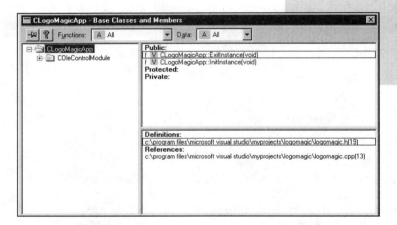

Figure 10-3
The CLogo-MagicApp – Base Classes and Members window.

The CLogoMagicApp class inherits most of its functionality from another class from the MFC library. Point to the CLogoMagicApp listing in the Workspace window and click your right mouse button. Select the Base Classes command from the shortcut menu to open the Microsoft Visual C++ dialog box shown in Figure 10-2.

This Microsoft Visual C++ dialog box asks whether you want to change the LogoMagic project's build settings so that project builds generate browser information files. Click on the Yes button, and build settings are changed and the project is rebuilt. When the rebuild is finished, Visual C++ displays the CLogoMagicApp–Base Classes and Members window, shown in Figure 10-3.

As you can see in the left pane, the CLogoMagicApp class is derived from the COleControlModule class. All MFC ActiveX controls must be derived from the COleControlModule class. This top-level class provides member functions and variables used to manage your control.

The COleControl Class

Point to the CLogoMagicCtrl listing in the Workspace window and click your right mouse button. Select the Base Classes command from the shortcut menu. In the Microsoft Visual C++ dialog box that appears, you can see that the CLogoMagicCtrl class is derived from the COle-Control class.

Alternatively, double-click on the CLogoMagicCtrl listing on the ClassView page of the Workspace window and the Document window displays the LogoMagicCtrl.h file at the beginning of the CLogoMagicCtrl class declaration. You can see at the beginning of this declaration that the CLogo-MagicCtrl class is derived from the COleControl class.

All MFC ActiveX controls must include a class derived from the COle-Control class, which provides features that are essential for COM objects. These features include:

1. Support for in-place activation

2. Ability to fire events

3. Implementation of a dispatch map

In addition to these three important features, this class, often referred to simply as the control class, is where you add most of the functionality to your ActiveX control, as explained in Chapter 11.

In-Place Activation

ActiveX controls can be inserted into Web pages, Windows active desktops, Word documents, Excel documents, and a large array of other ActiveX control containers. Because of in-place activation support, users are able to activate a control wherever it sits and execute the tasks that the control is designed to carry out. Through the COleControl class, LogoMagic inherits the necessary overhead for in-place activation. A control in its active state can interact fully with users, control containers, and the Windows operating system. These interactions are carried out through events and dispatch maps.

Events

The COleControl class provides LogoMagic with the capability to send, or "fire," messages, called events, to other software components and control containers. These events are used to notify other software when something important happens in the control such as a mouse click.

Dispatch Maps

Dispatch maps are a mechanism for implementing Automation, which provides ways to call methods and to access properties across applications. Some programming environments can only access and manipulate software components if they provide Automation. For instance, scripting languages such as VBScript and JScript are only able to access Automation components. ActiveX controls are defined as Automation components and must include a dispatch map.

A dispatch map exposes a set of functions, also known as methods, and attributes, also known as properties, to the control user through an interface. Properties allow a control container or a control user to manipulate the ActiveX control in various ways. For instance, a user can change a control's appearance, some of its values, or make requests, such as accessing data encapsulated by a control.

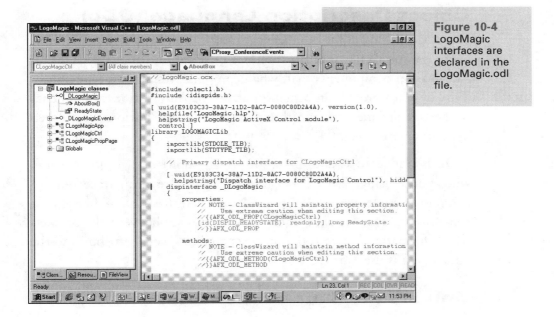

Figure 10-4
LogoMagic
interfaces are
declared in the
LogoMagic.odl
file.

LogoMagic Interfaces

Interfaces are one of the central design features of ActiveX controls in particular and for objects that conform to the COM specification in general. The Classview page of the LogoMagic project Workspace window lists two interfaces, _DLogoMagic and _DLogoMagicEvents. Double-click on _DLogoMagic, the primary dispatch interface for LogoMagic, in the Workspace window; in response Visual C++ loads the LogoMagic.odl file and displays the declaration of the DLogoMagic interface in the Document window, as shown in Figure 10-4.

Note

By convention, dispatch interface names begin with a capital D for Dispatch. Visual C++ adds an underscore (_) before the capital D in dispatch interface names. The underscore makes the interface invisible to users of some programming environments such as Visual Basic.

Object Description Language (ODL)

The LogoMagic.odl file is an Object Description Language (ODL) file. ODL is a special flavor of the Interface Description Language (IDL) for Automation components that, when compiled, results in a type library. Type libraries provide information about an Automation component's properties and methods to other components, applications, and development environments.

ODL is similar to C and C++. You usually don't need to know ODL when you're using Visual C++ because it takes care of interface and dispatch map implementation for you. Nevertheless, you should be able to recognize, and understand, some of what you see between the brackets ([]). Information between the brackets applies specific attributes to the library that is used for creating the interface.

Universally Unique Identifier (UUID)

The uuid listing between the brackets contains attribute specifications for LogoMagic's primary dispatch interface, known as _DLogoMagic. The uuid acronym (typically in uppercase as UUID) stands for universally unique identifier, which is a unique 128-bit value created by Visual C++. This unique number, reproduced below, actually identifies the _DLogoMagic interface.

```
uuid(E9103C34-38AF-11D2-8AC7-0080C80D2A4)
```

The number created for the _DLogoMagic interface in your LogoMagic ActiveX control is sure to be different from the one listed above. The interfaces for your LogoMagic software are unique in the world, even if the code for your LogoMagic is exactly the same as the code in this book.

The display of a UUID typically takes the form of a group of 8 hexadecimal numbers, followed by three groups of 4 hexadecimal numbers, followed by one group of 12 hexadecimal numbers.

An algorithm generates the UUID, using your computer's unique networking card number (if it has one), the date and time at the moment of the number's generation, and a random seed. The result is a 16-byte or 128-bit number that is almost certain to be unique in the world for at least the next couple of millennia.

UUIDs are used as interface names by computers, whereas labels, such as _DLogoMagic, are for human recognition. Words and combinations of words, constrained to some reasonable length, could never produce even close to the number of unique combinations as the UUID system. There may be two or more interfaces in the world with the _DLogoMagic label, but every one of them has a unique 128-bit number. In fact, each person who creates a LogoMagic software component will use the _DLogoMagic label as the primary dispatch interface, but each 128-bit number that names the respective interface will be unique.

You may also hear the term **GUID**. A GUID, globally unique identifier, is the Microsoft implementation of the UUID, universally unique identifier. The UUID is part of the Distributed Computing Environment (DCE) initiative.

All software components based on the COM specification must implement the IUnknown interface. Is the UUID different in each implementation of the IUnknown interface? No! All IUnknown interfaces must be the same interface in so all IUnknown interfaces must be identified by the same UUID. Interfaces identified by different UUIDs are different interfaces, even if their human readable names are the same. The IUnknown interface is a standard interface defined in the COM specification. The definition of the IUnknown interface, found in the Unknwn.h file, is set to one UUID, listed below.

```
00000000-0000-0000-C000-000000000046
```

The 128-bit number above uniquely identifies all IUnknown interfaces.

Other Attributes

After `uuid`, you should see the `helpstring` attribute listed between the brackets containing the attribute specifications for the LogoMagic primary dispatch interface. This attribute, reproduced below, specifies a character string that describes the interface.

```
helpstring("Dispatch interface for LogoMagic Control")
```

The last attribute listed is the `hidden` attribute. This attribute hides the _DLogoMagic interface from Web browsers, but not from other controls, control containers, or operating systems.

Dispatch Maps Revisited

The declaration of the _DLogoMagic dispatch interface continues after the list of attributes. You should see the next line of code, followed by a pair of brackets ({}) enclosing detailed dispatch map information.

```
dispinterface _DLogoMagic
```

The body of the declaration is broken up into two areas of code by the `properties` and `methods` keywords. The code following `properties` provides interface support for the ActiveX control's properties, and the code following `methods` provides interface support for its methods.

Currently, the LogoMagic software component has one default property and one method. The one property is the ReadyState property, which is assigned the ActiveX control's state of readiness. The ready state values and their definitions depend on the particular ActiveX control. The method is the `AboutBox()` method, which is used to display the control's About dialog box. The `AboutBox()` method is exposed to the "outside world" through the LogoMagic control's primary dispatch interface. You should see the following line of code below the `methods` keyword in the _DLogoMagic interface declaration:

```
[id(DISPID_ABOUTBOX)] void AboutBox();
```

This statement sets up the map, or association, between the method's dispatch identifier, found listed between the brackets ([]), and the method itself, with its complete declaration to the right of the dispatch identifier. The id attribute listed between the brackets ([]) should be followed by the dispatch identifier that you or Visual C++ wants to assign to the method that will follow. In this case, the DISPID_ABOUTBOX constant predefines the number. Predefined dispatch identifiers for various standard window components are listed in the OLECTL.H include file. As you'll see in Chapter 11, Visual C++ typically creates and maintains the code in the dispatch maps for you.

Note

> If you double-click on the _DLogoMagicEvents listing on the ClassView page of the Workspace window, the LogoMagic.odl file is opened to the _DLogoMagicEvents event dispatch interface. Its definition is structured the same way as the _DLogoMagic interface definition.

See the dispatch map for the AboutBox() method in action. Click on the Execute Program button on the Build MiniBar toolbar or select the Execute TSTCON32.EXE command from the Build menu to run the ActiveX Control Test Container. Click on the New Control button on the ActiveX Control Test Container toolbar or select the Insert New Control command from the Edit menu. The Insert Control dialog box appears. Select LogoMagic Control from the ActiveX control list and click on the OK button. The LogoMagic ActiveX control should be displayed in the ActiveX Control Test Container window. Finally, while LogoMagic remains selected, click on the Invoke Methods toolbar button or select the Invoke Methods command from the Control menu. The Invoke Methods dialog box is shown in Figure 10-5.

Figure 10-5
Call the AboutBox()
method through the
Invoke Methods
dialog box.

Figure 10-6
Invoke the default
About LogoMagic
Control dialog box.

The only method currently available through the LogoMagic interfaces is the AboutBox() method listed in the Method Name drop-down list on the Invoke Methods dialog box. Click on the Invoke button to open the About LogoMagic Control dialog box, shown in Figure 10-6.

The About LogoMagic Control dialog box is defined in the LogoMagic project's resource file. Click on the OK button on the About LogoMagic Control dialog box and then click on the Close button on the Invoke Methods dialog box. Then switch to the Visual C++ integrated development environment (IDE). Click on the ResourceView tab in the Workspace window to switch to the ResourceView page and open the LogoMagic resources tree so that you can see the Dialog folder. Open the Dialog folder tree and double-click on the IDD_ABOUTBOX_LOGO-MAGIC listing. The About LogoMagic Control dialog box displays in the Visual C++ resource editor, as shown in Figure 10-7.

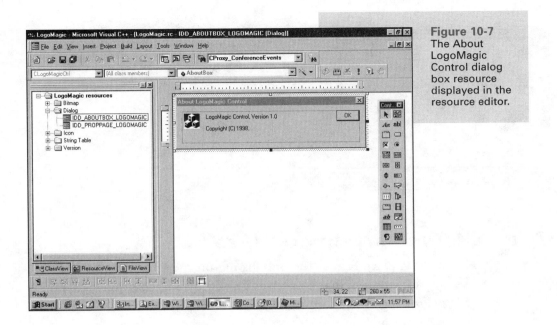

Visual C++ sets up the default dialog box for you. In Chapter 11, you learn how to use the resource editor to modify the dialog box to your own liking.

A Final Look at the ODL File

If you browse through the LogoMagic.odl file you should see two more UUIDs listed. You've explored the declarations of the two dispatch interfaces. What could these universally unique identifiers be used for?

ActiveX control interface names must be unique, but so must other names—the name of the control itself, for instance. The UUID included in the declaration at the top of the file is the name for the LogoMagic's control module, and the one included in the declaration at the bottom of the file is the name for the control itself. The control module is the top-level object in a MFC ActiveX control and is, as you've already seen, an object created from a class derived from the COleControlModule class—in this case, the CLogoMagicApp class. The name of the entire control, however, is mapped onto the control object in a MFC ActiveX control, which is derived from the COleControl class. The LogoMagic control object is the CLogoMagicCtrl class.

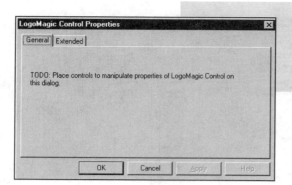

Figure 10-8
The General page of the LogoMagic Control Properties dialog box.

The COlePropertyPage Class

CLogoMagicPropPage is the only listing on the ClassView page of the Workspace window that you haven't explored yet. Point to the CLogo-MagicPropPage listing in the Workspace window and click your right mouse button. Select the Base Classes command from the shortcut menu. In the Microsoft Visual C++ dialog box that appears, you can see that the CLogoMagicPropPage class is derived from the COleProperty-Page class.

Objects created from classes derived from the COlePropertyPage class graphically display control properties. View the LogoMagic ActiveX control property page. Return to the ActiveX Control Test Container window running the LogoMagic ActiveX control. Make sure that LogoMagic remains selected and then click on the Properties toolbar button, or select the Properties command from the Edit menu. Figure 10-8 shows the General page of the LogoMagic Control Properties dialog box.

The Properties dialog box is where users can view and sometimes edit an ActiveX control's properties. Currently, LogoMagic has no properties, so none are displayed. Click on the OK or Cancel button to close the dialog box.

Like the About dialog box, the LogoMagic Control Properties dialog box is defined in the LogoMagic resource file. Switch to the Visual C++ IDE to take a quick look at its resource. Make sure that the Workspace

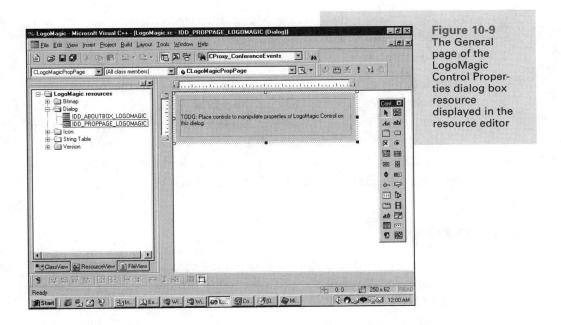

window displays the ResourceView page. Double-click on the IDD_PROPPAGE_LOGOMAGIC listing under the dialog box folder, and the resource for the General page of the LogoMagic Control Properties dialog box displays in the Visual C++ resource editor, as shown in Figure 10-9.

After you add properties to the LogoMagic in Chapter 11, you learn how to use the resource editor to modify the page to display the property values.

CLogoMagicCtrl Class Definition

The CLogoMagicCtrl class is where you add most, if not all, of your custom code to the LogoMagic software component. Look at the open tree under the CLogoMagicCtrl listing in the ClassView page of the Workspace window. You should see the AboutBox() method listed under CLogoMagicCtrl. Double-click on the AboutBox() listing, and the LogoMagicCtrl.cpp file loads and displays in the Document window at the AboutBox() method definition. Recall that the AboutBox() method is available through the _DLogoMagic interface. In fact, it's the only method currently added to the LogoMagic dispatch map and that is available through a LogoMagic control interface.

After looking at the two statements used to display the About Logo-Magic dialog box, double-click on the OnDraw() listing in the Workspace window. The Document window displays the two statements that the default MFC ActiveX control code uses to draw an oval. You learn more about many of the other functions as you modify the LogoMagic to display your company logo (and more) in Chapter 11.

Summary

ActiveX controls and COM are some of the most exciting topics in programming today. They are also potentially difficult subjects to master. Visual C++ and the MFC library make it easy for you to realize the full potential of these component software technologies. This chapter revealed the architecture of the LogoMagic ActiveX control created with the help of the MFC ActiveX ControlWizard in Chapter 9. You learned how the architecture conforms to the COM specifications. With this knowledge, you can modify the LogoMagic framework into a unique and useful ActiveX component.

CHAPTER 11

Customizing LogoMagic

Visual C++ and the MFC ActiveX ControlWizard provide you with the tools to quickly create an ActiveX control with all the necessary mechanisms and interfaces in place, allowing you to focus on adding the code that makes your control unique. In this chapter, you modify the Logo-Magic ActiveX control so that it displays your company logo, which can be transferred from a file residing anywhere on the Internet or intranets. In fact, the logo can reside anywhere on the entire computing enterprise.

Displaying a Logo

The primary purpose of the LogoMagic control is to display business or company logos in a consistent manner across a wide variety of places. Users can drop the LogoMagic control displaying their company graphic into Web pages, Active Desktops, Word documents, Excel spreadsheets, and anything else that acts as a container for ActiveX controls. Different users will want to provide different images depicting their company logos for the LogoMagic control to display. Begin your

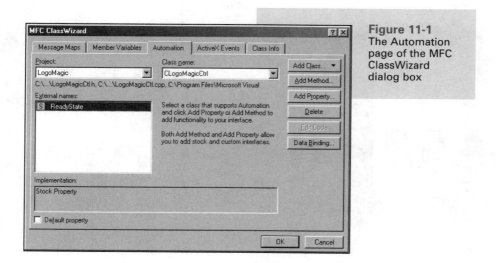

Figure 11-1
The Automation
page of the MFC
ClassWizard
dialog box

customization of the LogoMagic control by adding an image path property that users will be able to view and modify through the control's property sheet.

Creating an ImagePath Property

Use the ClassWizard to add properties to your control. With the Logo-Magic project loaded in your workspace, select the ClassWizard command from the View menu to open the MFC ClassWizard dialog box. Click on the Automation tab to display the Automation page shown in Figure 11-1.

LogoMagic control properties should be encapsulated by the control's central object, the CLogoMagicCtrl object. Select CLogoMagicCtrl in the Class Name drop-down list. You should see the ReadyState stock property listed in the External Names list. The MFC ActiveX Control-Wizard added this property to the LogoMagic control when you created it in Chapter 9.

Add Property

External name:	Image	OK
Type:	BSTR	Cancel
Get function:	GetImage	
Set function:	SetImage	

Implementation

○ Stock   ○ Member variable   ● Get/Set methods

Parameter list:

Name	Type

Figure 11-2
Add properties to
your control through
the Add Property
dialog box.

To add a new property, click on the Add Property button on the Automation page of the MFC ClassWizard dialog box. The Add Property dialog box appears, as shown in Figure 11-2.

Select the Get/Set Methods radio button on the Add Property dialog box. Then type the name of the property that you're adding, **ImagePath**, into the External Name text box and drop-down list. Next, select the type of data returned by the get function, the BSTR type, in the Type drop-down list. The Get Function and Set Function text boxes on the Add Property dialog box should automatically read GetImagePath and SetImagePath, respectively. Keep these method names. Click on the OK button to add the ImagePath property to the External Names list; the C to the left of the names indicates that ImagePath is a custom property. Click on the OK button on the MFC ClassWizard dialog box.

Expand the DLogoMagic interface tree in the ClassView page of the Workspace window. The ImagePath property was added. If you expand the CLogoMagicCtrl class tree, you can see that the `GetImagePath()` and `SetImagePath()` methods were added.

Figure 11-3
Add property
variables through the
Add Member Variable
dialog box.

You added the ImagePath property, but now you need to assign the property value to a variable. An ActiveX component property is, at its most fundamental level, a private data variable. Add the image property variable, m_propImage, to the CLogoMagicCtrl class.

Expand the tree on the ClassView page of the Workspace window so that LogoMagic control's various classes and interfaces are listed. Point to CLogoMagicCtrl and click your right mouse button to display the shortcut menu. Select the Add Member Variable command, and the Add Member Variable dialog box appears, as shown in Figure 11-3.

Type the property's data type, **CBitmapProperty**, into the Variable Type text box of the Add Member Variable dialog box. Then type the variable name, **m_propImage,** into the Variable Name text box and set the variable's access to private by selecting the Private radio button in the Access area of the Add Member Variable dialog box. Click on the OK button to add the image property variable to the CLogoMagicCtrl class.

The LogoMagic control supports the bitmap image file format, so you might think that you should type the CBitmap class into the Variable Type text box. However, how would users assign their particular bitmap image to the variable? Advanced ActiveX controls (and those are what you want, right?) solve this and other problems by using special property classes.

The CBitmapProperty Class

You create the special property class, CBitmapProperty, which is used by the LogoMagic control ImagePath property. The CBitmapProperty class is derived from the MFC library CCachedDataPathProperty class. Point

Figure 11-4
Add a new class
to your project
through the New
Class dialog box.

to the LogoMagic classes listing on the ClassPath page of the Workspace window and click on your right mouse button. Select the New Class command from the shortcut menu to open the New Class dialog box shown in Figure 11-4.

Select MFC Class from the Class Type drop-down list on the New Class dialog box because your new class, CBitmapProperty, will be derived from an MFC class. Type in the name of the new class in the Name text box at the top of the Class Information area. Keep the default file name BitmapProperty.cpp. Finally, select CCachedDataPathProperty from the Base Class drop-down list and click on the OK button. CBitmapProperty should be added to the list under LogoMagic classes on the ClassView page of the Workspace window.

The CBitmapProperty class constructor must be modified so that CBitmapProperty objects can obtain pointers to the instantiating control object. Double-click on CBitmapProperty listed on the ClassView page of the Workspace window to open the `BitmapProperty.h` file in the Visual C++ document window. Find the CBitmapProperty class constructor declaration, shown below, listed under the "Constructor" remark and a `public` keyword.

```
CBitmapProperty();
```

Add a parameter to the constructor named `pControl`, a pointer to the control, declared as a COleControl class data type. Recall that COle-Control is a base class of the CLogoMagicCtrl class. Finally, assign NULL to the pointer by default. The modified class constructor declaration should look like this:

```
CBitmapProperty(COleControl* pControl = NULL);
```

Next, modify the CBitmapProperty class constructor definition. Open the BitmapProperty.cpp file to the CBitmapProperty class constructor definition. You need to do this step manually because the constructor declaration doesn't currently match its definition. Modify the code defining CBitmapProperty class constructor so that it looks like this:

```
CBitmapProperty(COleControl* pControl) : CCachedDataPathProperty(pControl),
  m_dlState(dlNone)
{
}
```

The implementation of the CBitmapProperty class constructor uses multiple inheritance. CBitmapProperty inherits the CCachedDataPath-Property class constructor that takes a pointer to its associated control, which is in turn inherited from the CDataPathProperty class constructor of the same type. And the CBitmapProperty class constructor also inherits from `m_dlState`.

You should be scratching your head right now wondering how it can be that the CBitmapProperty class constructor inherits from `m_dlState`. What is an `m_dlState`, anyway?

`m_dlState` is a variable name with the DLState enumerated structure assigned to it. You haven't added these to the CBitmapProperty class yet (you add them shortly), so it's not surprising that you don't recognize them. Nevertheless, how is it that they can be used in the definition of a class constructor?

Recall first, that C++ classes can use multiple inheritance and, second, that structure, including enumerated structure, can be recognized as classes in C++. They are pure data classes, but classes nonetheless.

DLState enumerates five possible download states. Declare the enumerated structure named DLState and its variable named m_dlState with the five steps of reading a bitmap file enumerated, as shown here:

```
enum DLState
{
  dlNone,
  dlFileHeader,
  dlInfoHeader,
  dlColorTable,
  dlDone
} m_dlState;
```

Open the BitmapProperty.h file and add the preceding code under the "Attributes" remark and the public keyword. Table 11.1 describes the download state enumeration constants. Notice that the m_dlState object inherited by the CBitmapProperty class constructor is created with dlNone assigned to it, creating a default initial condition that says that none of the bitmap data has been transferred yet.

Table 11.1 Download State Enumeration Constants

Enumeration Constant	Description
dlNone	None of the file has been transferred yet. Begin by trying to read the bitmap file header.
dlFileHeader	The bitmap file header has been transferred. Next, try to read the bitmap info header.
dlInfoHeader	The bitmap info header has been transferred. Next, try to read the color table.
dlColorTable	The color table has been transferred. Next, try to read some image data.
dlDone	File transfer is complete.

The CCachedDataPathProperty Class

The CCachedDataPathProperty class is part of the MFC library. Objects instantiated from the CCachedDataPathProperty class, including CBitmapProperty objects, implement mechanisms that transfer data asynchronously while saving the data to memory.

The CCachedDataPathProperty class itself implements only one data member and no functions; the rest are inherited from its base classes. The m_cache data member is declared with the CMemFile class as its data type. The m_cache variable is assigned a CMemFile object encapsulating the cache where the image data are saved in computer memory.

The CCachedDataPathProperty class inherits functions for getting or setting the path to retrievable data from the CDataPathProperty class, and the CCachedDataPathProperty class transfer mechanisms are inherited from the CAsyncMonikerFile class.

Overriding the OnDataAvailable() Function

The transfer mechanisms inherited from the CAysncMonikerFile class include the CreateBindStatusCallback() function that creates a COM object implementing the IBindStatusCallback interface and the OnDataAvailable() function that is one of the methods pointed to by the IBindStatusCallback interface.

Override the OnDataAvailable() function so you can customize it to recognize bitmap data. Select the ClassWizard command from the View menu, and the MFC ClassWizard dialog box appears. Click on the Message Maps tab to display the Message Maps page and select the CBitmapProperty class from the Class Name drop-down list. Finally, select OnDataAvailable in the Messages list and click on the Add Function button. OnDataAvailable is added to the Member Functions list of the MFC ClassWizard dialog box shown in Figure 11-5.

Click on the Edit Code button, and Visual C++ takes you to the OnDataAvailable() function source code that you just added to the CBitmapProperty class. The method signature should look like this:

```
void CBitmapProperty::OnDataAvailable(DWORD dwSize, DWORD bscfFlag)
```

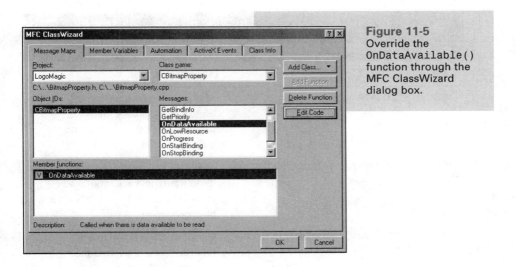

Figure 11-5
Override the
OnDataAvailable()
function through the
MFC ClassWizard
dialog box.

The first parameter of the OnDataAvailable() function, dwSize, is assigned the cumulative number of bytes of data available since your control began the transfer. The bscfFlag parameter is assigned a BSCF enumeration constant. The BSCF data type stands for Bind Status Callback Function and is defined by the typedef declaration reproduced here:

```
typedef {
    BSCF_FIRSTDATANOTIFICATION,
    BSCF_INTERMEDIATEDATANOTIFICATION
    BSCF_LASTDATANOTIFICATION,
    BSCF_DATAFULLYAVAILABLE,
    BSCF_AVAILABLEDATASIZEUNKNOWN
} BSCF;
```

The BSCF constant assigned to the bscfFlag variable indicates the status of the data transfer. For instance, the BSCF_DATAFULLYAVAILABLE constant indicates that the data transfer is complete and that of the data are available and ready to be used. Table 11.2 describes the five BSCF enumerated constants.

Table 11.2 Bind Status Callback Function (BSCF) Enumeration Constants

Enumeration Constant	Description
BSCF_FIRSTDATANOTIFICATION	Identifies the first call to the IBindStatusCallback interface OnDataAvailable() method for a bind operation.
BSCF_INTERMEDIATEDATANOTIFICATION	Identifies an intermediate call to the IBindStatusCallback interface OnDataAvailable() method for a bind operation.
BSCF_LASTDATANOTIFICATION	Identifies the last call to the IBindStatusCallback interface OnDataAvailable() method for a bind operation.
BSCF_DATAFULLYAVAILABLE	All of the requested data are available.
BSCF_AVAILABLEDATASIZEUNKNOWN	The size of the available data is unknown.

The first code to add to the overridden OnDataAvailable() function, shown next, tests whether the current call is the first call to the OnDataAvailable() method.

```
if (bscfFlag & BSCF_FIRSTDATANOTIFICATION)
  ResetData();
```

Note

Add this code to the OnDataAvailable() function right under the "TODO" remark and before the call to the CCachedData-PathProperty class implementation of the OnDataAvailable() function.

Recall that when you perform a bitwise AND, the resulting bit is on only if both bits that you are comparing are on. Otherwise, the resulting bit is turned off.

If the value assigned to the bscfFlag variable is the same as the BSCF_FIRSTDATANOTIFICATION constant, then a value of one or greater is generated, which is equivalent to being true in C++. Otherwise, a zero is generated, which is equivalent to being false in C++.

If it is the first call to the OnDataAvailable() function, then the Reset-Data() function is called. You override the ResetData() function shortly in the "Override the ResetData() Function" section to add new functionality. The CBitmapProperty class inherits the ResetData() function from the CDataPathProperty class. The function notifies clients that the control properties have changed and that the information loaded asynchronously is no longer valid. A call to the ResetData() function at the beginning of the download of a new bitmap invalidates any bitmap data previously loaded by the component.

The next statement in the OnDataAvailable() function should already be in place. The statement calls the CCachedDataPathProperty class implementation of the OnDataAvailable() function, as shown here:

```
CCachedDataPathProperty::OnDataAvailable(dwSize, bscfFlag);
```

Before you add the next statement to the OnDataAvailable() function, add a new member variable, named m_cbRead, to the CBitmapProperty class. The m_cbRead variable, which is assigned the total number of bytes currently read by the component, is used in the next statement.

Add the m_cbRead variable to the CBitmapProperty class by pointing to CBitmapProperty in the ClassView page of the Workspace window and clicking your right mouse button to open a shortcut menu. Select the Add Member Variable command from the shortcut menu to open the Add Member Variable dialog box as shown in Figure 11-6.

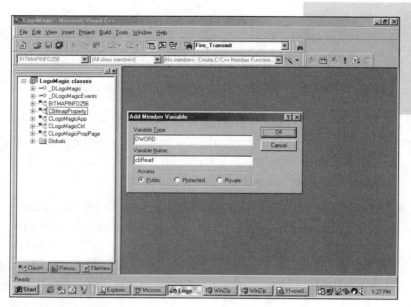

Figure 11-6
Add the
m_cbRead
variable through
the Add Member
Variable dialog
box.

The m_cbRead variable is a DWORD data type. Type **DWORD** into the Variable Type text box in the Add Member Variable dialog box. Then type in the name of the variable, **m_cbRead**, into the Variable Name text box. Finally, the m_cbRead variable is public so select the Public radio button in the Access area of the Add Member Variable dialog box, and then click on the OK button. The new CBitmapProperty member variable should appear in the ClassView page of the Workspace window.

With the m_cbRead variable added to the CBitmapProperty class, you can get back to implementing the overridden OnDataAvailable() function. Add the following new if...else statement after the call to the CCachedDataPathProperty class implementation of the OnDataAvailable() function. That function tests the size of the cumulative number of bytes of data available since your control began the transfer, which is assigned to the dwSize variable, against the total number of bytes read, which is assigned to the m_cbRead variable.

```
if (dwSize <= m_cbRead)
  return;
else
  dwSize -= m_cbRead;
```

If the cumulative number of bytes available is less than or equal to the number of bytes that have been read, then all the data have been transferred and the function can end. Otherwise, the number of bytes read is subtracted from the cumulative number of bytes available, and the result is assigned to the dwSize variable. That is, the bytes available are adjusted down because the number of bytes read came from the bytes that were available.

After going through these checks on bytes available and bytes read, the m_cbRead variable is assigned the total number of bytes left to transfer, including those bytes currently being transferred. That is, type in the following code that adds the number of bytes currently being read (m_cbRead) to the number of bytes currently available (dwSize).

```
m_cbRead += dwSize;
```

The next statement you add, shown here, declares a Boolean variable named bContinue that tests whether a while loop, which you add next, should continue looping.

```
BOOL bContinue = m_dlState != dlDone;
```

The download state assigned to the m_dlState variable is tested to see that it's not equal to dlDone. Recall that the CBitmapProperty class constructor inherited m_dlState, which is an enumerated structure named DLState. Also recall that dlDone is one of the five enumerated states in that structure, listed in Table 11.1, and it means that the file transfer is done. As long as the file transfer isn't finished, the bContinue variable is assigned true and the while loop executes. When the file transfer is complete, it's assigned false and the while loop is skipped.

The while loop does most of the work in the OnDataAvailable() function and includes most of the code. Because this loop has so much code, only its skeleton is shown:

```
while (bContinue)
{
  // lots of code
}
```

Add this code directly under the bContinue variable declaration that you just added. The code in the body of the while loop is presented here in segments. You can also refer to Listing 11.1 for the complete OnDataAvailable() function code.

Almost the whole body of the while loop is filled with a switch statement. The following is the skeleton of the switch statement:

```
switch (m_dlState)
{
  // lots of code
};
```

Add the switch statement code inside the while loop. The switch statement enables you to create five different processing schemes, depending on the five possible download states assigned to the m_dlState variable. Each possible state is presented here along with its associated code.

The first case statement is when dlNone is assigned to the m_dlState variable. At this point, none of the file has been transferred yet. Here's the complete case statement:

```
case dlNone:
  {
    BITMAPFILEHEADER bmfh;
    if (ReadStruct(dwSize, &bmfh, sizeof(bmfh)))
    {
      ASSERT(bmfh.bfType == 'B' | ('M' << 8));
      m_dlState = dlFileHeader;
    }
    else
    {
      bContinue = FALSE;
      break;
    }
  }
  break;
```

This first pass at transferring the bitmap file tries to read the bitmap file header. First, the bmfh variable is declared as a BITMAPFILEHEADER data type. BITMAPFILEHEADER is a data structure that contains information about the type, size, and layout of a device-independent bitmap (DIB) file. The BITMAPFILEHEADER structure declaration follows, and Table 11.3 describes each member of the structure.

```
typedef struct tagBITMAPFILEHEADER { // bmfh
  WORD     bfType;
  DWORD    bfSize;
  WORD     bfReserved1;
  WORD     bfReserved2;
  DWORD    bfOffBits;
} BITMAPFILEHEADER;
```

Table 11.3 Members of the BITMAPFILEHEADER Structure

Variable	Description
bfType	Specifies the file type, which must be BM for bitmap.
bfSize	Specifies the size, in bytes, of the bitmap file.
bfReserved1	Reserved; its value must be zero.
bfReserved2	Reserved; its value must be zero.
bfOffBits	Specifies the offset, in bytes, from the BITMAPFILEHEADER structure to the bitmap bits.

Next, an if statement tests a call to the ReadStruct() function, which you haven't implemented yet. You create the CBitmapProperty class ReadStruct() later this chapter in the section "Create the ReadStruct() Function." For now, it's enough to know that the ReadStruct() function reads a data structure of the type passed to the function's second parameter, in this case a BITMAPFILEHEADER structure. The first parameter is passed the number of bytes currently available for transfer, as assigned to the dwSize variable, and the third parameter is passed the size of the data structure, which is determined here by the sizeof operator.

The ReadStruct() function returns true if it reads a data structure and false if it doesn't; therefore, the body of the if statement executes if the function reads a bitmap file header data structure. The first statement in the body of the if statement checks that the character constants for B and M are assigned to the bfType variable. This must be true if the file doesn't contain a bitmap image. The second statement in the body of the if statement assigns the dlFileHeader enumerated constant to the m_dlState variable. This step indicates that the bitmap file header has been transferred.

If the if statement conditional is false, then the body of the else statement is executed. The first statement in the body of the else statement assigns FALSE to the bContinue variable, which results in the termination of the while loop. No sense in continuing if the file in question doesn't have a bitmap file header!

Assuming that a bitmap file header was downloaded successfully, the next case statement to be executed while the while loop is running occurs when dlFileHeader is assigned to the m_dlState variable, indicating that the file header has been transferred. The complete case statement follows.

```
case dlFileHeader:
  if (ReadStruct(dwSize, &m_bmInfo.bmiHeader, sizeof(m_bmInfo.bmiHeader)))
  {
    m_BitmapSize.cx = m_bmInfo.bmiHeader.biWidth;
    m_BitmapSize.cy = m_bmInfo.bmiHeader.biHeight;
    ASSERT_KINDOF(CLogoMagicCtrl, GetControl());
    ((CLogoMagicCtrl*)GetControl())->InformSize();
    m_dlState = dlInfoHeader;
  }
  else
  {
    bContinue = FALSE;
    break;
  }
  break;
```

The first line of code in the body of this case statement begins an if statement that checks the return of another call to the ReadStruct()

function; this time the ReadStruct() function is trying to read a bitmap information header. The LogoMagic control successfully downloads and displays a subset of all possible bitmap files: those with 256 colors or gray tones. Derive your own structure from the BITMAPINFO structure that declares a 256-color bitmap information header structure. The BITMAPINFO structure declaration follows, and Table 11.4 describes each member.

```
typedef struct tagBITMAPINFO {
  BITMAPINFOHEADER      bmiHeader;
  RGBQUAD               bmiColors[1];
} BITMAPINFO;
```

Table 11.4 Members of the BITMAPINFO Structure

Variable	Description
bmiHeader	Specifies a BITMAPINFOHEADER structure that contains information about the dimensions and color format of a device-independent bitmap (DIB)
bmiColors[1]	Specifies an array of RGBQUAD or DWORD data types that define the colors in the bitmap

The default number of colors in the BITMAPINFO structure's bmiColors array is one. Add the following structure to the top of the BitmapProperty.h file, before any of the CBitmapProperty class declarations:

```
struct BITMAPINFO256 : public BITMAPINFO
{
  RGBQUAD bmiOtherColors[255];
};
```

Your custom BITMAPINFO256 data structure is derived from BITMAPINFO. The bmiColors array is added to the two other variables inherited from BITMAPINFO. The bmiColors array is an array of 256 RGBQUAD data structure elements. Each RGBQUAD data structure defines a color, so the bmiColors array defines 256 colors. The RGBQUAD structure declaration follows, and Table 11.5 describes each member.

```
typedef struct tagRGBQUAD {
```

```
    BYTE    rgbBlue;
    BYTE    rgbGreen;
    BYTE    rgbRed;
    BYTE    rgbReserved;
} RGBQUAD;
```

Table 11.5 Members of the RGBQUAD Structure

Variable	Description
rgbBlue	Specifies the intensity of blue in the color.
rgbGreen	Specifies the intensity of green in the color.
rgbRed	Specifies the intensity of red in the color.
rgbReserved	Reserved; the value must be zero.

Now that you've defined the BITMAPINFO256 data structure, add a member variable named m_bmInfo to the CBitmapProperty class with a BITMAPINFO256 data type. Point to CBitmapProperty on the ClassView page of the Workspace window and click your right mouse button to open the shortcut menu. Select the Add Member Variable command from the shortcut menu to open the Add Member Variable dialog box as shown in Figure 11-7.

Type **BITMAPINFO256** into the Variable Type text box in the Add Member Variable dialog box. Then type in the name of the variable, **m_bmInfo**, into the Variable Name text box. Finally, the m_bmInfo variable is public, so select the Public radio button in the Access area of the Add Member Variable dialog box and then click on the OK button. The new CBitmapProperty member variable should appear in the ClassView page of the Workspace window.

With the m_bmInfo variable added to the CBitmapProperty class, you need to add one more member variable to the CBitmapProperty class before you can get back to implementing the dlFileHeader case statement. In this case statement, you find out the size of the bitmap from

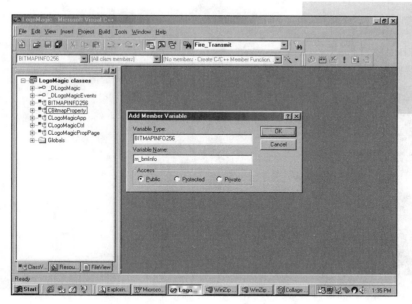

Figure 11-7
Add the
`m_bmInfo`
variable through
the Add Member
Variable dialog
box.

the bitmap information header. You want the CBitmapProperty object to maintain this information.

Add a member variable named `m_BitmapSize`, with a CSize data type, to the CBitmapProperty class. Point to CBitmapProperty on the ClassView page of the Workspace window and click your right mouse button to open the shortcut menu. Select the Add Member Variable command from the shortcut menu to open the Add Member Variable dialog box as shown in Figure 11-8.

Type **CSize** into the Variable Type text box in the Add Member Variable dialog box. Then type in the name of the variable, **m_BitmapSize**, into the Variable Name text box. Finally, the `m_BitmapSize` variable is public, so select the Public radio button in the Access area of the Add Member Variable dialog box and then click on the OK button. The new CBitmapProperty member variable should appear in the ClassView page of the Workspace window.

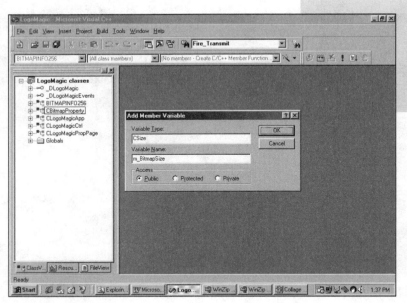

Figure 11-8
Add the
m_BitmapSize
variable through
the Add Member
Variable dialog
box.

With both the m_bmInfo and m_BitmapSize variables added to the CBitmap-Property class, you can get back to implementing the dlFileHeader case statement. Recall that you left off at the call to the ReadStruct() function in the first line of the if statement. The call assigns the bitmap file's bitmap information header to the variable passed to the function's second parameter, in this case the bmiHeader member variable of the BITMAPINFO256 structure. Remember that the m_bmInfo variable is declared a BITMAPINFO256 data type and that this structure is extended from the BITMAPINFO structure. The bmiHeader variable is declared a BITMAPINFOHEADER type in the BITMAPINFO structure. The BITMAPINFOHEADER structure declaration follows, and Table 11.6 describes each member.

```
typedef struct tagBITMAPINFOHEADER{
  DWORD  biSize;
  LONG   biWidth;
  LONG   biHeight;
  WORD   biPlanes;
  WORD   biBitCount;
  DWORD  biCompression;
  DWORD  biSizeImage;
  LONG   biXPelsPerMeter;
```

```
LONG    biYPelsPerMeter;
DWORD   biClrUsed;
DWORD   biClrImportant;
} BITMAPINFOHEADER;
```

Table 11.6 Members of the BITMAPINFOHEADER Structure

Variable	Description
biSize	Specifies the size of the structure in bytes.
biWidth	Specifies the width of the bitmap in pixels.
biHeight	Specifies the height of the bitmap in pixels.
biPlanes	Specifies the number of planes for the target device.
biBitCount	Specifies the number of bits per pixel.
biCompression	Specifies the type of compression for a bottom-up compressed bitmap. Top-down device-independent bitmaps (DIBs) cannot be compressed.
biSizeImage	Specifies the size of the image in bytes.
biXPelsPerMeter	Specifies the horizontal resolution, in pixels per meter, of the target device for the bitmap.
biYPelsPerMeter	Specifies the vertical resolution, in pixels per meter, of the target device for the bitmap.
biClrUsed	Specifies the number of color indexes in the color table that are actually used by the bitmap.
biClrImportant	Specifies the number of color indexes that are required for displaying the bitmap.

If the ReadStruct() function successfully reads the bitmap information header, then it returns true and the body of the if statement is executed. The first two statements in the body of the if statement assign the width and height of the bitmap found in the bitmap information header (biWidth and biHeight, respectively) to the width and height variables (cx and cy, respectively) encapsulated in the CSize object assigned to the m_BitmapSize variable.

The third statement in the body of the if statement uses ASSERT_KINDOF, which is an MFC macro. This macro takes two parameters. The first is the name of a CObject derived class, and the second takes a pointer to a class object. The ASSERT_KINDOF macro makes sure that the object pointed to is either an object of the specified class or an object of a class derived from the specified class. When the call to the macro is successful, the next line of code, which accesses the control object, CLogoMagicCtrl, can be executed with confidence.

You need to get a pointer to the CLogoMagicCtrl object so that its InformSize() function can be called. You haven't yet added this function to the CLogoMagicCtrl class; you do so later this chapter in the section "Create the InformSize() Function," but it's enough to know now that this call tells the control the size of the bitmap file being transferred.

> **Note**
>
> **You must include the LogoMagicCtl.h file at the top of the BitmapProperty.cpp file now that you've included a reference to the CLogoMagicCtrl class. Add the following line of code right after the include for the LogoMagicCtl.h file.**
>
> ```
> #include "LogoMagicCtl.h"
> ```

The final statement in the body of the if statement assigns the dlInfo-Header enumerated constant to the m_dlState variable, indicating that the information header has been transferred successfully. Otherwise, if the body of the if statement conditional returns a false, the else statement is executed. The code in the body of the else statement assigns FALSE to the bContinue variable, which results in the end of while loop execution.

Assuming that the body of the if statement executes and successfully transfers the bitmap information header, the case dlInfoHeader statement is the next to be executed. The complete case statement follows.

```
case dlInfoHeader:
  if (ReadStruct(dwSize, &m_bmInfo.bmiColors, sizeof(RGBQUAD) * (1 <<
m_bmInfo.bmiHeader.biBitCount)))
  {
    CWindowDC screenDC(NULL);
    m_Bitmap.CreateCompatibleBitmap(&screenDC, m_BitmapSize.cx, m_Bitmap-
Size.cy);
    m_dlState = dlColorTable;
  }
  else
  {
    bContinue = FALSE;
    break;
  }
  break;
```

The code in this case statement reads the color table from the bitmap information header. The first line of code begins an if statement that calls the ReadStruct() function. If the call successfully reads the color table, it returns true and the body of the if statement is executed. Otherwise, the function returns false, and the else statement is executed, assigning FALSE to the bContinue variable, resulting in the end of execution of the while loop.

The body of the if statement creates a buffer for the bitmap. First a windows device context variable is declared, and then a compatible bitmap is created by calling the CBitmap class CreateCompatibleBitmap() function. You haven't created the m_Bitmap variable yet, so now is a good time to do so.

Add the CBitmapProperty class member variable named m_Bitmap, with a CBitmap data type. Point to CBitmapProperty on the ClassView page of the Workspace window and click your right mouse button to open the shortcut menu. Select the Add Member Variable command from the shortcut menu to open the Add Member Variable dialog box as shown in Figure 11-9.

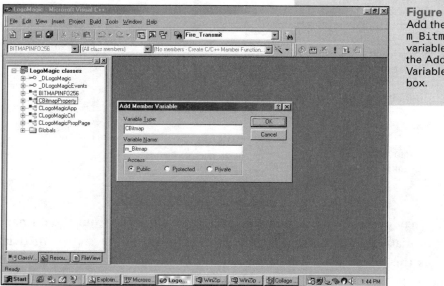

Figure 11-9
Add the
`m_Bitmap`
variable through
the Add Member
Variable dialog
box.

Type **CBitmap** into the Variable Type text box in the Add Member Variable dialog box. Then type in the name of the variable, **m_Bitmap**, into the Variable Name text box. Finally, the `m_Bitmap` variable is public, so select the Public radio button in the Access area of the Add Member Variable dialog box and then click on the OK button. The new CBitmapProperty member variable should appear in the ClassView page of the Workspace window.

You pass the `CreateCompatibleBitmap()` function the screen device context you just created and the width and height, in pixels, of the bitmap that were assigned to the `m_BitmapSize` variable when the information header was read.

The last statement in the body of the `if` statement assigns the `dlColor-Table` enumerated constant to the `m_dlState` variable, indicating that the color table was successfully transferred. Assuming that the body of the `if` statement executes and successfully transfers the color table, the `case` `dlColorTable` statement is the next to be executed. The complete `case` statement follows.

```
case dlColorTable:
  {
    BYTE* pb = NULL;
    int nLines = ReadArray(dwSize, (void **)&pb,
      ((((m_bmInfo.bmiHeader.biBitCount * m_BitmapSize.cx) + 31) / 32) * 4),
        m_BitmapSize.cy - m_nScanLine);
    if (nLines > 0)
    {
      CWindowDC screenDC(NULL);
      CDC dc;
      dc.CreateCompatibleDC(&screenDC);
      CBitmap* pBitmap = dc.SelectObject(&m_Bitmap);
      SetDIBits(dc.m_hDC, (HBITMAP)m_Bitmap.m_hObject, m_nScanLine, nLines,
        pb, &m_bmInfo, DIB_RGB_COLORS);
      m_nScanLine += nLines;
      GetControl()->Invalidate(FALSE);
    }
    else
    {
      bContinue = FALSE;
      break;
    }
    delete [] pb;
    if (m_nScanLine == m_BitmapSize.cy)
      m_dlState = dlDone;
  }
  break;
```

This statement is the last of the five case statements that you add to the OnDataAvailable() function's while loop. Its purpose is to transfer pixels. The first line of code declares the pb variable, which is a pointer to a BYTE. This variable is used during data transfer.

Next, a call is made to the CBitmapProperty class ReadArray() function. You haven't added this function but you do later this chapter in the "Create the ReadArray() Function" section. The ReadArray() function is where the actual data transfer is carried out. You pass the first parameter the amount of data to read, in bytes. The second parameter receives a pointer to the transferred data. The third parameter takes the size of each element, and the fourth parameter takes the maximum number of elements.

The m_nScanLine variable in the fourth parameter of the ReadArray() function is a CBitmapProperty class member variable that you haven't

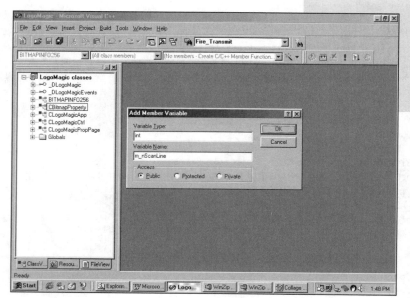

Figure 11-10
Add the
m_nScanLine
variable through
the Add Member
Variable dialog
box.

added yet. This member variable gets assigned the number of scan lines found in the array containing device-independent color data.

Add the m_nScanLine variable to the CBitmapProperty class with an int data type. Point to CBitmapProperty on the ClassView page of the Workspace window and click your right mouse button to open the shortcut menu. Select the Add Member Variable command from the shortcut menu to open the Add Member Variable dialog box as shown in Figure 11-10.

Type **int** into the Variable Type text box in the Add Member Variable dialog box. Then type in the name of the variable, **m_nScanLine**, into the Variable Name text box. Finally, the m_nScanLine variable is public so select the Public radio button in the Access area of the Add Member Variable dialog box and then click on the OK button. The new CBitmapProperty member variable should appear in the ClassView page of the Workspace window.

The ReadArray() function returns the number of elements transferred. This number gets assigned to the nLines local variable. The integer assigned to the nLines variable is used by the if...else statement that follows. If the number of lines transferred is greater than zero, then the body of the if statement is executed. Otherwise, the else statement is executed.

The code in the body of the if statement creates a compatible screen device context and a local pointer to the CBitmap object assigned to the m_Bitmap variable. But this step only leads up to the main event, which is to call the SetDIBits() function to set the pixels in the transferred bitmap data using the color data found previously in the color table. The declaration for the SetDIBits() function follows, and Table 11.7 describes each parameter.

```
int SetDIBits( HDC hdc,
  HBITMAP hbmp,
  UINT uStartScan,
  UINT cScanLines,
  CONST VOID *lpvBits,
  CONST BITMAPINFO *lpbmi,
  UINT fuColorUse
);
```

Table 11.7 Parameters of the SetDIBits() function

Parameter	Description
hdc	Handle to a device context.
hbmp	Handle to the bitmap that is to be altered using the color data from the specified device-independent bitmap's (DIBs) color table.
uStartScan	Specifies the starting scan line for the device-independent color data in the array pointed to by the lpvBits parameter.
cScanLines	Specifies the number of scan lines found in the array containing device-independent color data.
*lpvBits	Pointer to the device-independent bitmap (DIB) color data, stored as an array of bytes.
*lpbmi	Pointer to a BITMAPINFO data structure that contains information about the device-independent bitmap (DIB).
fuColorUse	Specifies whether the bmiColors member variable of the BITMAPINFO data structure was assigned a value and, if it was, specifies whether it's using explicit red, green, and blue (RGB) values or palette indexes. Either the DIB_RGB_COLORS constant or the DIB_PAL_COLORS is assigned to the variable.

The next statement adds the number of scan lines just set in the bitmap, assigned to the nLines variable, to the total number of scan lines transferred so far, which is assigned to the m_nScanLine variable.

Finally, a pointer to the CLogoMagicCtrl object is returned, and a call is made to the object's Invalidate() function, inherited from the CWnd class. The Invalidate() function invalidates the entire client area of the component's graphical user interface, initiating the repainting of the area with the new bitmap data. FALSE is passed to the function, telling it not to erase the background in the client area.

The first line of code after the if...else statement deletes the pointer to the BYTE array assigned to the pb variable. Then an if statement tests whether the number of scan lines transferred equals the number of pixels in the bitmap's vertical direction. If it's true, then the entire bitmap has been transferred and the operation is finished. The dlDone enumerated constant is assigned to the m_dlState variable.

You are finished coding the central functionality of the CBitmapProperty class. Listing 11.1 shows the code of the finished OnDataAvailable() function; the new code you added appears in bold.

Listing 11.1 CBitmapProperty Class OnDataAvailable() **Function in BitmapProperty.cpp**

```
void CBitmapProperty::OnDataAvailable(DWORD dwSize, DWORD bscfFlag)
{
    // TODO: Add your specialized code here and/or call the base class
    if (bscfFlag & BSCF_FIRSTDATANOTIFICATION)
        ResetData();

    CCachedDataPathProperty::OnDataAvailable(dwSize, bscfFlag);

    if (dwSize <= m_cbRead)
        return;
    else
        dwSize -= m_cbRead;
    m_cbRead += dwSize;

    BOOL bContinue = m_dlState != dlDone;
    while (bContinue)
    {
```

```
switch (m_dlState)
{
case dlNone:
  {
    BITMAPFILEHEADER bmfh;
    if (ReadStruct(dwSize, &bmfh, sizeof(bmfh)))
    {
      ASSERT(bmfh.bfType == 'B' ¦ ('M' << 8));
      m_dlState = dlFileHeader;
    }
    else
    {
      bContinue = FALSE;
      break;
    }
  }
  break;

case dlFileHeader:
  if (ReadStruct(dwSize, &m_bmInfo.bmiHeader, sizeof(m_bmInfo.bmi-
Header)))
    {
      m_BitmapSize.cx = m_bmInfo.bmiHeader.biWidth;
      m_BitmapSize.cy = m_bmInfo.bmiHeader.biHeight;
      ASSERT_KINDOF(CLogoMagicCtrl, GetControl());
      ((CLogoMagicCtrl*)GetControl())->InformSize();
      m_dlState = dlInfoHeader;
    }
    else
    {
      bContinue = FALSE;
      break;
    }
    break;

case dlInfoHeader:
  if (ReadStruct(dwSize, &m_bmInfo.bmiColors, sizeof(RGBQUAD) * (1 <<
m_bmInfo.bmiHeader.biBitCount)))
    {
      CWindowDC screenDC(NULL);
      m_Bitmap.CreateCompatibleBitmap(&screenDC, m_BitmapSize.cx,
m_BitmapSize.cy);
      m_dlState = dlColorTable;
    }
    else
    {
      bContinue = FALSE;
      break;
    }
```

```
                  break;

              case dlColorTable:
                {
                  BYTE* pb = NULL;
                  int nLines = ReadArray(dwSize, (void **)&pb,
                    (((((m_bmInfo.bmiHeader.biBitCount * m_BitmapSize.cx) + 31) / 32)
* 4),
                        m_BitmapSize.cy - m_nScanLine);
                  if (nLines > 0)
                  {
                    CWindowDC screenDC(NULL);
                    CDC dc;
                    dc.CreateCompatibleDC(&screenDC);
                    CBitmap* pBitmap = dc.SelectObject(&m_Bitmap);
                    SetDIBits(dc.m_hDC, (HBITMAP)m_Bitmap.m_hObject, m_nScanLine,
nLines,
                      pb, &m_bmInfo, DIB_RGB_COLORS);
                    m_nScanLine += nLines;
                    GetControl()->Invalidate(FALSE);
                  }
                  else
                  {
                    bContinue = FALSE;
                    break;
                  }
                  delete [] pb;
                  if (m_nScanLine == m_BitmapSize.cy)
                    m_dlState = dlDone;
                }
                break;

            };
            bContinue = bContinue && (m_dlState != dlDone);
          }
          ASSERT_KINDOF(CLogoMagicCtrl, GetControl());
          ((CLogoMagicCtrl*)GetControl())->InformDlStatus(m_dlState);
        }
```

Overriding the ResetData() Function

You've implemented the OnDataAvailable() function in the CBitmapProperty class, which is a centrally important function for transferring bitmap
files. However, the OnDataAvailable() function calls several functions that

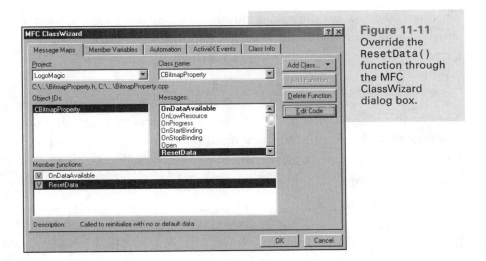

Figure 11-11
Override the
ResetData()
function through
the MFC
ClassWizard
dialog box.

you need to add to the CBitmapProperty. One such function is the Reset-Data() function that you override. The CCachedDataPathProperty class inherits the ResetData() function from the CDataPathProperty class. Recall that a call to the ResetData() function invalidates any bitmap data previous loaded by the component.

To override the ResetData() function, select the ClassWizard command from the View menu to open the MFC ClassWizard dialog box. Click on the Message Maps tab to display the Message Maps page and select the CBitmapProperty class from the Class Name drop-down list. Finally, select ResetData in the Messages list and click on the Add Function button. ResetData is added to the Member Functions list of the MFC ClassWizard dialog box, as shown in Figure 11-11.

Click on the Edit Code button, and Visual C++ takes you to the Reset-Data() function source code that you just added to the CBitmapProperty class. Add the following code to the ResetData() function immediately after the code added by Visual C++ calling the CCachedDataPathProperty object ResetData() function.

```
m_dlState = dlNone;
```

This statement assigns the `dlNone` enumerated constant to the `m_dlState` variable, indicating that none of the current bitmap file has been transferred. Next, type in the following `if` statement:

```
if (m_Bitmap.m_hObject != NULL)
    m_Bitmap.DeleteObject();
```

The conditional tests whether a CBitmap object remains assigned to the `m_Bitmap` variable. If one is, then it's deleted through a call to the CBitmap object's `DeleteObject()` function. Add the following line:

```
m_Cache.SetLength(0);
```

This statement calls the `SetLength()` function of the CCachedDataPathProperty class `m_Cache` member variable and sets the length of the cached file to zero. Next set the number of scan lines transferred to zero by assigning zero to the `m_nScanLine` variable with the following statement:

```
m_nScanLine = 0;
```

Finally, set the number of bytes of data being transferred to zero by assigning zero to the `m_cbRead` variable with the following statement.

```
m_cbRead = 0;
```

That's the complete `ResetData()` function. You can see that it deletes objects and sets variables to zero. Listing 11.2 shows the finished `ResetData()` function; the code you added appears in bold.

Listing 11.2 CBitmapProperty Class `ResetData()` Function in BitmapProperty.cpp

```
void CBitmapProperty::ResetData()
{
  // TODO: Add your specialized code here and/or call the base class
  CCachedDataPathProperty::ResetData();
  m_dlState = dlNone;
  if (m_Bitmap.m_hObject != NULL)
    m_Bitmap.DeleteObject();

  m_Cache.SetLength(0);
  m_nScanLine = 0;
  m_cbRead = 0;
}
```

Creating the ReadStruct() Function

The ReadStruct() function reads a data structure of the type passed to the function's second parameter, and it's called three times from the OnDataAvailable() function. It's called to read the bitmap file header, the bitmap information header, and the color table. It's time to write the ReadStruct() function.

Point to CBitmapProperty in the ClassView page of the Workspace window and click your right mouse button to display a shortcut menu. Select the Add Member Function command to open the Add Member Function dialog box as shown in Figure 11-12.

The ReadStruct() function returns true or false. Type **BOOL** into the Function Type text box in the Add Member Function dialog box. The ReadStruct() function takes three parameters. Type the following line into the Function Declaration text box:

```
ReadStruct(DWORD& rdwSize, void* pb, int cLen)
```

The first parameter, rdwSize, takes the number of bytes available for transfer. The second parameter, pb, takes a pointer to the type of data structure that will be transferred. The third parameter, cLen, is passed the size of the data structure that will be transferred.

The ReadStruct() function is public, so select the Public radio button in the Access area of the Add Member Function dialog box. Finally, leave the Static and Virtual check boxes at the bottom of the dialog box unchecked, and then click on the OK button. The ReadStruct() function should be added to the tree under CBitmapProperty in the

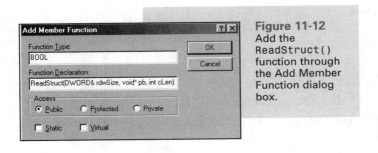

Figure 11-12
Add the ReadStruct() function through the Add Member Function dialog box.

ClassView page of the Workspace window. Double-click on that listing, and the BitmapProperty.cpp file opens in the Visual C++ document window displaying the ReadStruct() function definition. The first line of code you add to the function, which follows, calls the AfxTransferFile-Content() function.

```
AfxTransferFileContent(this, &m_Cache, rdwSize);
```

This function is part of the application framework. You need to override the function by typing the code in Listing 11.3 into the CBitmapProperty class. Don't add a function declaration to the class's header file.

> **Note**
>
> **Be sure to add the** AfxTransferFileContent() **function definition before the** ReadStruct() **function definition in the BitmapProperty.cpp file.**

Listing 11.3 CBitmapProperty Class AfxTransferFile-Content() **Function in BitmapProperty.cpp**

```
DWORD AfxTransferFileContent(CFile* pFrom, CFile* pTo, DWORD dwAmount)
{
  BYTE buff[1024];
  DWORD dwRead = 0;
  DWORD dwActual = 1;
  while ((dwAmount > 0) && (dwActual > 0))
  {
    dwActual = pFrom->Read(buff, min(dwAmount, 1024));
    pTo->Write(buff, dwActual);

    dwAmount -= dwActual;
    dwRead += dwActual;
  }
  return dwRead;
}
```

The first parameter to the AfxTransferFileContent() function takes a pointer to the file that the transfer is being initiated from, and the second parameter takes a pointer to the file that is writing the bitmap data to the other file.

Now that you've added the `AfxTransferFileContent()` function, go back to the body of the `ReadStruct()` function and add the following statement that sets the number of bytes currently being transferred, assigned to the `rdwSize` variable, to zero:

```
rdwSize = 0;
```

Add this statement right after the call to the `AfxTransferFileContent()` function. Next, get the length of the memory file encapsulated by the CMemFile object assigned to the `m_Cache` variable:

```
int cCache = m_Cache.GetLength();
```

The CMemFile class inherits the `GetLength()` function from the CFile class. The function returns the length of the memory file and assigns the value to the `cCache` local variable. The following `if...else` statement tests the value assigned to the `cCache` variable against the value assigned to the `cLen` variable, which is the size of the data structure that's being transferred. There must be at least as much memory as there is file to put in it. Under these conditions, the body of the `if` statement is executed, and the file is transferred. Otherwise, the `else` statement is executed, and the transfer is terminated.

```
if (cCache >= cLen)
{
  m_Cache.SeekToBegin();
  VERIFY(m_Cache.Read(pb, cLen) == (UINT)cLen);
  if (cCache > cLen)
  {
    CMemFile memFile;
    AfxTransferFileContent(&m_Cache, &memFile, cCache - cLen);
    m_Cache.SetLength(0);
    memFile.SeekToBegin();
    AfxTransferFileContent(&memFile, &m_Cache, cCache - cLen);
  }
  else
  {
    m_Cache.SetLength(0);
  }
  return TRUE;
}
else
{
  return FALSE;
}
```

Listing 11.4 shows the complete ReadStruct() function code; your additions appear in bold.

Listing 11.4 CBitmapProperty Class ReadStruct()
Function in BitmapProperty.cpp

```
BOOL CBitmapProperty::ReadStruct(DWORD& rdwSize, void* pb, int cLen)
{
  AfxTransferFileContent(this, &m_Cache, rdwSize);
  rdwSize = 0;
  int cCache = m_Cache.GetLength();
  if (cCache >= cLen)
  {
    m_Cache.SeekToBegin();
    VERIFY(m_Cache.Read(pb, cLen) == (UINT)cLen);
    if (cCache > cLen)
    {
      CMemFile memFile;
      AfxTransferFileContent(&m_Cache, &memFile, cCache - cLen);
      m_Cache.SetLength(0);
      memFile.SeekToBegin();
      AfxTransferFileContent(&memFile, &m_Cache, cCache - cLen);
    }
    else
    {
      m_Cache.SetLength(0);
    }
    return TRUE;
  }
  else
  {
    return FALSE;
  }
}
```

Creating the ReadArray() Function

The ReadArray() function is where the actual data transfer is carried out when it's called from the case dlColorTable statement in the OnDataAvailable() function. Add the function to the CBitmapProperty class.

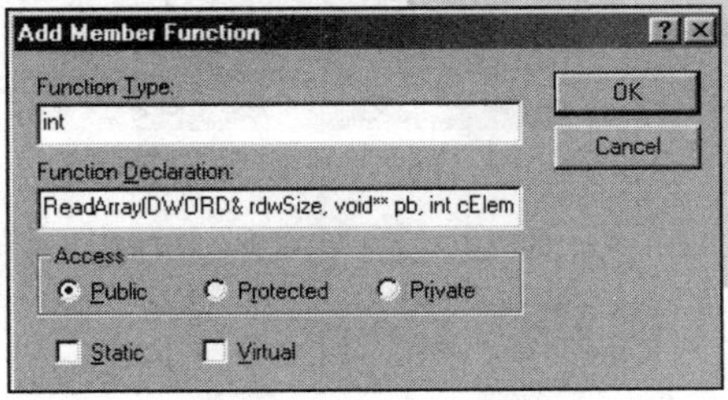

Figure 11-13
Add the
ReadArray()
function through the
Add Member
Function dialog box.

Point to CBitmapProperty in the ClassView page of the Workspace window and click your right mouse button to display a shortcut menu. Select the Add Member Function command to open the Add Member Function dialog box as shown in Figure 11-13.

The ReadArray() function returns an integer value, which is the number of elements transferred. Type **int** into the Function Type text box in the Add Member Function dialog box. The ReadArray() function takes four parameters. Type the following line into the Function Declaration text box:

```
ReadArray(DWORD& rdwSize, void** pb, int cElem, int cMax)
```

The first parameter takes the amount of data to read, in bytes. The second parameter takes a pointer to the transferred data, and the third parameter takes the size of each element. Finally, the fourth parameter takes the maximum number of elements.

The ReadArray() function is public, so select the Public radio button in the Access area of the Add Member Function dialog box and then click on the OK button. The ReadArray() function should be added to the tree under CBitmapProperty in the ClassView page of the Workspace window. Double-click on that listing and the BitmapProperty.cpp file opens in the Visual C++ document window displaying the ReadArray() function definition.

Add the code in Listing 11.5 to the ReadArray() function in the CBitmapProperty class. The listing includes the complete code for the function; the code you add appears in bold.

Listing 11.5 CBitmapProperty Class `ReadArray()` **Function in BitmapProperty.cpp**

```cpp
int CBitmapProperty::ReadArray(DWORD& rdwSize, void** pb, int cElem, int cMax)
{
    AfxTransferFileContent(this, &m_Cache, rdwSize);
    rdwSize = 0;
    int nElems = 0;
    int cCache = m_Cache.GetLength();
    if (cCache >= cElem)
    {
        m_Cache.SeekToBegin();
        nElems = min(cCache / cElem, cMax);
        int cSize = nElems * cElem;
        ASSERT(cSize <= cCache);
        *pb = new BYTE[cSize];
        ASSERT(m_Cache.Read(*pb, cSize) == (UINT)cSize);
        if (cCache > cSize)
        {
            CMemFile memFile;
            AfxTransferFileContent(&m_Cache, &memFile, cCache - cSize);
            m_Cache.SetLength(0);
            memFile.SeekToBegin();
            AfxTransferFileContent(&memFile, &m_Cache, cCache - cSize);
        }
        else
        {
            m_Cache.SetLength(0);
        }
    }
    return nElems;
}
```

The CLogoMagicCtrl Class

With the CBitmapProperty class complete, you can focus on customizing the CLogoMagicCtrl class. This class, when instantiated, is the core of the LogoMagic component that actually displays the bitmap that the CBitmapProperty object worked so hard to transfer.

Adding the AutoSize Property

The LogoMagic control automatically changes the size of its graphics interface to match the size of the bitmap image that is displayed there. Add an AutoSize property that includes the `m_bAutoSize` member variable, which is assigned the size of the current bitmap.

Select the ClassWizard command from the View menu to open the MFC ClassWizard dialog box. Click on the Automation tab to display the Automation page of the MFC ClassWizard dialog box. Select CLogoMagicCtrl in the Class Name drop-down list; then click on the Add Property button to open the Add Property dialog box as shown in Figure 11-14.

Select the Member Variable radio button on the Add Property dialog box. Then type in the name of the property that you're adding, `AutoPath`, into the External Name text box and drop-down list. Next, select the type of data returned by the get function, the BOOL type, in the Type drop-down list. Modify the variable name provided by Visual C++ in the Variable Name text box to read `m_bAutoSize`. This variable is assigned true if the user wants the control to automatically resize and false otherwise. Keep the notification function name provided by Visual C++, OnAutoSizeChanged, displayed in the Notification Function text box. Click on the OK button to add the AutoSize property to the External

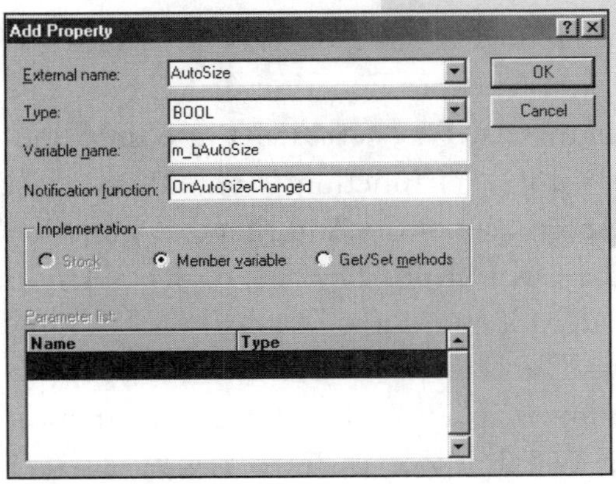

Figure 11-14
Add the AutoSize property through the Add Property dialog box.

Figure 11-15
Add the AutoSize()
function through the
Add Member Function
dialog box.

Names list; the C at the left indicates that AutoSize is a custom property. Click on the Edit Code button to close the MFC ClassWizard dialog box and go to the OnAutoSizeChanged() function in the CLogoMagicCtrl class.

Add the following if statement immediately after the "TODO" remark in the OnAutoSizeChanged() function and before the call to the SetModifiedFlag() function.

```
if(m_bAutoSize)
  AutoSize();
```

If true is assigned to the m_bAutoSize variable, then the AutoSize() function is called, which actually sets the control size. Add the AutoSize() function to the CLogoMagicCtrl class.

Point to CLogoMagicCtrl in the ClassView page of the Workspace window and click your right mouse button to display a shortcut menu. Select the Add Member Function command to open the Add Member Function dialog box as shown in Figure 11-15.

The AutoSize() function doesn't return a value, so type **void** into the Function Type text box in the Add Member Function dialog box. The AutoSize() function takes no parameters. Type **AutoSize()** into the Function Declaration text box. The AutoSize() function is public, so select the Public radio button in the Access area of the Add Member Function dialog box and then click on the OK button. The AutoSize() function should be added to the tree under CLogoMagicCtrl in the ClassView page of the Workspace window. The LogoMagicCtrl.cpp file opens in the Visual C++ document window displaying the AutoSize() function definition. Add the following two lines of code to the AutoSize() function definition:

Figure 11-16
Add the InformSize()
function through the
Add Member Function
dialog box.

```
ASSERT(m_bAutoSize);
SetControlSize(m_propImage.m_BitmapSize.cx, m_propImage.m_BitmapSize.cy);
```

The first statement checks the m_bAutoSize variable to be sure that it's assigned a valid value. The second statement calls the SetControlSize() function inherited from the COleControl class. This function sets the size of the control window.

Creating the InformSize() Function

The InformSize() function informs the LogoMagic control about the size of the bitmap file being transferred. Recall that, after reading the bitmap information header, the OnDataAvailable() function in the CBitmapProperty class calls the InformSize() function. Now you will add the InformSize() function to the CLogoMagicCtrl class.

Point to CLogoMagicCtrl in the ClassView page of the Workspace window and click your right mouse button to display a shortcut menu. Select the Add Member Function command to open the Add Member Function dialog box as shown in Figure 11-16.

The InformSize() function doesn't return a value, so type **void** into the Function Type text box in the Add Member Function dialog box. The InformSize() function takes no parameters. Type **InformSize()** into the Function Declaration text box. The InformSize() function is public, so select the Public radio button in the Access area of the Add Member Function dialog box and then click on the OK button. The InformSize() function should be added to the tree under CLogoMagicCtrl in the ClassView page of the Workspace window. The LogoMagicCtrl.cpp file opens in the Visual C++ document window displaying the InformSize()

function definition. Add the following three lines of code to the Inform-
Size() function definition:

```
if (m_bAutoSize)
  AutoSize();
InternalSetReadyState(READYSTATE_INTERACTIVE);
```

If true is assigned to the m_bAutoSize variable, then the AutoSize() function is called, setting the control size. Then the InternalSetReadyState()
function, inherited from the COleControl class, is called. This function
sets the readiness state of the control. Table 11.8 lists the constants available for setting a control's readiness state.

Table 11.8 Readiness State Constants

Constant	Description
READYSTATE_UNINITIALIZED	Default initialization state.
READYSTATE_LOADING	Control is currently loading its properties.
READYSTATE_LOADED	Control has been initialized.
READYSTATE_INTERACTIVE	Control has enough data to be interactive, but not all asynchronous data are loaded.
READYSTATE_COMPLETE	Control has all its data.

Creating the InformDlStatus() Function

The InformDlSize() function informs the LogoMagic control about the
state of the transfer process in progress. Recall that the OnDataAvailable()
function in the CBitmapProperty class calls this function at the end of
each pass through the while loop. Add the InformDlSize() function to
the CLogoMagicCtrl class. You need to add this function manually
because Visual C++ has a problem with adding the parameter that the
function needs through the Add Member Function dialog box.

Open the LogoMagicCtl.h file and add the following declaration below
the "Dispatch and event IDs" remark and under the public keyword:

```
void InformDlStatus(CBitmapProperty::DLState dlState);
```

Next, open the LogoMagicCtl.cpp file and add the complete `Inform-DlStatus()` function in Listing 11.6.

> ## Listing 11.6 CLogoMagicCtrl Class `InformDlStatus()` Function in LogoMagicCtl.cpp

```cpp
void CLogoMagicCtrl::InformDlStatus(CBitmapProperty::DLState dlState)
{
  Invalidate(FALSE);
  if (dlState == CBitmapProperty::DLState::dlDone)
    InternalSetReadyState(READYSTATE_COMPLETE);
}
```

Modifying the OnDraw() Function

Most of the work to display your logo bitmap to the LogoMagic control graphics interface occurs in the CLogoMagicCtrl class `OnDraw()` method. Replace the two lines of default code added by Visual C++ under the "TODO" remark with the code highlighted in bold face type in Listing 11.7.

> ## Listing 11.7 CLogoMagicCtrl Class `OnDraw()` Function in LogoMagicCtl.cpp

```cpp
void CLogoMagicCtrl::OnDraw(CDC* pdc, const CRect& rcBounds, const CRect& rcInvalid)
{
  // TODO: Replace the following code with your own drawing code.
  if (m_propImage.m_Bitmap.m_hObject != NULL)
  {
    CWindowDC screenDC(NULL);
    CDC dc;
    dc.CreateCompatibleDC(&screenDC);
    CBitmap* pBitmap = dc.SelectObject(&m_propImage.m_Bitmap);

    int cx(min(rcBounds.Width(), m_propImage.m_BitmapSize.cx));
    int cy(min(rcBounds.Height(), m_propImage.m_BitmapSize.cy));

    pdc->BitBlt(rcBounds.left, rcBounds.top, cx, cy, &dc, 0, 0, SRCCOPY);
    if (cx < rcBounds.Width())
    pdc->PatBlt(cx, rcBounds.top, rcBounds.Width() - cx, rcBounds.Height(),
BLACKNESS);
    if (cy < rcBounds.Height())
```

```
        pdc->PatBlt(rcBounds.left, cy, rcBounds.Width(), rcBounds.Height() -
cy, BLACKNESS);

    if (!IsOptimizedDraw())
    {
        dc.SelectObject(pBitmap);
    }
  }
  else
  {
    pdc->PatBlt(rcBounds.left, rcBounds.top,
        rcBounds.Width(), rcBounds.Height(), BLACKNESS);
  }
}
```

If a bitmap image hasn't been transferred to the LogoMagic control, then the conditional expression in the first `if` statement is false and the body of the `else` statement is executed. The result is that the control's window is filled with black. Otherwise, if the control does contain a bitmap file then the body of the first `if` statement is executed and the bitmap is displayed to the control's graphics interface.

The CLogoMagicPropPage Class

Your last task is to connect the LogoMagic property page with the LogoMagic control AutoSize and ImagePath properties. First you need to add a couple of controls to the LogoMagic property page interface. Open the Visual C++ Workspace window to the ResourceView page, open the tree under the Dialog folder in the LogoMagic resources folder, and double-click on IID_PROPPAGE_LOGOMAGIC. The property page dialog control displays in the resource editor as shown in Figure 11-17.

Select the placeholding Static Text control on the property page and delete the control by selecting the Delete command from the Edit menu or by pressing the delete key on your keyboard. Add a new Static Text control by clicking on the Static Text button (the one with the "Aa" label) on the Control toolbar and then by clicking on the property page dialog control.

Figure 11-17
The LogoMagic property page displayed in the Visual C++ resource editor

By placing the mouse pointer inside the highlighted rectangle around the text "Static", and pressing and holding the left mouse button, you can move that text label around the resource area. Move the Static Text control so that its upper-left corner is about 7 pixels to the right and 9 pixels down (7, 9) from the dialog's upper-left corner. These coordinates are displayed at the bottom right of the Visual C++ window in the status bar. The pair of numbers on the left is the distance of the upper-left corner of the currently selected control from the upper-left corner of the control in which the former is embedded. The pair of numbers on the right is the size of the currently selected control.

Tip

Use the arrow keys on your keyboard for fine adjustments to the position of controls in the resource editor.

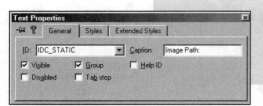

Figure 11-18
The Static Text control's General page of the Text Properties dialog box

While pointing to the new Static Text control, click your right mouse button to open a shortcut menu. Select the Properties command from the shortcut menu to open the Text Properties dialog box. Click on the General tab to display the General page of the Text Properties dialog box shown in Figure 11-18.

Change the text in the Caption text box on the General page of the Text Properties dialog box to read Image Path: and then close the dialog box.

Add an Edit Box control by clicking on the Edit Box button on the Control toolbar (the button with the "ab|"on it) and then clicking on the properties page dialog in the resource editor. Move the control so that its upper-left corner is 48 pixels to the right and 7 pixels down (48, 7) from the upper-left corner of the dialog. Resize the Edit Box control so that it's 195 pixels across and 13 pixels (195, 13) in the vertical direction. This is done by placing the cursor over one of the small black squares embedded in the highlighted frame around the edit box. The mouse cursor will change to a set of arrows, indicating the adjustment permitted at that location. Then press and hold the left button and drag the edge of the text box out to the desired size.

Tip

Use the arrow keys while holding down a Shift key for fine adjustments to the size of the currently selected control in the resource editor.

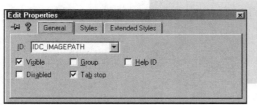

Figure 11-19
The Edit Box control's
General page of the
Edit Properties dialog
box

Figure 11-20
The Check Box control's
General page of the Check
Box Properties dialog box

While pointing to the new Edit Box control, click your right mouse button to open a shortcut menu. Select the Properties command from the shortcut menu to open the Edit Properties dialog box. Click on the General tab to display the General page of the Edit Properties dialog box shown in Figure 11-19.

Change the identifier in the ID combo box on the General page of the Edit Properties dialog box to read IDC_IMAGEPATH and then close the dialog box.

Finally, add a Check Box control to the property page by clicking on the Check Box button on the Control toolbar and then clicking on the properties page dialog in the resource editor. Move the control so that its upper-left corner is 7 pixels to the right and 26 pixels down (7, 26) from the upper-left corner of the dialog.

While pointing to the new Check Box control, click your right mouse button to open a shortcut menu. Select the Properties command from the shortcut menu to open the Check Box Properties dialog box. Click on the General tab to display the General page of the Check Box Properties dialog box shown in Figure 11-20.

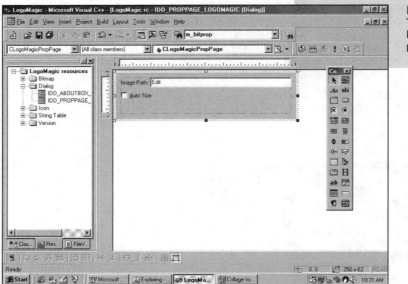

Figure 11-21
The completed
LogoMagic
property page

Change the identifier in the ID combo box on the General page of the
Check Box Properties dialog box to read IDC_AUTOSIZE and change
the text in the Caption text box to read &Auto Size. Close the dialog
box. The finished property page should look like Figure 11-21.

You'll notice that the A in Auto Size is underlined. The "&" is used to
indicate a hot focus key. When this page is in use, when someone presses
ALT+A, the highlight immediately switches to this checkbox.

Now connect the controls on the property page with the LogoMagic
control ImagePath and AutoSize properties. Select the ClassWizard
command from the View menu to open the MFC ClassWizard dialog
box. Click on the Member Variables tab. Make sure that ClogoMagicPropPage is selected in the Class Name drop-down list.

Associate member variables with the control identifiers of the controls
you just added to the property page. Make sure that the member variable names are the same as those associated with the same properties in
the CLogoMagicCtrl class.

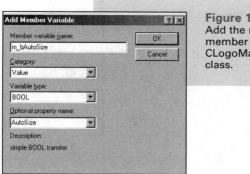

Figure 11-22
Add the m_bAutoSize member variable to the CLogoMagicPropPage class.

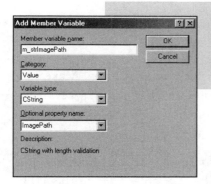

Figure 11-23
Add the m_strImagePath member variable to the CLogoMagicPropPage class.

Highlight the IDC_AUTOSIZE control identifier in the Control IDs list and then click on the Add Variable button. The Add Member Variable dialog box appears, as shown in Figure 11-22.

Type `m_bAutoSize` in the Member Variable Name text box. Make sure that `Value` is selected in the Category drop-down list and that `BOOL` is selected in the Variable Type drop-down list. Type `AutoSize` in the Optional Property Name text box and then click on the OK button.

This time highlight the IDC_IMAGEPATH control identifier in the Control IDs list and then click on the Add Variable button. The Add Member Variable dialog box appears, as shown in Figure 11-23.

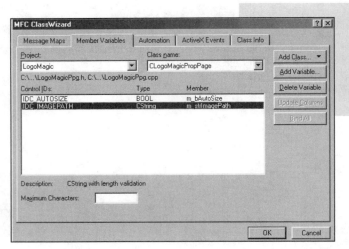

Figure 11-24
Connect the property
page with LogoMagic
properties through the
Member Variables page
of the MFC ClassWizard
dialog box.

Type **m_strImagePath** in the Member Variable Name text box. Make sure
that value is selected in the Category drop-down list and that CString is
selected in the Variable Type drop-down list. Type **ImagePath** in the
Optional Property Name text box and then click on the OK button.

You've added the member variables associated with the AutoSize and
ImagePath properties through the Member Variables page of the MFC
ClassWizard dialog box, which should currently look like Figure 11-24.

Click on the OK button on the MFC ClassWizard dialog box, and the
Wizard adds the appropriate code to your LogoMagic project. With this
step, you've completed the LogoMagic project.

Building and Running LogoMagic

Build the LogoMagic project by clicking on the Build button on the
Visual C++ toolbar. After the program is built, click on the Execute button on the Visual C++ toolbar to open the Executable for Debug Session dialog box shown in Figure 11-25.

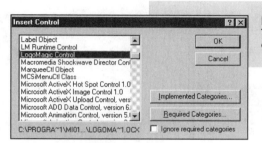

Figure 11-25
The Executable for
Debug Session
dialog box

Figure 11-26
The Insert Control
dialog box

Click on the button with the right-pointing arrowhead that sits to the right of the Executable File Name text box and select ActiveX Control Text Container from the menu. Click on the OK button to launch the ActiveX Control Text Container program.

Insert the LogoMagic control in the text container. Click on the New Control button on the test container's toolbar or select the Insert New Control command from the Edit menu to open the Insert Control dialog box shown in Figure 11-26.

Select LogoMagic Control in the list on the Insert Control dialog box and click on the OK button. The LogoMagic control should appear in the ActiveX Control Test Container window as a black box, as shown in Figure 11-27.

Point to the LogoMagic control and click your right mouse button to open a shortcut menu. Select the Properties command from the shortcut menu to open the LogoMagic Control Properties dialog box. Click on the General tab to display the General page of the Logo-

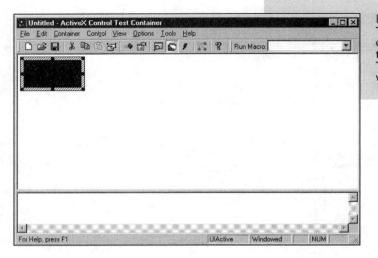

Figure 11-27
The LogoMagic
control inserted in
the ActiveX Control
Test Container
window

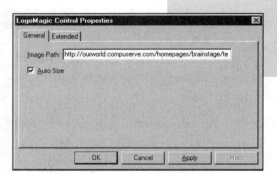

Figure 11-28
The LogoMagic
Control Properties
dialog box

Magic Control Properties dialog box, which displays the control's property sheet that you created as shown in Figure 11-28.

Type the following Web address—to the teddy.bmp file—into the Image Path text box on the LogoMagic Control Properties dialog box:

```
http://ourworld.compuserve.com/homepages/brainstage/teddy0.bmp
```

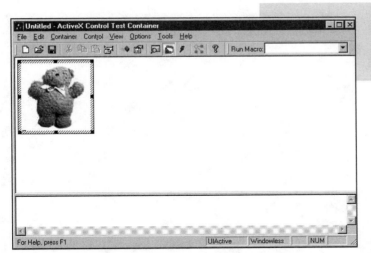

Figure 11-29
The LogoMagic
control displaying
the teddy0.bmp file

Click on the OK button. An image of a teddy bear transfers across the Internet and displays in your LogoMagic control, as shown in Figure 11-29.

Summary

In this chapter, you created an ActiveX control implementing a sophisticated image property. ActiveX controls are software components that can run anywhere on the computing enterprise. In fact, they can communicate among themselves no matter where they are on the enterprise thanks to Distributed COM (DCOM). You learn about DCOM in Project 3, but first deploy your new ActiveX control, the LogoMagic control, in Chapter 12.

CHAPTER 12

Testing LogoMagic

Visual C++ provides special integrated tools for testing and debugging ActiveX controls such as LogoMagic. In this chapter, you run the LogoMagic control in the Visual C++ debugger and use some of the tools that enable you to expose ActiveX control internal mechanisms. Then you build a final release version of the LogoMagic control and deploy it using InstallShield.

Exploring LogoMagic Using the Debugger

The Visual C++ debugger has special built-in facilities for debugging ActiveX controls. The debugger works with the ActiveX Control Test Container application, installed with Visual C++, to provide you with extensive ActiveX control testing and debugging capabilities, which include the ability to test control, property, method, event, data-binding, and persistence functionality.

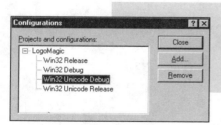

Figure 12-1
According to the Configurations dialog box, Visual C++ is set to create the debug version of a 32-bit Windows program that implements Unicode.

To debug your ActiveX control, you must use the debug build configuration when you build the control. Make sure that the currently active configuration of the LogoMagic project is set to build the 32-bit Windows debug version of the control. The build should also be set to compile Unicode code. ActiveX controls are designed to run on the enterprise regardless of the spoken or written language. View the LogoMagic project build configuration by selecting the Configurations command from the Build menu. The Configurations dialog box appears in Figure 12-1.

You build a release version of the LogoMagic control later in this chapter in the "Building the Release Version" section. For now, you want a build that contains debug information so that you can use the Visual C++ debugger and the ActiveX Control Test Container application to explore the internal operation of the LogoMagic ActiveX control.

Change the active build configuration of your LogoMagic project if it isn't set to create the 32-bit Windows Unicode debug version of the LogoMagic control. Select the Set Active Configuration command from the Build menu to open the Set Active Project Configuration dialog box, shown in Figure 12-2.

Select LogoMagic – Win32 Unicode Debug from the Project configurations list in the Set Active Project Configuration dialog box and then click on the OK button. Click on the Build button on the toolbar or select the Build LogoMagic.ocx command from the Build menu to build a debug version of the LogoMagic control.

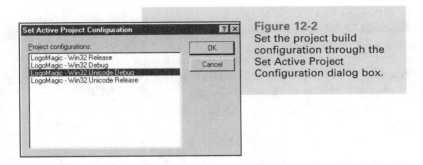

Figure 12-2
Set the project build
configuration through the
Set Active Project
Configuration dialog box.

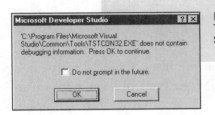

Figure 12-3
The Microsoft Developer
Studio dialog box

Start a Visual C++ debugging session with the LogoMagic ActiveX control by opening the Start Debug submenu on the Build menu; then select the Go command. The Executable for Debug Session dialog box appears if you haven't yet run the ActiveX Control Test Container application from the LogoMagic project. If this dialog box appears, click on the right-pointing arrowhead button that sits to the right of the Executable file name text box and select the ActiveX Control Test Container command from the menu; then click on the OK button. Otherwise, a Microsoft Developer Studio dialog box appears, as shown in Figure 12-3.

The Microsoft Developer Studio dialog box appears to tell you that the ActiveX Control Test Container application doesn't contain debugging information. That's all right because you aren't debugging the ActiveX Control Test Container application. You're debugging the LogoMagic ActiveX control that will go into the container. Click on the OK button to close the dialog box; Visual C++ enters into debug mode, and the ActiveX Control Test Container application appears.

> The Microsoft Developer Studio dialog box displays the path and name of the executable file containing the ActiveX Control Test Container application. The application's executable file is named TSTCON32.EXE and it's typically found in the C:\Program Files\Microsoft Visual Studio\Common\Tools\ folder.

Adding LogoMagic to the Test Container

Insert the LogoMagic control in the test container. Click on the New Control button on the test container's toolbar or select the Insert New Control command from the Edit menu to open the Insert Control dialog box, shown in Figure 12-4.

Select LogoMagic Control in the list on the Insert Control dialog box and click on the OK button. The LogoMagic control should appear in the ActiveX Control Test Container window as a black box, as shown in Figure 12-5.

Setting Breakpoints

The image property is the principal feature of the LogoMagic control, and the OnDataAvailable() function in the CBitmapProperty class implements much of the property's functionality. Explore the image property's code in action. Switch to the Visual C++ window to add a breakpoint in the CBitmapProperty class OnDataAvailable() function.

Double-click on OnDataAvailable() listed under CBitmapProperty in the ClassView page of the Workspace window, and the BitmapProperty.cpp file displays in the Visual C++ document window at the OnDataAvailable() function. Click on the first line of code after the "TODO" remark in the OnDataAvailable() function, which is the first line of the following if statement:

```
if (bscfFlag & BSCF_FIRSTDATANOTIFICATION)
```

Next, click on the Insert/Remove Breakpoint button on the Build Mini-Bar toolbar or, while pointing to the same line of code, right-click to open a shortcut menu and then select the Insert/Remove Breakpoint

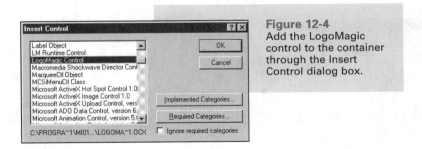

Figure 12-4
Add the LogoMagic control to the container through the Insert Control dialog box.

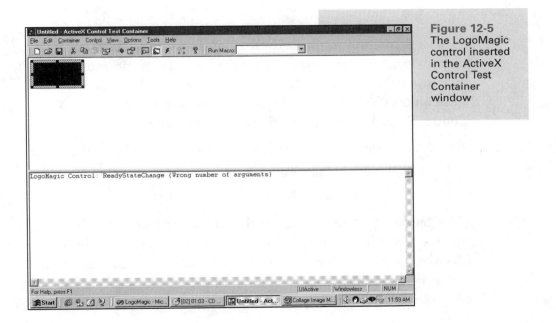

Figure 12-5
The LogoMagic control inserted in the ActiveX Control Test Container window

command. A red dot displays to the left of the line of code where the breakpoint is inserted.

Transferring Bitmap

Switch back to the ActiveX Control Test Container application to begin transferring the bitmap file. Open the LogoMagic control property sheet. While the LogoMagic control is selected, click on the Properties command on the Edit menu or point to the edge of the

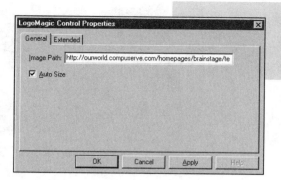

Figure 12-6
The LogoMagic
Control Properties
dialog box

LogoMagic control in the ActiveX Control Test Container and right-click to open a shortcut menu; select the Properties command from the shortcut menu. The LogoMagic Control Properties dialog box appears. Click on the General tab to display the General page of the LogoMagic Control Properties dialog box, shown in Figure 12-6.

Type the following Web address (to the teddy.bmp file) into the Image Path text box on the LogoMagic Control Properties dialog box:

```
http://ourworld.compuserve.com/homepages/brainstage/teddy0.bmp
```

Click on the OK button. An assertion is thrown by the ActiveX Control Test Container application due to the breakpoint, and the Visual C++ debugger gains the focus with the yellow arrow pointing to the currently executing code at the breakpoint you inserted in the OnDataAvailable() function.

This should be the first data notification to the LogoMagic control. You can see it for yourself by pointing your mouse control over the bscfFlag, which is assigned the current state of the bind status callback function (see Table 11.2). A window appears, displaying the variable name and the value currently assigned to the variable. Now point to the BSCF_FIRSTDATANOTIFICATION constant. The value assigned to the constant should be the same as the value assigned to the variable. This way of looking at values on-the-fly is an elegant feature of the Visual C++ environment.

Click on the Step Over button on the Debug toolbar to execute the next statement. Notice that the pointer moves to the body of the if statement because the conditional was true. The data are reset through the ResetData() function. Click on the Step Over button again. This is a call to the base class OnDataAvailable() function. For fun, take a look at the current value assigned to the dwSize variable by pointing to the variable. If you're transferring the teddy0.bmp file, dwSize should be 4222. Click on the Step Over button on the Debug toolbar.

The if statement currently being executed checks to see that the amount of data read is more than or equal to the amount of data in the bitmap file. Look at the value assigned to the m_cbRead variable. It should be 0 because no data have been transferred yet. The conditional is false, so the body of the if statement is skipped, and the else statement is executed. Click on the Step Over button.

The statement in the body of the else statement is executed. The value assigned to the dwSize variable remains at 4222 because 0, the value assigned to the m_cbRead variable, is subtracted. Click on the Step Over button.

The size of the data currently being transferred is added to the amount already read and is assigned to the m_cbRead variable. Click on the Step Over button and then point to the m_cbRead variable. It should be assigned 4222 now. The statement currently pointed to checks to see that the current transfer, or download, state is not equal to the dlDone constant. Point to the m_dlState variable, and you can see that the current state is dlNone, which is clearly not the same as dlDone. Therefore, when you click on the Step Over button, a 1 (true) is assigned to the bContinue variable. Click on the Step Over button.

Executing the while Loop

With 1 assigned to the bContinue variable, the while loop conditional is true, and the while loop executes. Click on the Step Over button again and execution moves to the body of the while loop at the beginning of the switch statement.

Recall that the `dlNone` enumerated constant is currently assigned to the `m_dlState` variable, which means that none of the bitmap file currently being transferred has been transferred yet. Click on the Step Over button and execution moves to the body of the `case dlNone` statement.

Executing the case dlNone Statement

The `case dlNone` statement is where the bitmap file header is downloaded. The `bmfh` variable is declared as a BITMAPFILEHEADER data type. A call to the `ReadStruct()` function transfers the bitmap file header and assigns it to the `bmfh` variable.

Perhaps you'd like to see the size of the bitmap file header assigned to the `bmfh` variable? Highlight the `sizeof(bmfh)` expression in the `Read-Struct()` function call; then point to the highlight and click and drag your mouse until the pointer is pointing inside the Watch window at the bottom of the Visual C++ window. Release your mouse button.

You just dragged-and-dropped an expression from the source code in the Document window to the Watch window. The Watch window displays the value of an expression, which is 14 bytes in this case. Click on the Step Over button on the Debug toolbar.

Note

Notice that before dragging the entire `sizeof(bmfh)` expression to the Watch window, pointing to the `sizeof` keyword displays nothing, but pointing to `bmfh` shows that a data structure is assigned to the variable (the {...} indicates this). You display the result of an expression by highlighting it in the code and pointing to it with your mouse pointer. You can use this technique to get instant feedback on all sorts of information.

The call to the `ReadStruct()` function successfully transferred the bitmap file header and returned true, so the next statement to execute is in the body of the `if` statement. Point to the `bmfh` part of the `bmfh.bfType` member variable in the call to the ASSERT macro. You see that a data structure is assigned to the variable. But pointing to bfType displays nothing. Highlight the entire bmfh.bfType to display the value, 19778, assigned to the member variable. What does this number mean? In fact, what is that strange expression to the right of the equivalence operator?

Begin investigating to find answers to these questions by highlighting 'B'. Be sure to include the single quotes in the highlight. Then point to the highlighted 'B' character constant. Visual C++ shows you that the 'B' character constant equals 66 in decimal. Do the same with the 'M' character constant, and you'll see that it equals 77 in decimal.

The bits representing the 'M' character constant, which are arrayed in the binary equivalent of 77 in decimal, are left-shifted eight bits. That's what the 'M' << 8 expression means. Highlight the entire 'M' << 8 expression, and Visual C++ displays 19712 in decimal.

Wow! When the binary equivalent of 77 in decimal is left-shifted eight bits, the value of the resulting bit array is equivalent to 19712 in decimal. Add this value to 77, which is the numeric representation of the 'B' character constant, and you get 19778. In fact, performing a binary OR operation on the 'B' and left-shifted 'M' character constants does just that. Highlight the entire expression 'B' | 'M' << 8, and Visual C++ displays 19778!

You can see that features of the Visual C++ debugger make exploring your running code like an expedition of discovery. That funny-looking code to the right of the equivalence operator creates the number 19778, which is equivalent to the 'B' and 'M' character constants sitting side by side in memory, which is distinctly different from the "BM" string. When the bfType variable is assigned the 'B' and 'M' character constants side by side in memory, the file header is to a bitmap image file, which must be true for the ASSERT macro to be happy and let execution go on to the next statement. Click on the Step Over button on the Debug toolbar.

The next statement, which assigns the dlFileHeader enumerated constant to the m_dlState variable, is pointed to for execution. The ASSERT macro was happy because a bitmap file header was, indeed, downloaded.

The current statement sets the download state to indicate that the file header was successfully transferred. Click on the Step Over button.

Point to the m_dlState variable now, and you see that it's assigned the dlFileHeader constant. The yellow arrow points to the else statement. Because the if statement executed successfully, when you click on the Step Over button again—go ahead and do it!—the arrow points to the break keyword at the end of the case dlNone statement. Click on the Step Over button yet again.

Execution is not longer in the body of the switch statement, and the yellow arrow points to the last statement in the body of the while statement. This statement checks to see that the current state isn't the finished state represented by the dlDone constant, and it makes sure that true is assigned to the bContinue variable. If both conditions are true, then 1 remains assigned to the bContinue variable and the while loop continues looping. Otherwise, the 0 is assigned to the bContinue variable, and the loop quits executing.

Click on the Step Over button and execution goes to the end of the while loop. You can point to the bContinue variable and see that it's assigned 1; therefore, the loop will continue executing. Click on the Step Over button again and execution moves to the beginning of the while loop, where the value assigned to the bContinue variable determines whether the loop continues. Click on the Step Over button on the Debug toolbar, and the yellow arrow points to the switch statement. Finally, click one last time on the Step Over button, and program execution goes to the first statement in the body of the case dlFileHeader statement because the dlFileHeader constant is assigned to the m_dlState variable.

Next the LogoMagic control reads the bitmap information header. You can continue stepping through the code as much as you like on your own. You have the skills. Enjoy the exploration.

When you're finished exploring, click on the Stop Debugging button on the Debug toolbar or select the Stop Debugging command from the Debug menu.

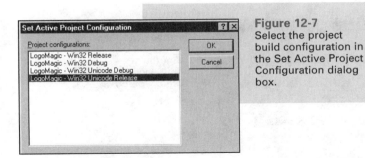

Figure 12-7
Select the project
build configuration in
the Set Active Project
Configuration dialog
box.

Building the Release Version

Now that you're finished exploring or debugging the LogoMagic control, build a 32-bit Windows Unicode release version for deployment. Select the Set Active Configuration command from the Build menu to open the Set Active Project Configuration dialog box, shown in Figure 12-7.

Select LogoMagic - Win32 Unicode Release in the Set Active Project Configuration dialog box Project Configurations list; then click on the OK button. Build the release version of the LogoMagic control by clicking on the Build button on the Build MiniBar toolbar or select the Build LogoMagic.ocx command from the Build menu.

Deploying LogoMagic with InstallShield

Use InstallShield to create a setup program for distributing the Logo-Magic control over the Internet. Of course, you can also distribute the control on floppy disk or CD-ROM. InstallShield provides an advanced setup program so you don't need to spend a significant amount of time creating your own.

 See the "Setting Up InstallShield" section in Chapter 7, "Testing QuickBrowse," for instructions on installing the InstallShield program from your Visual C++ CD-ROM.

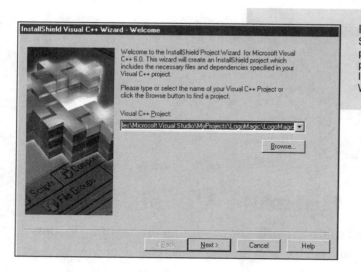

Figure 12-8
Select the LogoMagic project in the Welcome page of the InstallShield Visual C++ Wizard dialog box.

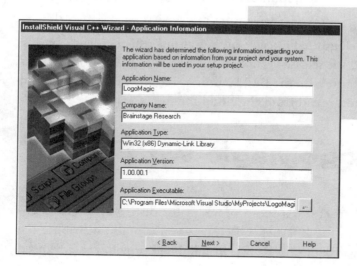

Figure 12-9
Enter information about your application in the Application Information page of the InstallShield Visual C++ Wizard dialog box.

Using the InstallShield Wizard

Deploy the LogoMagic control with InstallShield by using the InstallShield Wizard. Start up Visual C++ and load the LogoMagic project. Then select the InstallShield Wizard command from the Tools menu. The Welcome page of the InstallShield Visual C++ Wizard dialog box is shown in Figure 12-8.

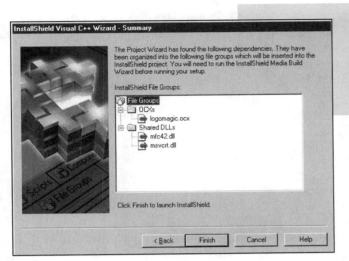

Figure 12-10
Review the files that
are included in your
project on the
Summary page of the
InstallShield Visual C++
Wizard dialog box.

By default, the LogoMagic project should be selected in the Visual C++ Project text box and drop-down list on the Wizard's Welcome page. Type in or select the LogoMagic project if it isn't selected already. Then click on the Next button to go to the Application Information page, shown in Figure 12-9.

Most of the default information displayed in the Application Information page is good. However, you might want to make some modifications. Type those in. And be absolutely sure that the LogoMagic.ocx file referenced in the Application Executable text box is the release version of the LogoMagic control. The file should be in the Release folder inside the LogoMagic folder. Typically, the file's full path is C:\Program Files\Microsoft Visual Studio\MyProjects\LogoMagic\ReleaseU\Logo-Magic.ocx. If the file is not in the Release folder, you can select the appropriate file by clicking on the ellipsis button to the right of the Application Executable text box; the Open dialog box appears. Find the release version of the LogoMagic.ocx file, select it, and click on the Open button. When you're satisfied with the information contained in the Application Information page, click on the Next button to go to the Summary page of the InstallShield Visual C++ Wizard dialog box, shown in Figure 12-10.

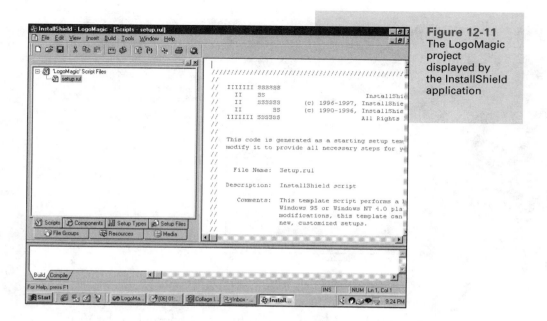

Figure 12-11
The LogoMagic
project
displayed by
the InstallShield
application

The Wizard gathers your control file and its support files, such as MFC dynamic link library files, and displays them in the Summary page of the InstallShield Visual C++ Wizard dialog box. You told the Install-Shield Wizard the control file (or files) that you want to deploy. The Wizard is smart enough to know which support files the control file needs. If the Summary page is missing a file or files that you want to deploy, go back to earlier pages by clicking on the Back button. Otherwise, click on the Finish button; the Wizard launches InstallShield, as shown in Figure 12-11.

InstallShield is a powerful application that provides a wide range of options for you. It's beyond the scope of this book to go into full details on this program, but you can find excellent guides from the Install-Shield Help menu, including the Getting Started and Getting Results online books.

When you are satisfied with the project's setup program, you can build the LogoMagic project setup program by clicking on the Media Build

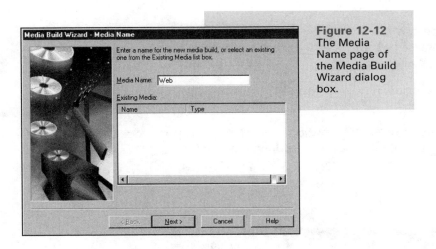

Figure 12-12
The Media
Name page of
the Media Build
Wizard dialog
box.

toolbar button or selecting the Media Build Wizard command from the Build menu. The Media Name page of the Media Build Wizard dialog box appears in Figure 12-12.

Type in a name designating the media you will be using to distribute your application, such as **Web**. Click on the Next button to open the Disk Type page of the Media Build Wizard dialog box, shown in Figure 12-13.

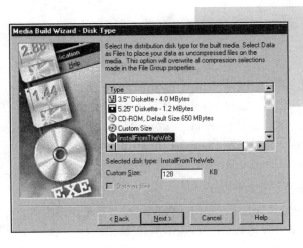

Figure 12-13
The Disk Type
page of the
Media Build
Wizard dialog
box

You can build the default setup program for the LogoMagic control put together by the InstallShield Wizard.

The Web is a distribution media. You can post your control on the Web for others to download.

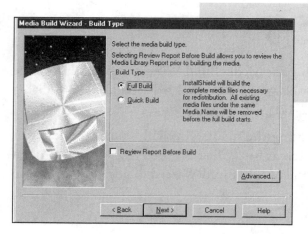

Figure 12-14
The Build Type page of the Media Build Wizard dialog box

The Type list on the Disk Type page displays several types of media from which you can deploy your application, including various floppy disk sizes, CD-ROMs, and the Web itself. Select InstallFrom TheWeb in the Type list. The Custom Size text box displays the amount of disk space available to you for deploying the LogoMagic control and auxiliary files. You probably have much more room than the default if you have a Web site. Click on the Next button to open the Build Type page of the Media Build Wizard dialog box, shown in Figure 12-14.

Select Full Build from the Build Type page of the Media Build Wizard dialog box. The full build gives you complete media files that are ready to distribute the LogoMagic control over the Web. Click on the

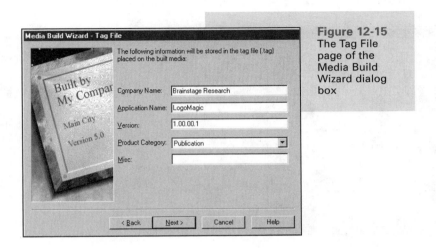

Figure 12-15
The Tag File page of the Media Build Wizard dialog box

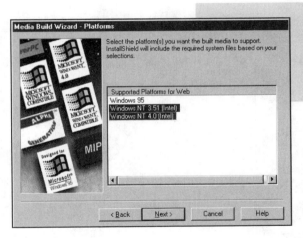

Figure 12-16
The Platforms page of the Media Build Wizard dialog box

Next button to open the Tag File page of the Media Build Wizard dialog box, shown in Figure 12-15.

Enter information about the application in the Tag File page. Select the appropriate product category in the Product Category drop-down list. Publication seems appropriate for the LogoMagic control. When you're satisfied with the information, click on the Next button to open the Platforms page of the Media Build Wizard dialog box, shown in Figure 12-16.

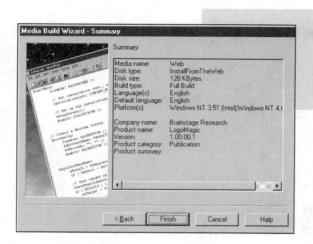

Figure 12-17
The Summary page of the Media Build Wizard dialog box

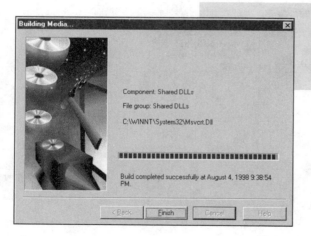

Figure 12-18
The Building Media dialog box at the end of a build

The LogoMagic control supports only Windows NT. Highlight Windows NT 3.51 (Intel) and Windows NT 4.0 (Intel) in the Supported Platforms for Web list; then click on the Next button to open the Summary page of the Media Build Wizard dialog box, shown in Figure 12-17.

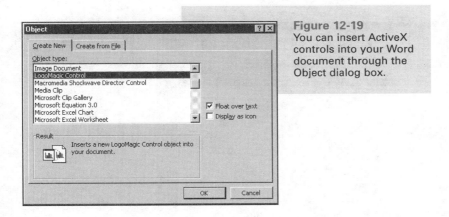

Figure 12-19
You can insert ActiveX
controls into your Word
document through the
Object dialog box.

Check over the contents of the Summary page to make sure that everything will be set up as you want it. If not, click on the Back button to go back to previous pages of the Wizard and change the information. Otherwise, click on the Finish button. InstallShield builds the media. When it's finished, the Building Media dialog box tells you that the build was a success, as shown in Figure 12-18.

Click on the Finish button. The media files are ready to deploy on the Web. You can use the Send Media To command on the Build menu to deploy the media files.

Using the LogoMagic Control

When users install the LogoMagic control on their machine, they can use it anywhere that they can use ActiveX controls. Typically, users will insert the control by selecting a command from a menu that opens a dialog box and then selecting the control from the dialog box. For instance, in Microsoft Word, selecting the Object command from the Insert menu opens the Object dialog box, shown in Figure 12-19.

Select LogoMagic Control from the Object type list and then click on the OK button. The control is inserted in the Word document. Now

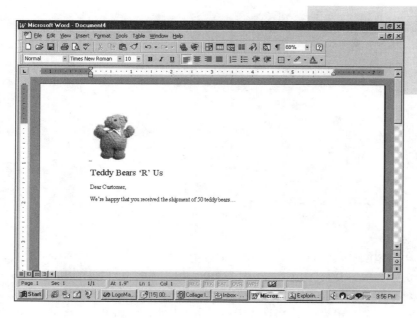

Figure 12-20
The LogoMagic
control in a
Microsoft Word
document.

you can set the Image Path on the LogoMagic control property sheet. Point to the LogoMagic control and right-click to display a shortcut menu. Open the LogoMagic Control Object submenu on the shortcut menu; then select the Properties command. The LogoMagic Control Properties dialog box appears. Type the path and bitmap image file name into the Image Path text box and click on the OK button to place your logo in the Word document. Figure 12-20 shows the result.

The same or similar procedure applies to a wide range of applications. For instance, FrontPage Express is a pared-down version of Microsoft FrontPage that you can get free by downloading the fully loaded version of Internet Explorer. You can use FrontPage Express to design Web pages. Insert the LogoMagic control in a Web page by opening the Other Components submenu on the FrontPage Express Insert menu and then selecting the ActiveX Control command. The ActiveX Control Properties dialog box is shown in Figure 12-21.

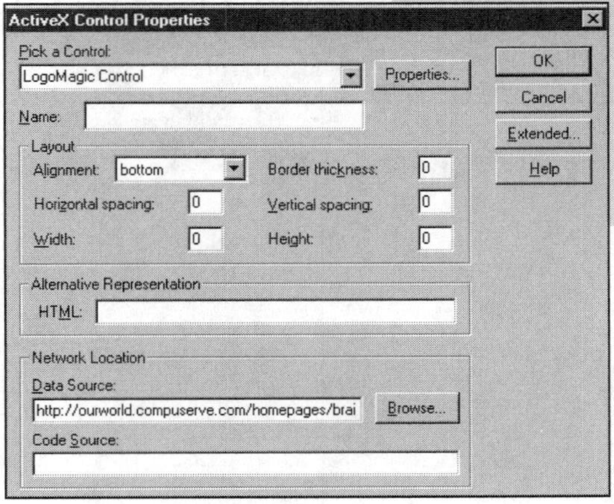

Figure 12-21
Insert ActiveX controls into Web documents through the FrontPage Express application ActiveX Control Properties dialog box

Select the LogoMagic Control from the Pick a Control drop-down list in the ActiveX Control Properties dialog box. You can fill out several options, but the only item you must include is the source of the bitmap image. Type the image source into the Data Source text box in the Network Location area or browse for the image through the Select a File dialog box by clicking on the Browse button. Click on the OK button, and the LogoMagic control with your company logo is inserted into your Web page, as shown in Figure 12-22.

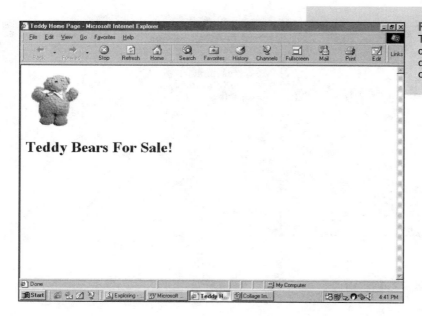

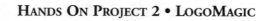

Figure 12-22
The LogoMagic control displaying a logo on a Web page.

Summary

In this chapter, you used the powerful Visual C++ debugger to explore the internal workings of the LogoMagic control image property, built a release version of the control, and created a setup program for deploying the control using InstallShield. You also saw that the LogoMagic control is truly for the enterprise. It can be inserted into a wide range of documents from the Web to the desktop. Project 3 tackles the final Web-programming step: creating software components that talk with one another across the enterprise.

Project 2 Summary

In the second project, you created the LogoMagic ActiveX control, which is a control that displays bitmap images from wherever they reside on the computing enterprise. The LogoMagic control can display company logos on Web pages, Word documents, Excel spreadsheets, Active Desktops, or anywhere an ActiveX control can be placed.

You answered queries presented by the MFC ActiveX ControlWizard, and the Wizard used the answers to create a complete ActiveX control with Microsoft Foundation Class (MFC) library support.

You also learned about the COM specification, and you created a bitmap property class from the CCachedDataPathProperty class in the MFC library.

You used visual design methods in the Visual C++ resource editor to create a property page where users can set the values of the LogoMagic control properties.

The LogoMagic project taught you how to create an enterprise-savvy ActiveX control that displays a company logo within a wide range of contexts. You learned how Visual C++ teams up with the MFC library and the MFC ActiveX ControlWizard to create a working ActiveX control so that you can focus on writing your custom code.

HANDS ON PROJECT 3

INSTANTPOST

- Create the frameworks for ATL-based software components using the ATL COM AppWizard.

- Insert objects and controls into the skeleton project created by the ATL COM AppWizard.

- Design the InstantPost ActiveX control graphic user interface using Visual C++ design tools.

- Learn the advantages of the Active Template Library (ATL) and when to use it.

- Learn about the Distributed Component Object Model (DCOM) specification.

- Implement distributed communication through connection points.

Project Overview

You begin this project by using the ATL COM AppWizard to rapidly pull together the skeleton of your new software component on the basis of a few queries. Visual C++ and the wizard take care of a lot of potentially complex overhead used to implement COM-based components.

You then add COM objects and controls to your project skeletons to begin adding real functionality. The Visual C++ integrated development environment provides preformed objects and controls from ATL that you simply insert into your project and modify to your own specifications. You add COM objects to the InstantPostServer component, and you add both objects and controls to the Instant-Post ActiveX control.

Next, insert a control into the InstantPost project that provides a dialog interface for the InstantPost control. Then use visual design methods in the Visual C++ resource editor to draw controls onto the dialog interface and modify their properties, creating a graphic user interface for the InstantPost ActiveX control. You then learn how to connect the new graphic interface with the rest of the control so that users can post and receive messages across the enterprise through the interface.

Next, find out what makes the ATL such a boon to developers of COM-based (and DCOM-based) software components, such as the standard objects and controls that the library offers. Use DCOM— COM with remote networking capabilities. DCOM is, in fact, simply the culmination of the original COM specification's goal to be location transparent. Understand DCOM and its sister networking specification, known as the Remote Procedure Calls (RPC) specification, and make the enterprise your computing environment.

Finally, implement the COM connection points facility to make real-time distributed communication a reality. This facility is notorious for being difficult to implement. However, Visual C++ provides tools that make it almost embarrassingly simple to implement connection points in your ATL-based software components. Get the InstantPost message posting system communicating by adding connection points to its components.

CHAPTER 13

What Is InstantPost?

InstantPost is an enterprise-wide, distributed message posting system that really consists of a Visual C++ project and a Visual Basic project. In the Visual C++ project you create the InstantPostServer component using the Active Template Library (ATL) and the ATL COM AppWizard, which were specifically developed to simplify the process of creating COM-based software components. The architecture of an ATL-based software component is much different from components based on the MFC library, such as the LogoMagic control. You create a client application, the InstantPost ActiveX control, which uses the InstantPostServer with Visual Basic. It's through the InstantPost controls, which can be placed anywhere on the enterprise, that users view messages posted by colleagues and where they can post their own messages. In contrast, the InstantPostServer runs invisibly on a server. It manages the various client connections from deployed InstantPost ActiveX controls, and it manages the posted messages from those clients. With InstantPost, you take the next step not only by deploying software components across the enterprise but also by virtually wiring the components together from wherever they are deployed. Place is no longer an issue.

Goals of the InstantPost Project

The InstantPost and InstantPostServer projects take you beyond creating ActiveX controls to getting them to communicate in real time across the computing enterprise. Any number of InstantPost ActiveX controls can be deployed and made to interact through the InstantPostServer component, like the two InstantPost controls shown in Figure 13-1.

Specifically, your goals in carrying out this project are these:

■ Create the framework for an ATL-based software component using the ATL COM AppWizard.

The ATL COM AppWizard quickly pulls together the skeleton of your new software component on the basis of a few queries. Visual C++ and the wizard take care of a lot of potentially complex overhead used to implement COM-based components.

■ Insert objects into the skeleton project created by the ATL COM AppWizard.

The initial code created using the ATL COM AppWizard is truly skeleton code. Unlike with projects created using the MFC ActiveX ControlWizard, if you compile these projects and run them, you won't see much at all. You need to add COM objects or controls to the skeleton to begin adding real functionality. The Visual C++ integrated development environment comes to the rescue with preformed objects and controls that you simply insert into your project and modify to your own specifications. You add COM objects to the InstantPostServer component.

■ Learn the advantages of the Active Template Library (ATL) and when to use it.

Find out what makes the ATL such a boon to developers of COM-based (and DCOM-based) software components.

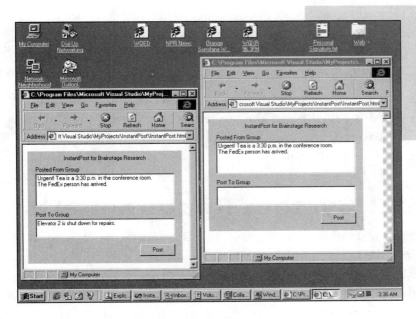

Figure 13-1
InstantPost controls displayed on Web pages interact through the InstantPost-Server component.

- Learn about the Distributed Component Object Model (DCOM) specification.

  DCOM is COM with remote networking capabilities. It is, in fact, simply the culmination of the original COM specification's goal to be location transparent. Understand DCOM and its sister networking specification, known as the Remote Procedure Calls (RPC) specification, and make the enterprise your computing environment.

- Implement distributed communication through connection points.

  Real-time distributed communication is accomplished by COM-based software components through the connection points facility. This facility is notorious for being difficult to implement. However, Visual C++ provides tools that make it almost embarrassingly simple to implement connection points in your

ATL-based software components. Get the InstantPost message posting system communicating by adding connection points to its components.

- Create the InstantPost ActiveX control using Visual Basic.

  The client language of choice for interactive components based on COM is Visual Basic. You create the InstantPost control using Visual Basic or, if you don't have Visual Basic, use the control provided on the CD-ROM.

InstantPost System Requirements

You can run InstantPost controls and the InstantPostServer component on one and the same computer running Windows 95, Windows 98, or Windows NT. However, posting messages to yourself has only limited application potential. Machines that you deploy these components on across the enterprise must support DCOM. Platforms such as Windows 98, Windows NT 4.0, and Windows NT 5.0 have DCOM support built in. On other platforms, such as Windows 95, support is available but you must install it.

Computers running applications built using ATL, like the InstantPost and InstantPostServer components, must have the ATL dynamic-link libraries. In addition, computers running the InstantPost ActiveX control built with MFC support must have the MFC dynamic-link libraries available to them.

InstantPost Customization Requirements

Visual C++ makes creating COM-based software components astonishingly easy once you are familiar with how those COM-based components are constructed. This is the primary hurdle to get over when creating software using the ATL COM AppWizard. You do a lot of customizing once you've finished the short question-and-answer period with the wizard. However, most of the customization involves knowing the right thing to do rather than any complicated coding strategy. Chapter 16, "Customizing InstantPost," takes you step by step through the process. Along with the other chapters, it will teach you how to use the power of Visual C++ to create software components that work together as a distributed application.

Summary

You are embarking on a project that reaches the pinnacle of COM programming, utilizing the COM connection points facility and DCOM. The InstantPost and InstantPostServer projects bring together all of the knowledge and skill that you've acquired by now to create distributed software components that interact with users and with each other. Use the techniques that you learn with this project to create entirely new types of distributed applications that reside on the computing enterprise.

CHAPTER 14

Creating InstantPost

Create COM-based components in moments and get the benefits of the Active Template Library (ATL) by using the ATL COM AppWizard. In this chapter you create the skeleton of the InstantPostServer component using the ATL COM AppWizard, which creates a component for you based on your answers to a set of queries. After you create the basic working component, it's a matter of adding or modifying code to transform InstantPostServer into your own custom component that will interact with InstantPost ActiveX controls to communicate anywhere across the computing enterprise.

Creating InstantPostServer Using the ATL COM AppWizard

The InstantPostServer component is the central management facility for the InstantPost distributed message posting application. You create the skeleton code for the InstantPostServer component in this chapter. In Chapter 16, "Customizing InstantPost," you finish the InstantPostServer

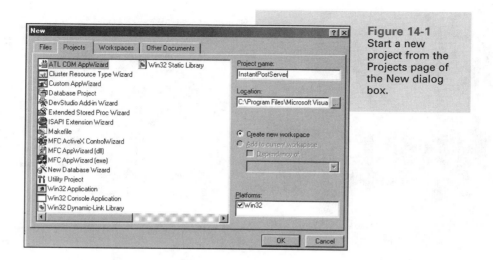

Figure 14-1
Start a new project from the Projects page of the New dialog box.

component by adding your own custom code and you create the InstantPost client using Visual Basic.

Start Microsoft Visual C++ if you haven't already, and then select the New command from the File menu. The New dialog box appears, as in Figure 14-1.

Click on the Projects tab to switch to the Projects page of the New dialog box if it isn't displayed already and then select ATL COM AppWizard. Type the project name, **InstantPostServer**, into the Project name text box and then click on the OK button. The Step 1 page of the ATL COM AppWizard dialog box appears, as in Figure 14-2.

You can choose between three types of COM server mechanisms: in-process, local out-of-process, or service.

Select the Dynamic Link Library (DLL) radio button in the Server Type area on the Step 1 page of the ATL COM AppWizard dialog box if you want your component to run in-process. ActiveX controls are dynamic-link library (DLL) programs that implement the in-process server. In-process servers are dynamically loaded at runtime by the operating system on behalf of programs calling functions in

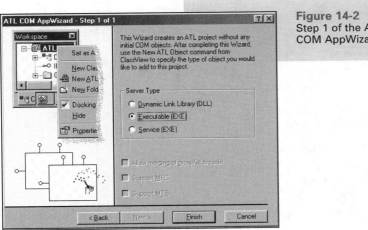

Figure 14-2
Step 1 of the ATL
COM AppWizard.

the control. The controls are always loaded into the same address space as the calling process, hence in-process.

Select the Executable (EXE) radio button if you want your component to run locally and out-of-process. This type of executable component runs in a separate process on the same machine as its client. It takes significantly more time to access local out-of-process servers because communication must switch between the client and server processes. However, this is the option to select if you want to be able to run the component as a stand-alone application.

Select the Service (EXE) radio button if you want your component to run as a Windows NT service. An executable component implementing the service mechanisms is installed in a registry database maintained by the Windows NT Service Control Manager. The component can be automatically started at boot time, or it can be started on demand through the Service Control Manager.

InstantPostServer is a local out-of-process server, so you want to select the Executable (EXE) radio button in the Server Type area on the Step 1 page of the ATL COM AppWizard dialog box. Click on the Finish button, and the New Project Information dialog box appears as in Figure 14-3.

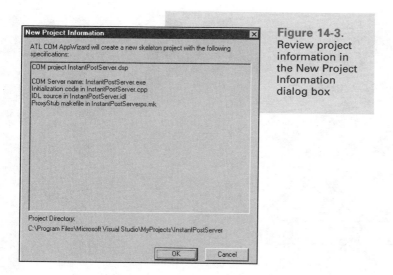

Figure 14-3.
Review project
information in
the New Project
Information
dialog box

Read over the information on the InstantPostServer project to be sure that you've made all of the correct selections. If you aren't satisfied with the selections, click on the Cancel button and you're taken back to the ATL COM AppWizard dialog box so that you can change your selections. Once you're satisfied, click on the OK button in the New Project Information dialog box; the wizard creates the skeleton InstantPost-Server component.

Adding COM Objects to InstantPostServer

The ATL COM AppWizard creates skeleton components that meet the COM specifications. However, the result lacks any COM objects. COM objects provide the interfaces and methods that are part of COM-based components. Visual C++ provides a simple way for you to add COM controls to your component.

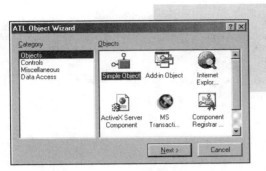

Figure 14-4
Add objects to your project through the ATL Object Wizard dialog box.

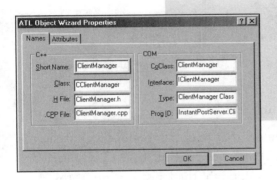

Figure 14-5
Name the elements associated with the added object through the Names page of the ATL Object Wizard Properties dialog box.

Adding the ClientManager Object

Select the New ATL Object command from the Insert menu and the ATL Object Wizard dialog box appears, as in Figure 14-4.

Select the Objects in the Category list on the ATL Object Wizard dialog box and then find and select Simple Object in the Objects list. Click on the Next button and the ATL Object Wizard Properties dialog box appears. Click on the Names tab to display the Names page of the ATL Object Wizard Properties dialog box, as in Figure 14-5.

Enter a name for the elements related to the Simple Object, `Client-Manager`, in the Short Name text box. The wizard automatically fills in the various text box values based on the name you entered into the Short Name text box.

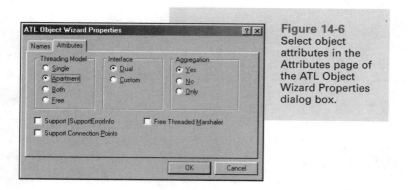

Figure 14-6
Select object attributes in the Attributes page of the ATL Object Wizard Properties dialog box.

Click on the Attributes tab to display the Attributes page of the ATL Object Wizard Properties dialog box, as in Figure 14-6

You have six choices to make on the Attributes page of the ATL Object Wizard Properties dialog box.

1. Your Component's Threading Model

Select the type of threading model that your component will use in the Threading Model area on the Attributes page of the ATL Object Wizard Properties dialog box. Oddly enough, the latest version of this page in Visual C++ retains out-of-date threading model terms that can be confusing. There are really two threading models: Single-Threaded Apartments (STAs) and Multithreaded Apartments (MTAs). Table 14.1 shows the relationship between the threading model terms on the Attributes page and the current threading models.

Table 14.1 Threading Models

Term on Attributes Page	Number of STAs	Number of MTAs
Single	1	0
Apartment	1 or more	0
Both	1 or more	1
Free	0	1

An *apartment* is the basic unit of thread safety used in the COM specification. Single-threaded apartments (STAs) may have only one thread executing per apartment, whereas multithreaded apartments (MTAs) may have more than one thread executing per apartment. A process may contain any number of STAs except in the single model, which is really thread-oblivious. A process may only have one MTA, but a process with one MTA may also contain any number of STAs.

Select the Single radio button if you want to use the legacy threading

The type of object you insert affects the number of threading model options available to you. ActiveX controls do not offer MTA support, and therefore you may select the Single model or the Apartment model.

model, which is really no threading model at all. The single threading model results in one thread and only one thread running in a process. A process and a thread are effectively the same thing here. There is no good reason to select this model, since, if you do, your component misses out on the advantages of using threads.

Select the Apartment radio button if you want to use the STA model, in which the component can run only one thread per apartment but can run many threads per process. This is the ideal selection for ActiveX controls and other components that you want to take advantage of threads but that you also want to take advantage of two special STA features: thread synchronization and window message queues. This is definitely the best choice for any component that receives user interaction through a graphic user interface.

Select the Both radio button if you want to use the full power of both the STA and MTA models. This is an excellent choice for components that can use MTAs. The component is able to use the MTA model for threads that should be able to communicate easily with one another within an apartment. Otherwise, it can use the STA model for threads that can run in separate apartments but remain within the same process.

Finally, select Free if you want the component to use only the MTA model. You may want to use this option in special cases. However, it is recommended that you thoroughly understand COM threading models before implementing components using this option. In particular, you will need to worry about thread synchronization and use mutual exclusion (mutex) objects, critical sections, semaphores, or events to make sure that they are synchronized.

Click on the Apartment radio button to get the best threading support for the ClientManager object.

2. The Types of Interfaces Your Component Supports

Choose between supporting only custom interfaces or both custom interfaces and the late-binding IDispatch interface. Custom interfaces provide direct method accessibility through a v-table. In contrast, accessing methods through the IDispatch interface takes several steps. Components implementing the IDispatch interface are called Automation objects. This facility provides a standard conduit between a client and component functionality. Also, unlike custom interfaces, it provides standardized access to component properties. Finally, the most compelling reason to add the IDispatch interface in your component is that scripting languages, such as JavaScript and VBScript, are only able to access and manipulate Automation objects. Generally, it's best to select a dual interface, both custom and IDispatch interfaces.

Click on the Dual radio button to add both custom and IDispatch interfaces to the ClientManager object.

3. Whether or Not Your Component Supports Aggregation

Aggregation is when an internal COM-based object's interfaces are exposed as interfaces of an external COM-based object. An internal COM-based object is an object embedded in another COM-based object, the external object. Aggregation works only among in-process components.

Select the Yes radio button in the Aggregation area on the Attributes page of the ATL Object Wizard Properties dialog box if you want the component to support aggregation.

Select the No radio button in the Aggregation area if you don't want the component to support aggregation.

Select the Only radio button in the Aggregation area if you want your component to only support aggregation. In other words, the component will only be able to expose its interfaces through another component.

For now, click on the Yes radio button so that the ClientManager object supports aggregation.

4. If Your Component Supports Error Handling through the ISupportErrorInfo Interface

Your component can provide rich error information through the ISupportErrorInfo interface. Client programs written using the MFC library utilize this interface, as do Visual Basic and Java Virtual Machines (Java VMs).

Leave the Support ISupportErrorInfo checkbox unchecked. The Client-Manager object does not support the ISupportErrorInfo interface.

5. If Your Component Supports Connection Points

Connection points are a COM service that support two-way communication between a client and an object. Components that support connection points typically notify clients by firing events when interesting things happen to them. ActiveX controls are connectable objects.

Leave the Support Connection Points check box unchecked.

6. If Your Component Supports a Free Threaded Marshaler

COM specifies that threads must always marshal interface pointers between apartments. This can create a performance problem when in-process components implement different threading models. The free-threaded marshaler provides an optimization for this circumstance.

The ClientManager object implements only the STA threading model. Therefore, leave the Free Threaded Marshaler check box on the Attributes page of the ATL Object Wizard Properties dialog box unchecked.

Click on the OK button and the ClientManager object is added to the InstantPostServer project.

Adding the PostManager Object

Select the New ATL Object command from the Insert menu and the ATL Object Wizard dialog box appears. Select the Objects in the Category list on the ATL Object Wizard dialog box and then find and select Simple Object in the Objects list. Click on the Next button and the ATL Object Wizard Properties dialog box appears. Click on the Names tab to display the Names page of the ATL Object Wizard Properties dialog box, as in Figure 14-7.

Enter **PostManager**, in the Short Name text box. The wizard automatically fills in the various text box values based on the name you entered into the Short Name text box.

Click on the Attributes tab to display the Attributes page of the ATL Object Wizard Properties dialog box, as in Figure 14-8.

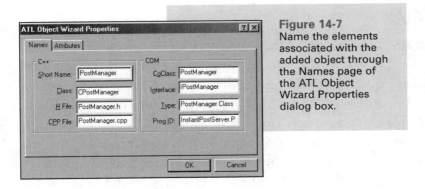

Figure 14-7
Name the elements associated with the added object through the Names page of the ATL Object Wizard Properties dialog box.

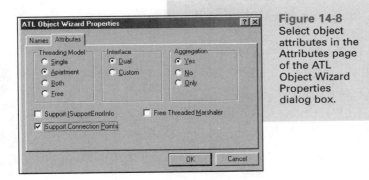

Figure 14-8
Select object attributes in the Attributes page of the ATL Object Wizard Properties dialog box.

Select the Apartment radio button on the Attributes page of the ATL Object Wizard Properties dialog box to get the best threading support for the PostManager object. Click on the Dual radio button to add both custom and IDispatch interfaces to the object. Click on the Yes radio button so that the PostManager object supports aggregation. Leave the Support ISupportErrorInfo check box unchecked. Check the Support Connection Points check box. And, finally, leave the Free Threaded Marshaler check box on the Attributes page of the ATL Object Wizard Properties dialog box unchecked. Click on the OK button and the Post-Manager object is added to the InstantPostServer project.

Summary

You created the skeleton of the InstantPostServer software component using the ATL COM AppWizard. You learned about the ATL COM AppWizard queries and how to customize your software component based on your answers. The wizard produced the infrastructure for your DCOM-based component. You then added COM objects to the InstantPostServer component that provided it with interfaces. You will finish creating the InstantPostServer software component in Chapter 16 by adding the working code behind the interfaces and between the skeletal elements that you created today. First, however, take a tour through the code you generated today to get an inside view of a DCOM-based component created using the ATL.

CHAPTER 15

InstantPost Architecture

InstantPost is the combination of two COM-based components with distinct architectures. You created the InstantPostServer component by using the Active Template Library (ATL), using the ATL COM App-Wizard, and inserting objects. The server component is executable and runs invisibly on a central machine. In contrast, the client component is an ActiveX control with a graphic user interface that you will write using Visual Basic in Chapter 16, "Customizing InstantPost." In this chapter you focus on what makes ATL so great for creating COM-based software components. You also look at the Distributed Component Object Model (DCOM) and how the InstantPost ActiveX control and the InstantPostServer component utilize the DCOM specification to communicate with one another. The InstantPost control and Instant-PostServer component are connectable objects that implement the COM connection points facility. Once you're finished, you will be ready to modify the code created by the ATL COM AppWizard so that you can build the final versions of the InstantPost and InstantPostServer components, which work together as a distributed message posting system.

The Active Template Library (ATL)

The Active Template Library, or ATL, is a library of template-based C++ classes that aid in the creation of small, fast COM objects for your software components. Perhaps most important, ATL provides stock implementations with key COM interfaces, connection points, and ActiveX controls. Microsoft developed ATL with the specific goal to make developing COM objects easy and flexible.

You already used many features of ATL in Chapter 14 when you created the InstantPost and InstantPostServer components. For instance, when you inserted various objects into the project skeletons, these were the ATL stock implementations of COM interfaces and, in the case of the InstantPostServer project, a stock implementation of an ActiveX control. It's the close collaboration between ATL and the Visual C++ integrated development environment that makes adding COM objects to your software components so easy.

C++ Templates

C++ templates are a mechanism for generating functions and classes based on type parameters. Templates enable you to design a single class that operates on data of many types so that you don't need to create a different class for each data type that you want the class to operate on. In fact, a class designed using templates can take data types not even thought of yet. Templates reduce source code size and increase code flexibility without reducing type safety.

Class declarations using templates look a bit strange at first. For instance, look at this class declaration:

```
template <class T > class MyClass
{
public:
  MyClass( void );
  ~MyClass( void );
  int MyClassFunction( T a, int b );
private:
  T myClassVariable;
};
```

Template classes begin with the `template` keyword followed by the class's parameters listed between a pair of brackets (<>). The `class` keyword and the `class` name follow the brackets.

The MyClass class has one parameter. The parameter is known as the type `T` parameter and can be passed any kind of data type including structures and classes. The data type passed to the type `T` parameter is substituted in all places you see `T` in the body of the class declaration. For instance, if the `char` data type is passed to the type `T` parameter, the Visual C++ compiler changes the class declaration into this form:

```
class MyClass
{
public:
  MyClass( void );
  ~MyClass( void );
  int MyClassFunction(char a, int b );
private:
  char myClassVariable;
};
```

Similarly, if you pass the type T parameter the CString class from the MFC library, then the compiler interprets the declaration in this way:

```
class MyClass
{
public:
  MyClass( void );
  ~MyClass( void );
  int MyClassFunction(CString a, int b );
private:
  CString myClassVariable;
};
```

The Standard Template Library (STL) was one of the first widely used and supported template libraries and is the library that inspired the design of Microsoft's ATL. In fact, STL is now a part of the Standard C++ Library included with all ANSI/ISO-compliant C++ compilers.

Smart Pointers

Smart pointers are classes that encapsulate pointers and override pointer operators to add new functionality to pointer operations. Smart pointers are typically implemented using template classes so that pointers of almost any data type can be encapsulated. Smart pointers are generally created to make programming using pointers safer and easier. Microsoft has created a set of smart pointer template classes that are included in ATL.

A Different Architecture

Components created using ATL are based on a very different architectural idea than those components created using the MFC classes, like the LogoMagic control in Project 2. MFC-based components have a strict object hierarchy and follow the document/view architecture. In contrast, ATL is a relatively flat library that loosens up the strict hierarchy found in MFC-based components, and the document/view architecture is gone. Both of these major architectural differences reflect the move away from large applications that do everything to small, distributed, and specialized software components that interact with other software components with different specialties.

Hidden Complexity

Visual C++ hides most of the code overhead required for COM objects. For instance, every COM object implements the IUnknown interface and its three standard methods: the QueryInterface(), AddRef(), and Release() methods. You can look as hard as you want in the ClassView page of the Workspace windows of the InstantPostServer project for the IUnknown interface and its functions, but you won't find them. The same thing is true for the IDispatch interface and a long list of other standard COM interfaces that your project might use. They are standardized and used often; why should you constantly rewrite them? ATL saves programmers time, enormous amounts of time, by simply providing the standard COM interfaces, but it also provides important support for COM facilities such as connectable objects and for writing ActiveX controls.

You made extensive use of ATL while creating the InstantPostServer component in Chapter 14, but you never actually saw the exotic template format with its angle brackets (<>). The cooperation between Visual C++ and ATL is so complete that you will never need to dive into the actual template declarations and definitions. The ATL Object Wizard and the tools Visual C++ provides for the easy implementation of properties, methods, and variables make the need to dive into the depths of the ATL source code a rare occasion.

Connectable Objects

The InstantPostServer component is a connectable object; it implements the COM connection points facility. This is one of the most important and one of the most notoriously difficult COM facilities to code. Connection points are important because they provide a means for components to fire and retrieve events that carry messages across any process or network. With the latest release of Visual C++, it's a breeze to add connection points to your components. In fact, you add them to the InstantPostServer component in Chapter 16, "Customizing InstantPost."

Recall that you sometimes checked a Support Connection Points check box on the Attributes page of the ATL Object Wizard Properties dialog box when you inserted an object into your ATL-based project. You did this for the PostManager object, but not for the ClientManager object, in the InstantPostServer project. You can see one of the results of checking the Support Connection Points check box if you look on the ClassView page of the Workspace window as it displays the InstantPostServer project. You should see a _IPostManagerEvents interface but not a _IClientManagerEvents interface. When you tell Visual C++ that you want an object to support connection points, it adds an event-generating interface to the object.

Note Do you wonder why the _IClientManagerEvents interface name begins with an underscore character (_)? Automation clients, such as the Visual Basic development environment, don't expose interfaces that begin with an underscore character. This is also true for property and method names.

Double-click the _IClientManagerEvents listing on the ClassView page of the Workspace window; the InstantPostServer.idl file displays in the document window at the _IClientManagerEvents interface declaration. The interface is declared as a dispinterface, or dispatch interface (IDispatch), type. This means that the interface is available through the COM Automation facility.

The COM Automation Facility

Automation is the COM facility that exposes application functionality for use by other programs. For instance, you can use JavaScript or VBScript in your Web pages to interact with ActiveX controls. This is all done through Automation. The properties, methods, and events exposed by an ActiveX control are all provided through the COM Automation facility, which is implemented through the IDispatch interface.

Double-click the IClientManager or IPostManager interface listed on the ClassView page of the Visual C++ Workspace window; the Instant-Post.idl file loads and displays at the interface definition. Both of these interfaces are derived from the IDispatch interface. In fact, the ATL COM AppWizard declares all interfaces as derived from the IDispatch interface when you select dual interfaces for your project. That way your component's interfaces are accessible through Automation by default even though you can use custom interfaces that aren't Automation-enabled if you want.

Note Actually, the custom interfaces that you add to components implementing dual interfaces benefit from the IDispatch interface. Clients can access a COM object through the custom interface or through Automation.

COM Automation and Binding

Clients that query interfaces derived from the IDispatch interface typically select a method, property, or event that they want to access. The process of accessing the object and calling a method, property, or event in that object is known as *binding*. Each method, property, or event associated with an IDispatch interface can be identified through its dispatch identifier, or DISPID. Clients bind through Automation by first getting the appropriate DISPID and then calling the IDispatch interface Invoke() method using the DISPID as one of the method's parameters. This is what is happening behind the scenes whenever you see a list of properties, events, and methods exposed by an ActiveX control through a programming tool such as Visual Basic.

The Distributed Component Object Model (DCOM)

The Distributed Component Object Model, or DCOM, is the name applied to the latest update of the COM specification, which realizes the location transparency goal that COM has been aiming at all along. With DCOM, it doesn't matter where a COM-based software component is located. You just use it. The DCOM protocol enables COM-based objects, like ActiveX controls, to communicate directly with each other across networks.

The primary thing that DCOM adds to the COM specification is a high-level network protocol that enables COM-based components to communicate across networks. The DCOM networking protocol sits on top of any existing networking protocol, of which there are many. The most popular existing networking protocol is the mainstay of the Internet which is based on, at various levels, the User Datagram Protocol (UDP), the Transmission Control Protocol (TCP), and the Internet Protocol (IP). However, the protocol layer just under DCOM is always the Remote Procedure Calls (RPC) protocol.

DCOM and RPC

DCOM and RPC have a very close relationship, to such an extent, in fact, that the DCOM network protocol is often called Object RPC (or ORPC). For instance, many of the authentication, authorization, and message integrity features of DCOM are inherited from RPC. DCOM extends the standard RPC protocol by the way that it calls remote objects and the way object references are represented, transmitted, and maintained.

DCOM Security Model

DCOM—and COM in general—has a security model that can be used to control activation, access, authentication, and identity. *Activation control* specifies who is permitted to launch components, *access control* limits access to a component's objects, *authentication control* ensures that a network transmission is authentic and protects data from unauthorized users, and *identity control* specifies the security credentials under which a component will execute. As mentioned previously, at the DCOM network protocol level, some of these controls are implemented through RPC.

Summary

Using the Visual C++ integrated development environment in conjunction with the Active Template Library (ATL) provides you with the tools you need to create COM-based distributed components not only with ease but also with the least overhead and the best performance. Creating software components using ATL and Visual C++ is ideal for widely distributed applications that are used on the computing enterprise. In Chapter 16, "Customizing InstantPost," you complete the InstantPost-Server component and you write the InstantPost ActiveX control. Then in Chapter 17, "Deploying InstantPost," you deploy the components on the enterprise and experience DCOM in action.

CHAPTER 16

Customizing InstantPost

You rapidly created the skeleton of the InstantPostServer project component using the ATL COM AppWizard, added COM objects to the skeleton, and explored the code. Now you are ready to modify the InstantPostServer component so that it works with the InstantPost ActiveX control to create a fully distributed message-posting application. Finally, you create the InstantPost ActiveX control using Visual Basic.

Customizing the InstantPostServer Component

The InstantPostServer component is the glue that holds your distributed application together. Begin your code customization with this component so that you'll be able to link the client code with some of the InstantPostServer code.

Modifying the CClientManager Object

Double-click on CClientManager listed on the ClassView page of the Workspace window to open the ClientManager.h file and display it in the Visual C++ document window. Add the `include` directive for the PostManager.h file right under the `include` directive for the resource.h file:

```
#include "PostManager.h"
```

The PostManager.h file contains the class definition for the CPostManager object, which will be added below. The CPostManager object manages the messages posted between the various InstantPost clients connected with the InstantPostServer. The ClientManager object manages the clients that communicate through InstantPostServer.

Remove IDispatchImpl from the CClientManager class declaration and replace it with IOleItemContainer so that the head of the CClientManager class declaration looks like this:

```
class ATL_NO_VTABLE CClientMangager :
  public CComObjectRootEx<CComSingleThreadModel>,
  public CComCoClass<CClientMangager, &CLSID_ClientMangager>,
  public IOleItemContainer
```

The InstantPost clients bind with the InstantPostServer using an item moniker. The IOleItemContainer interface provides the necessary functions for carrying this out.

Right under the CClientMangager header, at the beginning of the body of the CClientManager class declaration, type in the following private variable declaration:

```
private:
  CComObjectGlobal<CPostManager> m_connection;
```

The CPostManager object is assigned to the `m_connection` variable, which is globally accessible since it's declared using the CComObjectGlobal template. The object's global accessibility allows it to manage the messages posted from any and all InstantPost clients that connect with InstantPostServer.

In the COM map, replace the reference to the IClientManager interface with a reference to the IParseDisplayName interface and replace the reference to the IDispatch interface with a reference to the IOleItemContainer interface. The COM map should look like this after you make the changes:

```
BEGIN_COM_MAP(CClientMangager)
  COM_INTERFACE_ENTRY(IParseDisplayName)
  COM_INTERFACE_ENTRY(IOleItemContainer)
END_COM_MAP()
```

You add the IParseDisplayNames interface so that the CClientManager object can parse moniker names passed from InstantPost client components.

Add the following code right after the public keyword at the end of the body of the CClientManager class declaration:

```
// IParseDisplayName
  STDMETHOD(ParseDisplayName)(IBindCtx *pdc,
    LPOLESTR pszDisplayName, ULONG *pchEaten,
    IMoniker **ppmkOut);
//IOleContainer
  STDMETHOD(EnumObjects)(DWORD grfFlags, IEnumUnknown **ppenum);
  STDMETHOD(LockContainer)(BOOL fLock);
//IOleItemContainer
  STDMETHOD(GetObject)(LPOLESTR pszItem, DWORD dwSpeedNeeded,
    IBindCtx *pbc, REFIID riid, void **ppvObject);
  STDMETHOD(GetObjectStorage)(LPOLESTR pszItem, IBindCtx *pbc,
    REFIID riid, void **ppvStorage);
  STDMETHOD(IsRunning)(LPOLESTR pszItem);
```

These are the declarations for all of the methods that must be supported for the IParseDisplayName, IOleContainer, and IOleItemContainer interfaces.

Listing 16.1 displays the complete code in the ClientManager.h file with your modifications highlighted in boldfaced type.

Listing 16.1 ClientManager.h

```cpp
// ClientManager.h : Declaration of the CClientManager

#ifndef __CLIENTMANAGER_H_
#define __CLIENTMANAGER_H_

#include "resource.h"        // main symbols
#include "PostManager.h"


/////////////////////////////////////////////////////////////////////////////
// CClientManager
class ATL_NO_VTABLE CClientManager :
  public CComObjectRootEx<CComSingleThreadModel>,
  public CComCoClass<CClientMangager, &CLSID_ClientManager>,
  public IOleItemContainer
{
private:
  CComObjectGlobal<CPostManager> m_connection;

public:
  CClientManager()
  {
  }

DECLARE_REGISTRY_RESOURCEID(IDR_CLIENTMANAGER)

DECLARE_PROTECT_FINAL_CONSTRUCT()

BEGIN_COM_MAP(CClientManager)
  COM_INTERFACE_ENTRY(IParseDisplayName)
  COM_INTERFACE_ENTRY(IOleItemContainer)
END_COM_MAP()

// IClientManager
public:
// IParseDisplayName
  STDMETHOD(ParseDisplayName)(IBindCtx *pdc,
    LPOLESTR pszDisplayName, ULONG *pchEaten,
    IMoniker **ppmkOut);
//IOleContainer
  STDMETHOD(EnumObjects)(DWORD grfFlags, IEnumUnknown **ppenum);
  STDMETHOD(LockContainer)(BOOL fLock);
//IOleItemContainer
  STDMETHOD(GetObject)(LPOLESTR pszItem, DWORD dwSpeedNeeded,
    IBindCtx *pbc, REFIID riid, void **ppvObject);
```

```
  STDMETHOD(GetObjectStorage)(LPOLESTR pszItem, IBindCtx *pbc,
    REFIID riid, void **ppvStorage);
  STDMETHOD(IsRunning)(LPOLESTR pszItem);
};

#endif //__CLIENTMANAGER_H_
```

You finished modifying the header file for the CClientManager class. Next, implement the various methods declared for the new interfaces you added to the CClientManager class.

Open the ClientManager.cpp file in the Visual C++ document window by double-clicking on the file name listed in the FileView page of the Project window.

All of the methods declared by an interface implemented by the CClientManager class must be defined in the ClientManager.cpp file. The IParseDisplayName interface defines one method, the `ParseDiplay-Name()` method. Add the following code to the ClientManager.cpp file just under the "CClientManager" comment:

```
STDMETHODIMP CClientManager::ParseDisplayName(IBindCtx* pbc,
  LPOLESTR pszDisplayName, ULONG* pchEaten,
  IMoniker** ppmkOut)
{
  *pchEaten = wcslen(pszDisplayName);
  return CreateItemMoniker(L"!", pszDisplayName + 1, ppmkOut);
}
```

The IOleContainer interface defines two methods: the `EnumObjects()` and `LockContainer()` methods. InstantPostServer doesn't use either of these methods. Nevertheless, you need to add the method definitions. Add the following unimplemented method definitions:

```
STDMETHODIMP CClientManager::EnumObjects(DWORD grfFlags, IEnumUnknown**
ppenum)
{
  return E_NOTIMPL;
}

STDMETHODIMP CClientManager::LockContainer(BOOL fLock)
{
  return E_NOTIMPL;
}
```

You had to add the IOleContainer interface even though the application doesn't use its methods because the method you really want is part of the IOleItemContainer interface, which requires that the object implements the IOleContainer interface.

The IOleItemContainer interface defines three methods: the `GetObject()`, `GetObjectStorage()`, and `IsRunning()` methods. The `GetObject()` method is the one that InstantPostServer uses. It's through this method that the global CPostManager object is created and assigned to the `m_connection` variable. Add the `GetObject()` method definition, shown here, to the ClientManager.cpp file:

```
STDMETHODIMP CClientManager::GetObject(LPOLESTR pszItem, DWORD dwSpeedNeeded,
IBindCtx* pbc, REFIID riid, void** ppvObject)
{
  return m_connection.QueryInterface(riid, ppvObject);
}
```

Add the two other methods unimplemented, as shown here:

```
STDMETHODIMP CClientManager::GetObjectStorage(LPOLESTR pszItem, IBindCtx*
pbc, REFIID riid, void** ppvStorage)
{
  return E_NOTIMPL;
}

STDMETHODIMP CClientManager::IsRunning(LPOLESTR pszItem)
{
  return E_NOTIMPL;
}
```

Listing 16.2 shows the completed ClientManager.cpp file with the code you added or modified highlighted in boldfaced type.

Listing 16.2 ClientManager.cpp

```
// ClientManager.cpp : Implementation of CClientManager
#include "stdafx.h"
#include "InstantPostServer.h"
#include "ClientManager.h"


/////////////////////////////////////////////////////////////////////////////
// CClientManager

STDMETHODIMP CClientManager::ParseDisplayName(IBindCtx* pbc,
```

```
  LPOLESTR pszDisplayName, ULONG* pchEaten,
  IMoniker** ppmkOut)
{
  *pchEaten = wcslen(pszDisplayName);
  return CreateItemMoniker(L"!", pszDisplayName + 1, ppmkOut);
}

STDMETHODIMP CClientManager::EnumObjects(DWORD grfFlags, IEnumUnknown**
ppenum)
{
  return E_NOTIMPL;
}

STDMETHODIMP CClientManager::LockContainer(BOOL fLock)
{
  return E_NOTIMPL;
}

STDMETHODIMP CClientManager::GetObject(LPOLESTR pszItem, DWORD dwSpeedNeeded,
IBindCtx* pbc, REFIID riid, void** ppvObject)
{
  return m_connection.QueryInterface(riid, ppvObject);
}

STDMETHODIMP CClientManager::GetObjectStorage(LPOLESTR pszItem, IBindCtx*
pbc, REFIID riid, void** ppvStorage)
{
  return E_NOTIMPL;
}

STDMETHODIMP CClientManager::IsRunning(LPOLESTR pszItem)
{
  return E_NOTIMPL;
}
```

You've completed the modifications necessary to the code for the CClientManager object. This object manages the connections between the InstantPostServer and the various InstantPost client components communicating through the server. The center of the message posting activity, however, is the global CPostManager object.

Modifying the CPostManager Object

The PostManager object manages message posting in the InstantPost distributed application. Most of the working code in the InstantPostServer component is part of the PostManager object.

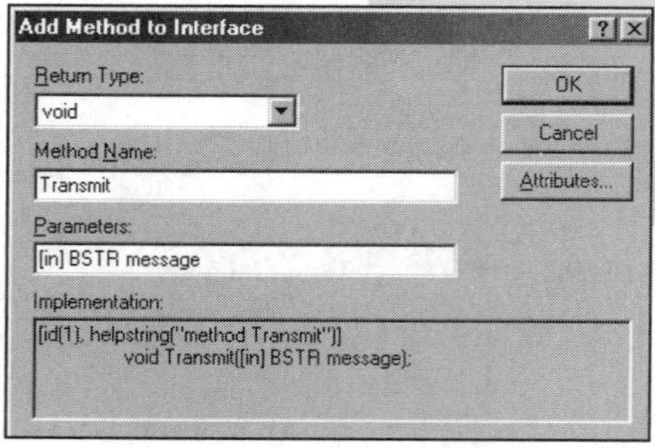

Figure 16-1
Add the Transmit()
method through the
Add Method to
Interface dialog box.

Adding Connectivity

Enable multiple clients to receive messages from the InstantPostServer through the implementation of connection points. You do four things:

1. Add a method to the _IPostManagerEvents interface for transmitting a message through an event.

2. Add a new method to the IPostManager interface that will actually broadcast the event created through the _IPostManagerEvents interface.

3. Implement the new method you declared in the IPostManager interface.

4. Implement a connection point through the new method you declared in the _IPostManagerEvents interface.

Adding the Transmit() Method to the _IPostManagerEvents Interface

Point to the _IPostManagerEvents interface on the ClassView page of the Workspace window and press your right mouse button; a shortcut menu appears. Select the Add Method command from the shortcut menu. The Add Method to Interface dialog box appears, as in Figure 16-1.

Select void from the Return Type drop-down list. Type `Transmit` into the Method Name text box and type `[in] BSTR message` in the Parameters text box. Click on the OK button.

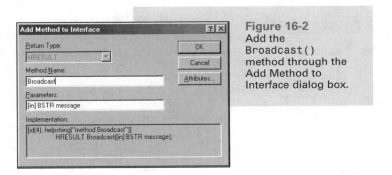

Figure 16-2
Add the Broadcast() method through the Add Method to Interface dialog box.

Adding the Broadcast() Method to the IPostManager Interface

Point to the IPostManager interface on the ClassView page of the Workspace window and press your right mouse button; a shortcut menu appears. Select the Add Method command from the shortcut menu. The Add Method to Interface dialog box appears, as in Figure 16-2.

Type **Broadcast** into the Method Name text box, and type **[in] BSTR message** in the Parameters text box. Click on the OK button.

Implementing the Broadcast() Method

Open the CPostManager tree on the ClassView page of the Workspace window and then open the IPostManager tree found under the CPostManager listing. Double-click on the Broadcast() method listing. The PostManager.cpp file opens in the document window to the Broadcast() method definition. Add the following line of code to the Broadcast() method definition right after the "TODO" remark:

```
Fire_Transmit(message);
```

The _IPostManagerEvents interface's Transmit() method is fired as an event through the connection point that you will implement in the next section, "Implementing the Connection Point." You must build the project here so that Visual C++ is able to find the Fire_Transmit() method call you just added to the Transmit() method definition. Click on the Build button on the toolbar or select the Build InstantPostServer.exe

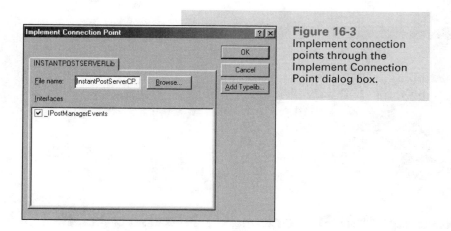

Figure 16-3
Implement connection
points through the
Implement Connection
Point dialog box.

command from the Build menu. When the build is finished, you are ready to implement the connection point.

Implementing the Connection Point

The Visual C++ integrated development environment has transformed implementing connection points, which was once a tedious task at best, into a matter of a few clicks of your mouse buttons.

Point to CPostManager on the ClassView page of the Workspace window and press your right mouse button. You should see the Implement Connection Point command listed. Select the Implement Connection Point command. The Implement Connection Point dialog box appears, as in Figure 16-3.

Visual C++ creates a new file for implementing connection points. Generally, the file takes the name of the project you're implementing the connection points in with a CP, for Connection Point, appended to the end. The File Name text box of the Implement Connection Point dialog box displays InstantPostServerCP.h by default. This name is fine.

Check the check box next to _IPostManagerEvents in the Interfaces list and click on the OK button. Visual C++ implements the _IPostManagerEvents interface connection point for you. The `Fire_Transmit()` method is defined in the new CProxy_IPostManagerEvents class created by Visual C++. That's it!

> **Note**
>
> Recompile your InstantPostServer project now. You will probably get an error pointing to the line in the connection point map with the _IPostManagerEvents interface identifier, found in the PostManager.h file. Visual C++ has a small bug when an events interface identifier is added to the connection point map. It adds an IID__IPostManagerEvents identifier when the IDL file defines it as DIID__IPostManagerEvents when, like for InstantPostServer, the application uses dual interfaces. Simply add a D to the beginning of the identifier name and recompile.

Modifying the WinMain() Function

Open the InstantPostServer.cpp file and scroll down until you find the `WinMain()` function. The function signature should look like this:

```
extern "C" int WINAPI _tWinMain(HINSTANCE hInstance,
    HINSTANCE /*hPrevInstance*/, LPTSTR lpCmdLine, int /*nShowCmd*/)
```

Scroll down through the `WinMain()` function until you see an `if` statement like this:

```
if (bRun)
{
  _Module.StartMonitor();
#if _WIN32_WINNT >= 0x0400 & defined(_ATL_FREE_THREADED)
  hRes = _Module.RegisterClassObjects(CLSCTX_LOCAL_SERVER,
    REGCLS_MULTIPLEUSE | REGCLS_SUSPENDED);
  ASSERTE(SUCCEEDED(hRes));
  hRes = CoResumeClassObjects();
#else
  hRes = _Module.RegisterClassObjects(CLSCTX_LOCAL_SERVER,
  REGCLS_MULTIPLEUSE);
#endif
  ASSERTE(SUCCEEDED(hRes));

  _Module.RevokeClassObjects();
  Sleep(dwPause); //wait for any threads to finish
}
```

Modify this `if` statement so that it looks like Listing 16.3. The new code is highlighted in bold type.

Listing 16.3 The Modified Portion of the `WinMain()`
Function in the InstantPostServer.cpp File

```
if (bRun)
{
  DWORD dwReg;
  CComObjectNoLock<CClientManager>* mgrClassObject = new
CComObjectNoLock<CClientManager>;
hRes = CoRegisterClassObject(CLSID_ClientManager, reinterpret_cast<IOleItem-
Container*>(mgrClassObject),
    CLSCTX_LOCAL_SERVER, REGCLS_MULTIPLEUSE, &dwReg);
  _ASSERTE(SUCCEEDED(hRes));

  MSG msg;
  while (GetMessage(&msg, 0, 0, 0))
    DispatchMessage(&msg);

  CoRevokeClassObject(dwReg);
}
```

Using InstantPost

The InstantPost client application is created using Visual Basic. If you don't have or use Visual Basic, don't worry. You can use the InstantPost client program included on the CD-ROM as long as you use the proper UUIDs. This is discussed in the next section, "Using the InstantPost Client on the CD-ROM." Otherwise, you can create a client program in Visual Basic as described in the section "Creating the InstantPost Client."

Using the InstantPost Client on the CD-ROM

To use the InstantPost client program that is already built for you, you must use the same UUIDs that were used for the interfaces in the Instant-PostServer component when the InstantPost client was created. The easiest way to do this is to use the InstantPostServer code from the CD-ROM. However, you can replace the UUIDs in your IDL file to get the same result. The IDL file used to create the type libraries that were referenced by the InstantPost control on the CD-ROM is shown in Listing 16.4.

Listing 16.4 The InstantPostServer.idl File with UUIDs Used by the InstantPost Client

```
// InstantPostServer.idl : IDL source for InstantPostServer.dll
//

// This file will be processed by the MIDL tool to
// produce the type library (InstantPostServer.tlb) and marshalling code.

import "oaidl.idl";
import "ocidl.idl";
                    [
                        object,
                        uuid(5ADF605D-3039-11D2-8AB3-0080C80D2A4A),
                        dual,
                        helpstring("IClientManager Interface"),
                        pointer_default(unique)
                    ]
interface IClientManager : IDispatch
                    {
                    };
                    [
                        object,
                        uuid(5ADF6061-3039-11D2-8AB3-0080C80D2A4A),
                        dual,
                        helpstring("IPostManager Interface"),
                        pointer_default(unique)
                    ]
interface IPostManager : IDispatch
                    {
                        [id(1), helpstring("method Broadcast")] HRESULT Broad-
cast([in] BSTR message);
                    };

[
uuid(5ADF6051-3039-11D2-8AB3-0080C80D2A4A),
        version(1.0),
helpstring("InstantPostServer 1.0 Type Library")
]
library INSTANTPOSTSERVERLib
{
importlib("stdole32.tlb");
importlib("stdole2.tlb");

                    [
                        uuid(5ADF6060-3039-11D2-8AB3-0080C80D2A4A),
                        helpstring("ClientManager Class")
```

```
                            ]
            coclass ClientManager
                            {
                                [default] interface IClientManager;
                        };
                        [
                            uuid(5ADF6063-3039-11D2-8AB3-0080C80D2A4A),
                            helpstring("_IPostManagerEvents Interface")
                        ]
            dispinterface _IPostManagerEvents
                            {
                                properties:
                                methods:
                                [id(1), helpstring("method Transmit")] void
            Transmit([in] BSTR message);
                            };

                        [
                            uuid(5ADF6062-3039-11D2-8AB3-0080C80D2A4A),
                            helpstring("PostManager Class")
                        ]
            coclass PostManager
                            {
                                [default] interface IPostManager;
                                [default, source] dispinterface _IPostManagerEvents;
                            };
            };
```

Once you replace your UUIDs in your InstantPostServer.idl file with the ones in Listing 16.4, build the project. Next, add the InstantPost.ocx files to a folder on your machine. Then skip to the section "Running the InstantPost Client."

Creating the InstantPost Client

Create the InstantPost ActiveX control using Visual Basic. Select ActiveX Control from the New page of the New Project dialog box that displays on starting Visual Basic, as shown in Figure 16-4, and then click on the OK button.

Alternatively, select the New Project command from the File menu to open the New Project dialog box. Then select the ActiveX Control and click on the OK button.

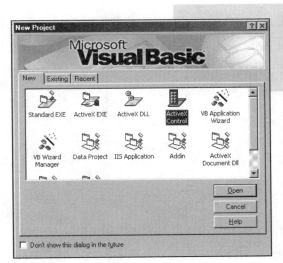

Figure 16-4
Select a new project type from the New page of the New Project dialog box.

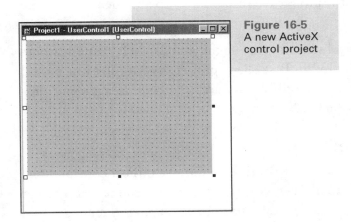

Figure 16-5
A new ActiveX control project

A new project appears and a blank user control is displayed, as in Figure 16-5.

The default size of the control's graphic user interface (4800 x 3600), displayed by default on the Visual Basic Standard toolbar, is fine for the InstantPost control, so leave it as is.

Save the project by clicking on the Save Project toolbar button. The Save File As dialog box appears, asking you to save the user control.

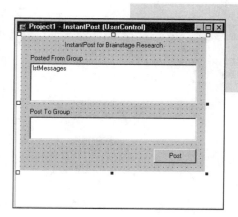

Name the user control file InstantPost.ctr, and then click on the Save button. The Save File As dialog box appears again, asking you to save the project. Name the project file InstantPost.vbp and then click on the Save button.

With the user control selected, change the user control's name attribute to InstantPost. The InstantPost client project is ready for you to add controls on the ActiveX control interface, add code to carry out processing, and make the OCX file.

Adding Controls

You need to add three major controls to the InstantPost control interface. Add a list box to display posts from the group connected through the InstantPost application, add a text box for typing in messages that you want to post to the group, and add a button that you click on to post a message. Once you finish adding these three elements, you add three labels. One is a title and the other two label the text boxes. The final InstantPost control interface should look similar to the one in Figure 16-6.

Click on the ListBox button displayed on the component toolbar and draw the list box where messages posted from the group will appear. Make the upper-left corner of the list box about 240 twips right of and

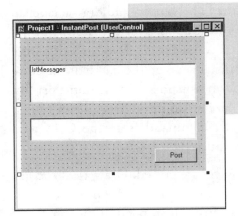

Figure 16-7
The InstantPost ActiveX control graphic user interface with its EditBox and CommandButton controls in place

720 twips down (240 x 720) from the upper-left corner of the control's interface. Make the list box cover about 4335 twips horizontally and 1035 twips vertically (4335 x 1035). Type **lstMessages** into the ListBox control's Name attribute.

Click on the TextBox button displayed on the component toolbar and draw the text box where users will type in messages they want to post to the group. Make the upper-left corner of the text box about 240 twips right of and 2160 twips down (240 x 2160) from the upper-left corner of the control's interface. Make the text box cover about 4335 twips horizontally and 615 twips vertically (4335 x 615). Type **txtMessages** into the TextBox control's name attribute and remove any text from its text attribute.

Click on the CommandButton button displayed on the component toolbar and draw a button on the InstantPost interface. Make the upper-left corner of the button about 3480 twips right of and 3000 twips down (3480 x 3000) from the upper-left corner of the control's interface. Make the button cover about 1095 twips horizontally and 375 twips vertically (1095 x 375). Type **cmdPost** into the CommandButton control's name attribute and type **Post** into its caption attribute.

The InstantPost graphic user interface should look similar to the one shown in Figure 16-7 at this point.

Add a title to the control. Click on the Label button and draw a label at the top of the control's interface. Draw it about 120 twips down from the top of the interface. Type text that you want displayed as a title into the control's Caption attribute. For instance, type the name of the control followed by your company or business name as in "**InstantPost for Brainstage Research**." Set the AutoSize attribute to True. Then center the title by selecting the Horizontally command from the Center in Form submenu under the Format menu.

Add a label to the list box where messages are posted. Draw a Label control over the top left of the lstMessages control. Draw it about 240 twips right and 480 twips down (240 x 480) from the top left of the interface. Type **Posted From Group** into the control's Caption attribute and set the AutoSize attribute to True.

Finally, add a label to the text box where users type in messages that they want to post. Draw a Label control over the top left of the txtMessages control. Draw it about 240 twips right and 1920 twips down (240 x 1920) from the top left of the interface. Type **Posted From Group** into the control's Caption attribute and set the AutoSize attribute to True.

Adding Code

Writing code for connecting with and interacting with a server is straightforward in Visual Basic. Add the following line of code to the General Declarations area:

```
Dim WithEvents post As PostManager
```

The WithEvents keyword tells Visual Basic that the object, in this case the PostManager object, fires events. The object, which you assigned as global in the InstantPostServer application, is assigned to the post variable.

Next add the main code so that it's executed when the ActiveX control is initialized. Under UserControl Initialize, add the following code:

```
Private Sub UserControl_Initialize()
  Dim obj As String
  obj = "clsid:5ADF6060-3039-11D2-8AB3-0080C80D2A4A:!"
  On Error GoTo failure
  Set post = GetObject(obj)
  cmdPost.Enabled = True
Exit Sub
Failure:
  MsgBox "Failed to connect with server " + Err.Description
End Sub
```

The ClientManager object's class identifier is assigned to the obj variable and passed to the GetObject() method. Use the UUID of your own ClientManager object if you created your own InstantPostServer code from scratch. The GetObject() method returns a moniker to the Post-Manager object, which is assigned to the post variable.

You want to post a message any time that you click on the Post button. Add the following code to cmdPost_Click():

```
Private Sub cmdPost_Click()
  post.Broadcast txtMessage
  txtMessage = ""
  txtMessage.SetFocus
End Sub
```

The current text in the txtMessage control is passed to the PostManager control's Broadcast() method. Next, the content of the txtMessage control is reset to an empty string and the focus is reset to the txtMessage control.

The last thing you need to do is add the connection point sink. This is the Transmit function that was declared on the _IPostManagerEvents interface but wasn't defined. It's defined in the client. Add the following code:

```
Private Sub post_Transmit(ByVal message As String)
  lstMessages.AddItem message
End Sub
```

When an event is fired, the InstantPost client intercepts it and displays the message in the lstMessages control.

The complete code for the InstantPost ActiveX control is shown in Listing 16.5.

Listing 16.5 The Visual Basic Code for the InstantPost ActiveX Control

```
Dim WithEvents post As PostManager

Private Sub cmdPost_Click()
  post.Broadcast txtMessage
  txtMessage = ""
  txtMessage.SetFocus
End Sub

Private Sub post_Transmit(ByVal message As String)
  lstMessages.AddItem message
End Sub

Private Sub UserControl_Initialize()
  Dim obj As String
  obj = "clsid:5ADF6060-3039-11D2-8AB3-0080C80D2A4A:!"
  On Error GoTo failure
  Set post = GetObject(obj)
  cmdPost.Enabled = True
Exit Sub
Failure:
  MsgBox "Failed to connect with server " + Err.Description
End Sub
```

Making the Control

To make the InstantPost ActiveX control you must include the correct references in the project and then make the project. Select the References command from the Project menu and the References dialog box appears, as in Figure 16-8.

Find InstantPostServer 1.0 Type Library in the Available References listing and check the check box next to the listing. Click on the OK button. Finally, select the Make InstantPost.ocx command from the File menu to make the InstantPost ActiveX control.

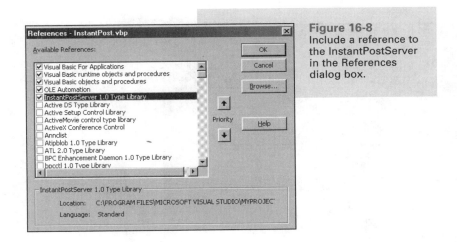

Figure 16-8
Include a reference to
the InstantPostServer
in the References
dialog box.

Running the InstantPost Client

Try out your new distributed message posting application. Run two instances of the InstantPost ActiveX control on your computer. Create an HTML file like the one in Listing 16.6. Be sure to enter the correct class identifier for the InstantPost control.

Listing 16.6 The InstantPost.html File

```
<HTML>
<BODY>
<OBJECT classid="clsid:6E2F7258-3D45-11D2-8AD4-0080C80D2A4A">
</OBJECT>
</BODY>
</HTML>
```

Open two instances of your Web browser and load the InstantPost.html file into each instance. Type into the Post To Group text boxes and press the Post buttons. You should see something like Figure 16-9.

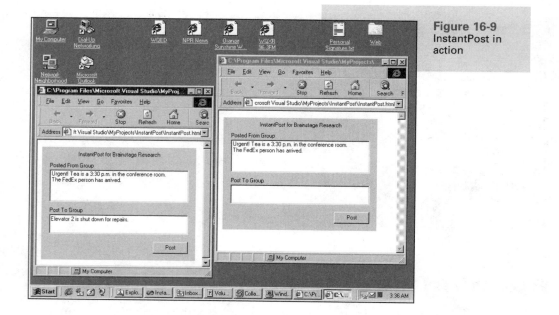

Figure 16-9
InstantPost in
action

Summary

You created an ActiveX control that interacts over the enterprise. The InstantPost project utilizes connection points, which are key to sending messages between controls during run-time. Connection points provide a means to fire and receive events between controls, and it's these events that carry messages. You've created a project that can run and interact across the enterprise, but you've yet to prove it. In the final Project 3 chapter, you learn how to deploy and run the InstantPost ActiveX control on the enterprise.

CHAPTER 17

Deploying InstantPost

Components developed following the DCOM specification run seamlessly across the computing enterprise. However, DCOM is a new technology, and a lot of legacy code out there doesn't know about DCOM. Learn how to take advantage of DCOM and deploy your software components across different platforms. Build a release version of the InstantPostServer component and deploy it, along with the InstantPost ActiveX control, to the enterprise using setup programs created with InstallShield.

Building Release Versions

By now you're a pro at building release versions of your software. As usual, make sure that the active configuration of your build is set to the 32-bit Windows platform release version. Since you are deploying these components on the enterprise, you want them to be as self-contained as possible. Therefore, select Win32 Release MinDependency in the Project Configurations list on the Set Active Project Configuration dialog box for minimum dependencies. Also be sure to make the final build of the InstantPostServer component before you make the final build of the InstantPost ActiveX control. Remember that the client control uses information from the server component during its build. You want these to be up to date.

InstantPost and DCOM

With the final builds of the InstantPost and InstantPostServer components, you are ready to deploy the distributed message posting application to the enterprise. The main difference between COM-based components that communicate within a process on a stand-alone computer and those that communicate across the enterprise is that the latter communicate through surrogate interfaces. That is, they communicate through proxy stubs. These stubs stand in for the component's actual interfaces, but they are able to communicate across networks. This is all taken care of for you by the hard work Visual C++ does behind the scenes when you're creating software components. However, you must tell the proxy stubs where to look for the component that they want to connect with. This is done through the Windows Registry.

The Windows Registry

Windows 95, Windows 98, and Windows NT are all 32-bit operating systems that have a 32-bit registry. The Registry is a database that contains system- and application-related information, including such things as the name of the program associated with a particular file extension and uninstall information. The Registry is actually made up of several database files containing information represented in a tree fashion, like folders and files in Windows Explorer.

You can look at and edit the Windows Registry using the Registry Editor, shown in Figure 17-1. Typically, you won't find this application listed on the Start menu. You can do a lot of damage to a system through

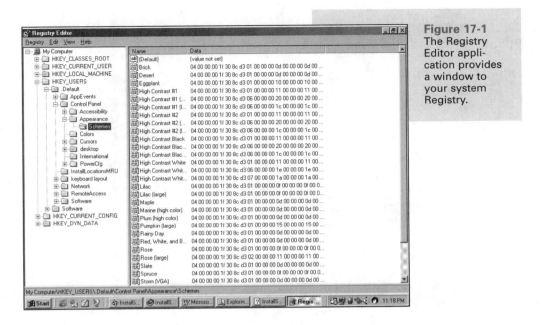

Figure 17-1
The Registry Editor application provides a window to your system Registry.

uninformed tampering with the Registry, so the Registry Editor remains hidden to all but the informed or the curious. Under Windows 95 and Windows 98, you can find the Registry Editor application in the Windows folder as the Regedit.exe file. Under Windows NT look in the Winnt folder.

A half dozen or so base keys display just under the My Computer root key listing. Among those is the HKEY_CLASSES_ROOT base key, which is the most important database key for registering DCOM-based software components.

Under the HKEY_CLASSES_ROOT base key are four keys important to the DCOM developer: the AppID, CLSID, TypeLib, and Interface keys. Data on a component's application identifier, class identifier, type library, and interfaces are stored under each of these keys, respectively. For instance, the InstantPostServer application identifier is listed under the AppID key in Figure 17-2. Notice that the full key name of the currently selected key displays in the status window at the bottom left of the Registry Editor window.

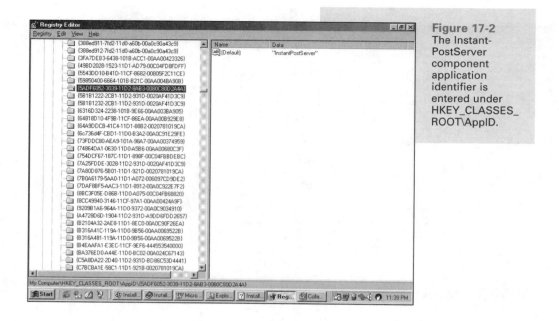

Figure 17-2
The Instant-PostServer component application identifier is entered under HKEY_CLASSES_ROOT\AppID.

The UUID (or GUID) listed for the InstantPostServer component's application identifier in Figure 17-2 is 5ADF6052-3039-11D2-8AB3-0080C80D2A4A. This is a unique number that is sure to be different from the number assigned to your InstantPostServer component.

Actually, most of these values are automatically registered by the self-registering features built into COM-based components created using Visual C++. When you install InstantPost ActiveX controls, however, you need to register the name of the computer that runs the remote server, the InstantPostServer component. You do this by adding the RemoteServerName name under the HKEY_CLASSES_ROOT\ AppID key in the registry and associating it with the name of the machine that runs the InstantPostServer component. For instance, if you were to use the Registry Editor to manually add the information to a Windows Registry that the InstantPostServer component runs on a computer named Whiskers, you would see something like Figure 17-3.

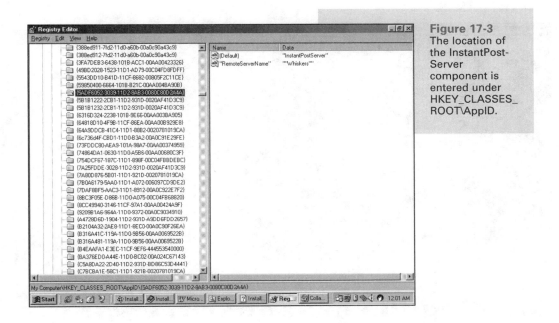

Figure 17-3
The location of the InstantPost-Server component is entered under HKEY_CLASSES_ ROOT\AppID.

Deploying InstantPost Using InstallShield

Use InstallShield to create a setup program for distributing the InstantPost ActiveX control and InstantPostServer component over the Internet. Of course, you can also distribute the control on floppy disk or CD-ROM. InstallShield provides you with an advanced setup program, so you don't need to spend a significant amount of time creating your own.

See the "Setting Up InstallShield" section in Chapter 7, "Testing QuickBrowse," for instructions on installing the InstallShield program from your Visual C++ CD-ROM.

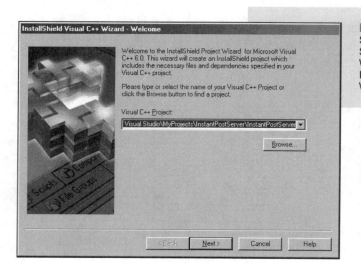

Figure 17-4
Select the InstantPost-
Server project in the
Welcome page of the
InstallShield Visual C++
Wizard dialog box.

Creating the InstantPostServer Setup Program

Deploy the InstantPostServer component with InstallShield by using the InstallShield Wizard. Start up Visual C++ and load the InstantPost-Server project. Then select the InstallShield Wizard command from the Tools menu. The Welcome page of the InstallShield Visual C++ Wizard dialog box appears, as in Figure 17-4.

By default, the InstantPostServer project should be selected in the Visual C++ Project text box and drop-down list on the Welcome page of the InstallShield Visual C++ Wizard dialog box. Type in or select the Instant-PostServer project if it isn't selected already. Then click on the Next button. The Application Information page appears, as in Figure 17-5.

Most of the default information displayed in the Application Information page is good. However, you might want to make some modifications. Type those in. And be absolutely sure that the InstantPostServer.exe file

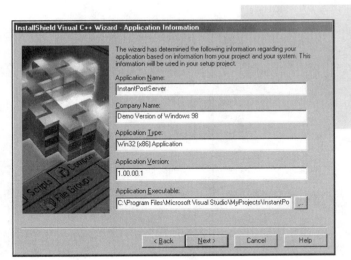

referenced in the Application Executable text box is the release version of the InstantPostServer component. The file should be in the Release-MinDependency folder inside the InstantPostServer folder. Typically, the file's full path is C:\Program Files\Microsoft Visual Studio\MyProjects\InstantPostServer\ReleaseMinDependency\InstantPostServer.exe. If the file is not in the ReleaseMinDependency folder, you can select the appropriate file by clicking on the ellipsis button to the right of the Application Executable text box to open the Open dialog box. Find the release version of the InstantPostServer.exe file, select it, and click on the Open button. Once you're satisfied with the information contained in the Application Information page, click on the Next button. The Summary page of the InstallShield Visual C++ Wizard dialog box appears, as in Figure 17-6.

The InstantPostServer component file is displayed in the Summary page of the InstallShield Visual C++ Wizard dialog box. The ATL-based component has no dependent files. Click on the Finish button; the wizard launches InstallShield as in Figure 17-7.

Figure 17-6
Review the files that are included in your project on the Summary page of the InstallShield Visual C++ Wizard dialog box.

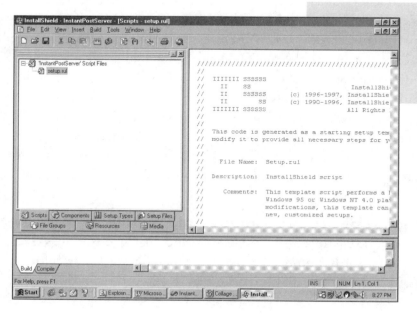

Figure 17-7
The InstantPost-Server project is displayed by the InstallShield application.

InstallShield is a powerful application that provides a wide range of options for you. It's beyond the scope of this book to go into full details on this program, but you can find excellent guides from the Install-Shield Help menu, including the Getting Started and Getting Results online books.

Once you are satisfied with the project's setup program, you can build the InstantPostServer project setup program by clicking on the Media Build toolbar button or selecting the Media Build Wizard command from the Build menu. The Media Name page of the Media Build Wizard dialog box appears, as in Figure 17-8.

Type in a name designating the medium you will be using to distribute your application, such as Web. Click on the Next button; the Disk Type page of the Media Build Wizard dialog box appears, as in Figure 17-9.

You can build the default setup program for the InstantPostServer put together by the InstallShield Wizard.

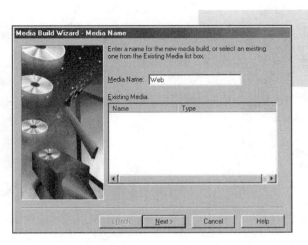

Figure 17-8
The Media Name page
of the Media Build
Wizard dialog box

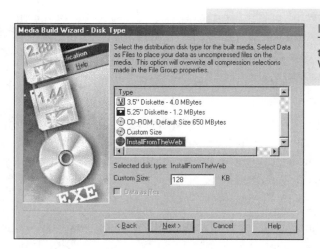

Figure 17-9
The Disk Type page of
the Media Build
Wizard dialog box

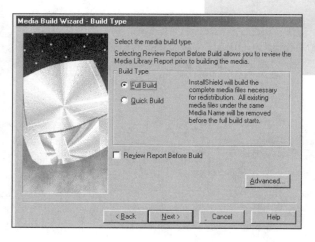

Figure 17-10
The Build Type page
of the Media Build
Wizard dialog box

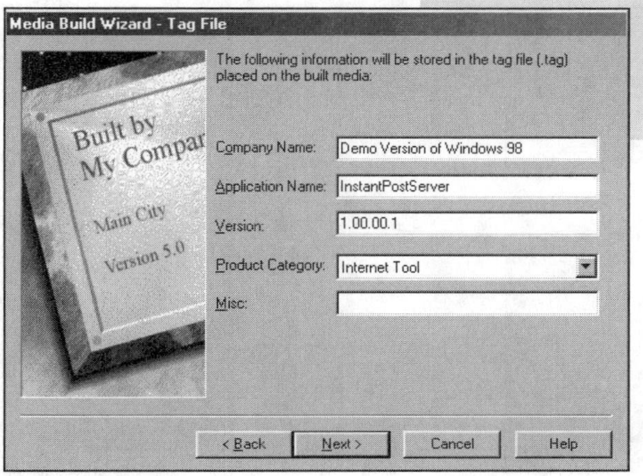

Figure 17-11
The Tag File page of the Media Build Wizard dialog box

The Type list on the Disk Type page displays several types of media that you can deploy your application from, including various floppy disk sizes, CD-ROMs, and the Web itself. Select InstallFromTheWeb in the Type list. The Custom Size text box displays the amount of disk space available to you for deploying the InstantPostServer component. You probably have much more room than the default if you have a Web site. Click on the Next button; the Build Type page of the Media Build Wizard dialog box appears, as in Figure 17-10.

Select Full Build from the Build Type page of the Media Build Wizard dialog box. The full build gives you complete media files ready for distributing the InstantPostServer component over the Web. Click on the Next button so that the Tag File page of the Media Build Wizard dialog box appears, as in Figure 17-11.

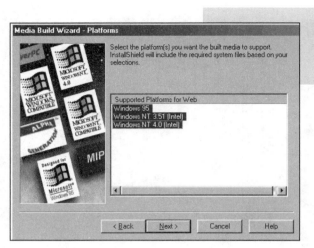

Figure 17-12
The Platforms page of
the Media Build
Wizard dialog box

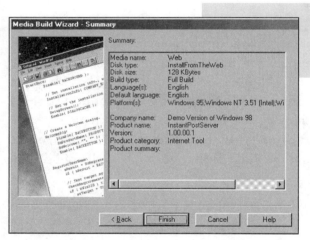

Figure 17-13
The Summary page of
the Media Build
Wizard dialog box

Enter information about the application in the Tag File page. Select the appropriate product category in the Product Category drop-down list. "Internet Tool" seems appropriate for the InstantPostServer component. When you're satisfied with the information, click the Next button. The Platforms page of the Media Build Wizard dialog box appears, as in Figure 17-12.

The InstantPostServer component can run on all of the 32-bit Windows platforms. Make sure that all of the platforms listed in the Supported

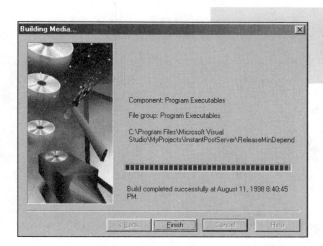

Figure 17-14
The Building Media
dialog box at the end
of a build

Platforms for Web list are highlighted and then click on the Next button. The Summary page of the Media Build Wizard dialog box appears, as in Figure 17-13.

Check over the contents of the Summary page to make sure that everything will be set up as you want it. If not, click on the Back button to go back to previous pages of the wizard and change the information. Otherwise, click on the Finish button. InstallShield builds the medium. When it's finished, the Building Media dialog box displays a message that the build was a success, as in Figure 17-14.

Click on the Finish button. The media files are ready to deploy on the Web. You can use the Send Media To command on the Build menu to deploy the media files.

Summary

You created release versions of the InstantPost and InstantPostServer components and deployed them on the enterprise. You've reached the pinnacle, the state-of-the-art, Visual C++ programming. Utilizing DCOM with COM-based software components that interact puts you right on the cutting edge. Your imagination is the only limit to the possibilities for new enterprise-wide applications.

Project 3 Summary

In Project 3, you used the ATL COM AppWizard to rapidly pull together the skeleton of your new software component on the basis of a few queries.

You added COM objects and controls to your project skeletons to flesh them out with real functionality. You inserted a control into the InstantPost project to provide a dialog interface for the Instant-Post control, and then you used visual design methods in the Visual C++ resource editor to draw controls onto the dialog interface and modify their properties. The result was a graphic user interface for the InstantPost ActiveX control.

You learned what makes the ATL such a boon to developers of COM-based (and DCOM-based) software components. You implemented the COM connection points facility to get real-time distributed communication between the InstantPost components.

The result of finishing Project 3 was learning all of these things and more. You created the InstantPost ActiveX control and the Instant-PostServer control. In combination, these software components make up an enterprise-wide, distributed message posting system. You took the ultimate step in Visual C++ programming not only by deploying software components across the enterprise but also by virtually wiring the components together from wherever they are deployed.

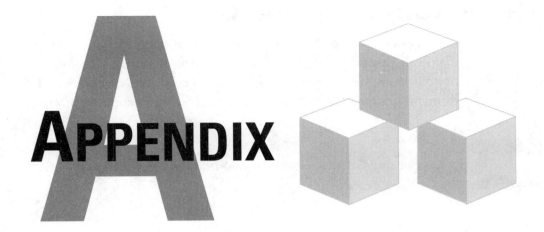

APPENDIX A

C++ in a Flash: The Language

C++ is a powerful object-oriented language, widely used in colleges, universities, and throughout the software industry. It's assumed that you know how to program in some language and that, at most, you need a brief course on object-oriented programming and the C++ language. This appendix briefly covers the C++ language syntax and how you use it. Appendix B, "C++ in a Flash: Object-Oriented Programming," provides a brief overview of object-oriented programming techniques.

Note

> Even if you already know C++, use this appendix as a handy reference to the C++ language.

C++ Inspired by the C

C++ looks similar to the C language on the surface; its syntax is nearly identical. However, C++ isn't C. C was the most widely used computer programming language, so it made sense to copy its syntax so that all of those programmers already using C would feel at home using C++.

 C++ is not C. In fact they are two quite separate languages.

If you already know the C language, the information in this appendix should look familiar. This appendix deals primarily with syntax. For instance, the addition operator (+) works the same in both C and C++, up to a point. In C++ you can do more with the addition operator, primarily due to your ability to override operators in C++. For instance, you can concatenate to strings using the addition operator. This expression:

```
"Wind is the sky " + "going somewhere."
```

results in this string:

```
"Wind is the sky going somewhere."
```

You learn about operators and overloading operators later in this appendix. First, you learn about the fundamental elements of a source code listing in C++.

Statements and Expressions

A statement in the C++ language is like a typical sentence in the English language; it's a unit of assertion. For instance, you might want to add the number of walkers to the number of runners in a marathon to know the total number of participants. You could do this in this way in C++, assuming there were 428 walkers and 117 runners:

```
totalParticipants = 428 + 117;
```

The number of walkers and runners are added together using the addition operator (+). The addition operator and the two operands, 428 and 117, form an expression. An expression is an operation that returns a value. The assignment operator (=) assigns the value returned from this expression to the `totalParticipants` variable. The combination of the addition and the assignment forms a complete statement, which is ended with a semicolon (;). All statements in C++ end with a semicolon.

Comments

Add comments to your C++ code using two different comment formats. Use this format to create a single line comment. The comment is everything written after the double-slashes (//).

```
// This is a single-line comment.
```

Use this format to create one or more lines of comments.

```
/* This is a multiline comment.

   It ends on the next line.
*/
```

Everything between the /* and the */ is considered comments by the C++ compiler. You can place these delimiters on the same line or across several lines.

Note

If you program in C, you recognize the comment format that begins with /* and ends with */. The comment format that starts with // and ends with a new line is not a part of the original C language, although most compilers now also support both formats in the C language.

Literals

A literal is an actual value that you want used in your C++ program. You can type in number, character, and string literals.

Number

There are two kinds of number literals: integer and floating-point. The simplest way to create integer literals is by typing an integer, such as 38. By default this is a signed integer. In other words, the integer is stored in memory in a way that allows it to be positive or negative. This is in contrast to unsigned integers, which are stored in memory in a way that only allows them to be positive numbers. You can specify that your integer is stored as an unsigned integer by appending an upper- or lowercase U to the number. For instance, 38U is an unsigned integer. On the other hand, you can guarantee that your integer is signed by preceding it with a plus or a minus sign, as in +38.

In Visual C++ long integers are the same size as regular integers. They both fill four bytes of memory; therefore the distinction isn't urgent. Typically you use a different data type to gain memory so that a larger number may be represented, or to save memory because only a small number needs to be used and you want your program to be memory efficient. Nevertheless, you might find occasion to use long integers. An integer is considered to be of the long type by the Visual C++ compiler if it's followed by an upper- or lowercase L. For instance, 38L is a long integer. You can also create a long and unsigned integer. You append upper- or lowercase U and L to the number like 38UL.

Create 64-bit (eight-byte) integers when you need to use monster numbers that don't each fit into four bytes of memory. Add i64 to the end of the number that you want represented as a 64-bit integer. For instance, 38i64 is a 64-bit integer.

Specify an octal literal by adding a leading zero (0) to an octal number. Recall that you count in octal from 0 to 7. So for instance, 038 is an error. The octal number 046 is the equivalent of the decimal integer 38.

Note

Use the Calculator accessory provided with Windows to translate numbers between different bases. Switch to the scientific calculator by selecting the Scientific command in the View menu. A checkmark should appear next to the Scientific command. Switch between bases by selecting the different radio buttons in the upper-left area of the scientific calculator.

Finally, specify a hexadecimal integer by preceding the number with zero (0) followed by an upper- or lowercase X. Recall that hexadecimal numbers are counted from 0 to F. That is, you count from 0 to 9, and then the hexadecimal equivalent of the decimal integer 10 is A, that of 11 is B, and so on. The hexadecimal equivalent of the decimal integer 15 is F. The hexadecimal number 0x26 is the equivalent of the decimal integer 38.

The Visual C++ integer literals are listed in Table A.1.

Table A.1 Integer Literals

Format	Description
number	Type int (4 bytes)
[+ ¦ [en]] number	Signed integer
number[u ¦ U]	Type unsigned (4 bytes)
number[l ¦ L]	Type long (4 bytes)
number[ul ¦ UL]	Type unsigned long (4 bytes)
numberi64	64-bit integer (8 bytes)
0octal	Octal integer
0[x ¦ X]hex	Hexadecimal integer

Much of the time your programs need to use fractional as well as whole numbers. The floating-point numbers fill this need. A floating-point number contains a decimal point (.) and can contain an exponent. These are floating-point numbers:

```
38.0
38.
3.8e1
```

The three numbers are equivalent. They are all 38. The last number is an exponent, represented by a number followed by an e, for exponent, that is followed by the number of tens to multiply the number by. Thus `3.8e1` is equivalent to `3.8 * 10` (3.8 multiplied by 10), or `38.0`.

You can force a number that isn't written with a decimal point to be a floating-point literal by appending an upper- or lowercase F to it. For instance, `38F` is a floating-point number.

The C++ language provides a floating-point number data type that stores the number in double the amount of memory space, eight bytes rather than four bytes, giving you a lot wider range of possible numbers. It is known as the double data type. You can force a number to be a double literal by appending an upper- or lowercase D to it, as in these examples:

```
38D
38.0d
```

The Visual C++ floating-point literals are listed in Table A.2.

Table A.2 Floating-Point Literals

Format	Description
[number].number	Type float (4 bytes)
number[f ¦ F]	Type float (4 bytes)
number[e ¦ E]number	Exponent
number[d ¦ D]	Type double (8 bytes)

Character

The simplest way to use characters in your C++ programs is to type a character surrounded by single quotes. For instance, to use a d, literally type 'd'.

You can also use d by typing an escape sequence using the ASCII number representation of the letter d. An escape sequence always begins with a backslash (\) that is followed by numbers or characters. When you create an escape sequence providing the ASCII representation of a character, you can use the ASCII number in octal or hexadecimal. For instance ,the octal ASCII character code for d is 144, and therefore the escape sequence for d reads \100. The hexadecimal escape sequence for d is \x064. A \x is required before a hexadecimal number.

Some characters are really not characters in the alphabet but represent some action such as ringing a bell or moving the cursor back a space. The C++ language provides special escape characters so that you can use these. For instance, you can ring a bell by using the \BEL character literal, and you can move the cursor back a space by using the \BS character literal. As with the letters in the alphabet, you can also use the ASCII number equivalents of these characters, such as \x007 for the bell and \x008 for the backspace. Table A.3 lists the character literals available to you in the C++ language.

String

Include strings in your C++ code by typing in zero or more characters surrounded by double quotes. This is a string:

```
"I like my C++ in the morning."
```

Two double quotes with zero characters in between ("") form an empty string. The formats for string literals in C++ are listed in Table A.4.

Table A.3 Character Literals

Format	ASCII (hex)	Description
`'character'`		Single character
`\ooo`		Octal value
`\xhhh`		Hexadecimal value
`\NUL`	0	Null character
`\BEL`	7	Alert
`\BS`	8	Backspace
`\HT`	9	Horizontal tab
`\LF`	A	Line feed
`\NL`	A	New line
`\VT`	B	Vertical tab
`\FF`	C	Form feed
`\CR`	D	Carriage return
`\"`	22	Double quote
`\'`	27	Single quote
`\?`	3F	Question mark
`\\`	5C	Backslash

Variables and Data Types

Variables are names, provided by you, the programmer, that represent locations in memory where values can be stored. A variable has a data type, a name, and a value.

Table A.4 String Literals

Format	Description
`"character(s)"`	String
`" "`	Empty string

Data Types

Each datum in a C++ program is of a certain type. You were introduced to many of the data types available in C++ in the previous section, "Literals." Table A.5 lists all of the fundamental data types available in the C++ language.

Table A.5 The C++ Fundamental Data Types	
Type	**Description**
char	Character data.
short int	Also simply short. Short integer data have 2 bytes of memory reserved for each integer.
int	Integer data have 4 bytes of memory reserved for each integer.
_intn	Sized integer data where you provide the amount of memory, n, that is reserved for each integer. You can provide an n of 8, 16, 32, or 64.
long int	Also simply long. Long integer data with 4 bytes of memory reserved for each integer.
float	Floating-point data with 4 bytes of memory reserved for each floating-point number.
double	Floating-point data with 8 bytes of memory reserved for each floating-point number.
long double	Floating-point data with 8 bytes of memory reserved for each floating-point number.

Names of Variables

You can provide variables with any name that you want. There are, however, some helpful guidelines to follow. Typically programmers find it useful to add a lowercase identifier to the beginning of their variable name that indicates the variable's data type. Some suggested prefixes are listed in Table A.6. When you use prefixes, it makes it easier to tell what is going on in your code. With a glance, you know what kinds of data are being used.

Follow the data type prefix with an uppercase letter that is the first letter of the variable name, like in the examples in Table A.6. Use words that make sense in the context of how the variable is used. For instance, if an integer variable is used to keep count, name the variable `iCount`. Capitalize the first letter of each word that you use in the variable name, as in `fltIceCream`.

Table A.6 Variable Prefixes Indicating a Variable's Data Type

Type	Prefix	Example
char	c	cShady
short int	n	nStuff
int	i	iCount
_intn	in	i64BigCount
long int	l	lDays
float	flt	fltIceCream
double	dbl	dblExposure

Declaring Variables

You must declare variables before you can use them in a program. A *variable declaration* is a statement that consists of a data type and a variable name ended, like all statements in C++, with a semicolon (;).

```
char cShady;
short nStuff;
float fltIceCream;
double dblExposure;
```

It's best to assign an initial value to a variable at the time of its declaration. That way you know what is assigned to the variable at all times.

You assign values to variables using the assignment operator (=).

```
char cShady = \NUL;
short nStuff = 0;
float fltIceCream = 0.0;
double dblExposure = 0.0;
```

Usually you'll initially assign zero or null to variables. However, there may be times you want to assign other initial values and there is nothing to stop you.

Expressions and Operators

An *expression* is an operation that returns a value, and an *operator* represents the particular type of operation carried out. The C++ language provides assignment, arithmetic, increment and decrement, comparison, logical, and bitwise operators.

Assignment

Use the assignment operator (=) to assign values to variables. Once a variable is declared, you can assign values to it as often as you like. Of course, when you assign a new value to a variable, the old value is erased. For instance, you can declare the fltIceCream variable and initially assign 0.0 to it, as in this statement:

```
float fltIceCream = 0.0;
```

A four-byte memory location is set aside for floating-point values pointed to by the fltIceCream variable name. The assignment operator (=) tells your computer to put the value 0.0 into that four-byte memory location. Since fltIceCream points to the location in memory, the value assigned to the variable doesn't get lost.

Now if you assign a new value to fltIceCream, as in this statement, the old value is erased and replaced by the new value:

```
fltIceCream = 31.0;
```

The four-byte memory location pointed to by fltIceCream now contains

`31.0`. The previous value, `0.0`, has vanished.

Arithmetic

Arithmetic operators are the workhorses of most programs. The five basic arithmetic operators available in the C++ language are listed in Table A.7.

Table A.7 Arithmetic Operators		
Operator	**Description**	**Example**
+	Addition	3 + 4
-	Subtraction	9 - 2
*	Multiplication	3 * 5
/	Division	8 / 2
%	Modulus	5 % 2

The arithmetic operators are known as binary operators because they take two operands, one on either side of the operator. All of the operators should be self explanatory except, perhaps, the modulus operator. An expression that uses the modulus operator (%) returns whatever is left after the number on the left has been divided as often as possible by the number on the right. Therefore, the expression `5 % 2` returns a `1`. You can divide 2 into 5 two times with a remainder of 1. It's the remainder that is returned by a modulus expression.

Increment and Decrement

You can increase or decrease an integer value assigned to a variable by one using the increment (++) and decrement (--) operators. These operators can appear before or after the variable they affect. When they are placed before the variable, they are known as prefixed increment or decrement operators.

```
++iCountUp     // prefixed increment operator
--iCountDown   // prefixed decrement operator
```

> The prefixed increment and decrement operators are also commonly referred to as pre-increment and pre-decrement operators.

The prefixed operators change the value assigned to their associated variables before the values are used.

When increment and decrement operators are placed after a variable, they are known as postfixed operators.

```
iCountUp++     // postfixed increment operator
iCountDown++   // postfixed decrement operator
```

The postfixed operators change the value assigned to their associated variables after the values are used.

> The postfixed increment and decrement operators are also commonly referred to as post-increment and post-decrement operators.

Suppose that you declare an integer counting variable named iCount and initially assign it a 0 value, as here:

```
int iCount = 0;
```

Then you apply the prefixed increment operator to the iCount variable and assign the result to an x variable:

```
x = ++iCount; // assigns 1 to x
```

The value assigned to the iCount variable, 0, is incremented to 1 before it's assigned to the x variable.

Next, you apply the prefixed decrement operator to the iCount variable and assign the result to a y variable:

```
y = --iCount; // assigns 0 to y
```

The value currently assigned to the iCount variable, 1, is decremented to 0 before it's assigned to the y variable.

Now you apply the postfixed increment operator to the iCount variable and assign the result to an x variable:

```
x = iCount++; // assigns 0 to x
```

The value assigned to the iCount variable, 0, is assigned to the x variable and then incremented to 1.

Finally, you apply the postfixed decrement operator to the iCount variable and assign the result to a y variable:

```
y = iCount--; // assigns 1 to y
```

The value assigned to the iCount variable, 1, is assigned to the y variable and then decremented to 0.

Comparison

You can use one of six C++ operators when you want to test for magnitude and equality. The comparison operators are all binary operators, and they are listed in Table A.8. Expressions using these operators return an int data type of either 1 if the expression is true or 0 if the expression is false.

Table A.8 Comparison Operators	
Operator	**Description**
==	Equal
!=	Not equal
<	Less than
>	Greater than
<=	Less than or equal to
>=	Greater than or equal to

Logical Operators

Create logical expressions using the AND, OR, and NOT operators. Usually you use the logical operators, listed in Table A.9, along with the comparison operators to check multiple conditions. The logical operators recognize only two states, true, represented by 1 (but also any nonzero integer), and false, represented by 0.

Expressions using the AND operator (&&) return an int data type of 1 (true) if its two operands are true. Otherwise, an int data type of 0 (false) is returned:

```
(7 > 2) && (3 == 3)  // is true
(7 < 2) && (3 == 3)  // is false
```

Expressions using the OR operator (¦¦) return an `int` data type of 1 (true) if either one or both of its operands are true. Otherwise, an `int` data type of 0 (false) is returned:

```
(7 > 2) ¦¦ (3 == 3)  // is true
(7 < 2) ¦¦ (3 == 3)  // is true
(7 > 2) ¦¦ (3 != 3)  // is true
(7 < 2) ¦¦ (3 != 3)  // is false
```

The NOT operator (!) is a unary operator; it takes only one operand. An expression using the NOT operator (!) returns an `int` data type of 1 (true) if its operand is true (nonzero). The expression returns an `int` data type of 0 (false) if its operand is false (0):

```
!(3 == 3)  // is false
!(3 != 3)  // is true
```

Table A.9 Logical Operators

Operator	Description
&&	AND
¦¦	OR
!	NOT

Bitwise Operators

Use bitwise operators to perform operations on individual bits in integers. The bitwise operators, listed in Table A.10, are binary operators.

The bitwise AND operator (&) compares each bit of its first operand to the corresponding bit of its second operand. If both bits are 1, the corresponding bit is set to 1. Otherwise, the corresponding bit is set to 0:

```
int iFirstNumber = 9;  // binary representation is 00001001
int iSecondNumber = 3; // binary representation is 00000011
x = iFirstNumber & iSecondNumber;  // x is assigned 1 or 00000001 in binary
```

The bitwise OR operator (¦), also known as the bitwise inclusive-OR operator, compares each bit of its first operand to the corresponding bit of its second operand. If ether bit is 1, the corresponding bit is set to 1. Otherwise, the corresponding bit is set to 0:

```
int iFirstNumber = 9;   // binary representation is 00001001
int iSecondNumber = 3; // binary representation is 00000011
x = iFirstNumber | iSecondNumber; // x is assigned 11 or 00001011 in binary
```

The bitwise XOR operator (^), also known as the bitwise exclusive-OR operator, compares each bit of its first operand to the corresponding bit of its second operand. If one bit is 0 and the other bit is 1, the corresponding bit is set to 1. Otherwise, the corresponding bit is set to 0:

```
int iFirstNumber = 9;   // binary representation is 00001001
int iSecondNumber = 3; // binary representation is 00000011
x = iFirstNumber ^ iSecondNumber;  // x is assigned 10 or 00001010 in binary
```

The C++ bitwise operators include two shift operators. The bitwise left shift operator (<<) shifts the first operand's bits left by the number of positions specified by the second operand:

```
int iNumber = 8; // binary representation is 00001000
iNumber << 2;    // ending value is 32 or 00100000 in binary
```

The bitwise right shift operator (>>) shifts the first operand's bits right by the number of positions specified by the second operand:

```
int iNumber = 8; // binary representation is 00001000
iNumber >> 2;    // ending value is 2 or 00000010 in binary
```

Table A.10 Bitwise Operators

Operator	Description
&	Bitwise AND
|	Bitwise OR
^	Bitwise XOR
<<	Bitwise left shift
>>	Bitwise right shift

Operator Precedence

Operator precedence determines the order that expressions are evaluated in a statement. In some cases, operator precedence has an effect on the result of a statement. For example, look at this statement:

```
x = 4 + 10 / 2;
```

The value assigned to the x variable depends on whether the expression with the addition operator (+) or the expression with the division operator (/) is evaluated first. The value can be either 7 or 9. You can predict the actual value assigned to the x variable due to the operator precedence built into the C++ language.

Operator precedence is shown in Table A.11. Operators at the beginning of the table have precedence over operators toward the end of the table. That is, operators listed at the top of Table A.11 are evaluated before operators listed below them. Notice that the addition operator (+) is listed below the division operator (/). That means that the preceding expression with the division operator is evaluated before the expression with the addition operator. The result of the statement is that 9 is assigned to the x variable.

You can change the order in which expressions are evaluated by using parentheses around the expressions you want evaluated first. Nest parentheses to make sure that expressions are evaluated in the order that you want them evaluated. The innermost expression surrounded by parentheses is evaluated first. This statement is the same as the preceding one except that parentheses were added around the expression with the addition operator so that it is evaluated first:

```
x = (4 + 10) / 2;
```

Now the statement results in the value 7 being assigned to the x variable. In addition to determining the order of evaluation, parentheses help to make your C++ source code easier to read.

Arrays

An *array* is a list of items. An array variable provides a number of slots in memory that each holds an item in a list. The data type of the variable determines the type of each item, or element, that the array can hold.

Declaring Array Variables

Declare an array variable that you can assign an array of integer values with this statement:

```
int iNumbers[10];
```

Like all variables, the array variable is declared using a data type (`int` in this case) and a name (`iNumbers`). Array variables have, in addition, at least one set of brackets surrounding a number indicating the number of elements the array can accept.

The `iNumbers` variable is ready to be assigned 10 different integers in 10 different memory slots. Arrays in C++ are zero (0) indexed. That means that the first slot in an array is accessed through `iNumbers[0]`, the next slot is accessed through `iNumbers[1]`, all the way to the last slot, which is `iNumbers[9]` in this case.

Accessing Array Elements

Once you create an array, you can access its elements by typing the array name followed by a pair of brackets surrounding the element number that you want to access. For instance, this statement assigns the third element (remember, the index number plus one since it's zero-based indexing) of the `iNumbers` array to the y variable:

```
y = iNumbers[2];
```

Changing Array Elements

You change elements in an array much the same way that you access them except that the array variable name and index number go on the left side of the assignment operator rather than the right. This statement assigns the number 5 to the eighth slot in the `iNumbers` array:

```
iNumbers[7] = 5;
```

Table A.11 Operator Precedence

Operator	Description
::	Scope resolution
::	Global
[]	Array subscript
()	Function call
()	Conversion
.	Member selection (object)
->	Member selection (pointer)
++	Postfix increment
--	Postfix decrement
new	Allocate object
delete	Deallocate object
delete[]	Deallocate object
++	Prefix increment
--	Prefix decrement
*	Dereference
&	Address-of
+	Unary plus
-	Arithmetic negation (unary)
!	Logical NOT
~	Bitwise complement
sizeof	Size of object
sizeof()	Size of type
typeid()	Type name
(type)	Type cast (conversion)
const_cast	Type cast (conversion)
dynamic_cast	Type cast (conversion)
reinterpret_cast	Type cast (conversion)
static_cast	Type cast (conversion)
.*	Apply pointer to class member (objects)
->*	Dereference pointer to class member
*	Multiplication

Table A.11 (*continued*)

Operator	Description
/	Division
%	Remainder (modulus)
+	Addition
-	Subtraction
<<	Bitwise left shift
>>	Bitwise right shift
<	Less than
>	Greater than
<=	Less than or equal to
>=	Greater than or equal to
==	Equality
!=	Inequality
&	Bitwise AND
^	Bitwise XOR
¦	Bitwise OR
&&	Logical AND
¦¦	Logical OR
e1?e2:e3	Conditional (ternary)
=	Assignment
*=	Multiplication assignment
/=	Division assignment
%=	Modulus assignment
+=	Addition assignment
-=	Subtraction assignment
<<=	Left-shift assignment
>>=	Right-shift assignment
&=	Bitwise AND assignment
¦=	Bitwise OR assignment
^=	Bitwise XOR assignment
,	Comma

Multidimensional Arrays

Create arrays of any number of dimensions simply by adding more bracket pairs. The iNumbers array, its declaration copied here, is a one-dimensional array of integer values:

```
int iNumbers[10];  // one-dimensional integer array
```

Create a two-dimensional array of integer values by adding another bracket pair enclosing the number of slots, as in the declaration here:

```
int iMoreNumbers[10][5];  // two-dimensional integer array
```

The iMoreNumbers integer array is a 10-by-five two-dimensional array. The first dimension contains 10 slots like in the one-dimensional iNumbers array. However, each of the 10 slots contains five slots for integers. Therefore, each of the first dimension's 10 slots can take five integers for a total of 50 integers. This statement assigns the integer 1960 to the first memory slot of the five slots available inside the first of 10 memory locations set aside for the variable's first dimension:

```
iMoreNumbers[0][0] = 1960;
```

The next statement assigns the integer 1977 to the second memory slot of the five slots available inside the first of 10 memory locations set aside for the iMoreNumbers variable's first dimension:

```
iMoreNumbers[0][1] = 1977;
```

You can fill up the five memory slots by continuing this count until you assign an integer to the fifth memory slot of the five slots available inside the first of the 10 first dimension memory locations, as in this statement:

```
iMoreNumbers[0][4] = 1947;
```

Fill memory slots in the second of the 10 first-dimension memory locations by placing a one between the first pair of brackets, as is done here:

```
iMoreNumbers[1][0] = 1919;
```

The preceding statement assigns the integer 1919 to the first of five slots in the second of the 10 first-dimension memory locations.

You follow the same procedures for variables of any number of dimensions. For instance, this statement declares a four-dimensional variable:

```
int iHypervariable[10][10][5][2];
```

The `iHypervariable` is a 10-by-10-by-five-by-two four-dimensional variable.

Block Statements

A *block statement* is a group of individual statements bundled together by a pair of braces ({}). You can create a block statement anywhere an individual statement can be used in a C++ program.

A block statement creates a new local scope for the statements inside it. This means that when you declare and use variables inside a block statement, those variables cease to exist after the block is finished executing. For example, this code excerpt includes two variables, x and y:

```
...
double x = 0.0;  // declare the x variable
x = 3.6;         // legal, it's in scope
{
  float y = 0.0;  // declare the y variable
  x = 93.0;       // legal, it's in scope
  y = 8.2;        // legal, it's in scope
}
x = 2.8;  // legal, it's in scope
y = 9.8;  // illegal, it's out of scope
...
```

The x variable is declared outside the block statement shown in the preceding code snippet. Variables remain in scope across all blocks nested inside the code block where a variable is declared. However, a variable does not exist once program execution has jumped outside the block statement it's declared in. The y variable shown exists only while the code between the braces ({}) is being executed.

The snippet of C++ code shown in this section is unusual. Block statements aren't typically set up this way. They are typically used with statements that control the flow of program execution. You learn about these conditional and loop statements in following sections.

if Conditionals

The if conditional statement enables you to control the statements executed in a program based on logical tests. The if conditional statement contains the if keyword followed by a Boolean test, which is followed by a statement. For instance, this is a simple if conditional statement:

```
if ( x > y )
  max = x;
```

The statement tests if the value assigned to the x variable is greater than the value assigned to the y variable. If it is, then the expression is true and the statement following the Boolean test is executed. That is, the value assigned to the x variable is assigned to the max variable. If the test is false, then the statement is passed over and the next statement in the code is executed.

The statement following the Boolean test is often a block statement. For instance, when this if conditional statement is true, a block statement is executed:

```
if ( x > y ) {
  max = x;
  min = y;
}
```

When false is returned from the Boolean test, the whole block statement is skipped and the next statement in the program code is executed.

Two other helpful keyword combinations can work together with the if keyword in conditional statements: the else and else if keyword combinations. For instance, if x isn't greater than y, then you might want to provide default operations:

```
if ( x > y ) {
  max = x;
  min = y;
}
else {
  max = y;
  min = x;
}
```

When the `if` statement is true, then the first block statement is executed and `else`, along with the statement following the `else` keyword, is ignored. However, when the `if` statement is false, the statement following the `else` keyword is always executed. In this case it's a block statement that's executed.

Sometimes you'll want to make further conditional evaluations after the initial `if` Boolean test. The `else if` keyword combination provides this ability in C++:

```
if ( x == y )
  z = 15;
else if ( y < x )
  z = 5;
else
  z = 20;
```

You can use `else if` as often as you need. (You can only use `if` and `else` once each.) However, if you find yourself using `else if` a lot, so that there is a long string of them, what you probably need to use is the `switch` conditional statement.

switch Conditionals

The `switch` conditional is handy when you need to test the value assigned to an integer variable against a list of integer constants or literals. You can do this with the `if` conditional, but you end up with a long list of `else if` statements. Test the value assigned to a variable with elegance and ease using the `switch` statement as in this example:

```
switch (iInput) {
  case 0:
    // do something
    break;
  case 1:
    // do something
    break;
  case 2:
  case 3:
    // do something
    break;
```

```
case 4:
  // do something
  break;
default:
  // do something
  break;
}
```

If the value assigned to iInput is 0, the statements following case 0: are executed until and including the break statement, which causes an immediate exit from the switch conditional. The same statements are executed if the value assigned to the iInput variable is either 2 or 3, since there is no break statement between case 2: and case 3:. Finally, if iInput is assigned a value that isn't included in the list of cases, 0 through 4 in the example, then the statements following default: are executed. The default isn't required.

 The break in the case statements isn't required. If the break keyword is left out, program execution simply keeps going. Be careful to not accidentally leave out a break!

for Loops

The for loop repeats a statement or block of statements a number of times until a condition is satisfied. The for loop consists of the for keyword, followed by a set of parentheses enclosing three important parts, which is followed by a block statement. The layout is shown here:

```
for (initialize; test; increment or decrement){
  statement;
}
```

The *initialize* section usually is an expression that initializes a counter variable for the loop. You can declare the variable and assign it an initial value in the initialize section, or you can declare the variable elsewhere and simply assign it an initial value in the initialize section.

The *test* section can be any expression but it typically tests the current value assigned to the counter variable and returns a Boolean value. If the expression returns true (a nonzero number), the block statement that follows the pair of parentheses is executed; otherwise, the loop stops and the program continues executing with the statement after the for loop.

The *increment or decrement* section can be any expression. However, it's commonly used to increment or decrement the value assigned to the counter variable by a set amount. The change in the counter's value is used to bring the state of the loop to completion by making the Boolean test fail.

The for loop is used frequently by C++ programmers. For instance, it's handy when assigning values to or from arrays:

```
int iNumbers[10];
for (int iCount = 0; iCount < 10; iCount++)
  iNumbers[iCount] = 10 - iCount;
```

You can nest for loops, as in this example, which initializes a two-dimensional array:

```
int iMoreNumbers[10][5];
for (int i = 0; i < 10; i++)
  for (int j = 0; j < 5; j++)
    iMoreNumbers[i][j] = i * j;
```

A common mistake when using the for loop is to put a semicolon (;) after the first line. This simply ends the loop with an empty statement so that the loop doesn't do anything. Make sure that you use semicolons only after the statement or statements in the block following the first line of the for loop.

while Loops

Use the while loop to repeat a statement or block of statements as long as a condition is true. The layout of the while loop looks like this:

```
while (test) {
  statement;
}
```

The test placed between the parentheses after the while keyword is a Boolean expression. If the expression returns true, then the body of the while loop, the statements following the first line of the while loop, are executed. Otherwise, they are passed over and the while loop ends.

The while loop is executed until its condition is false. The following example tests if the value assigned to the iCount variable is less than 10. If it is, then the statement that follows is executed, and the value assigned to the iCount variable is incremented by 2. The loop continues until the value equals 10 and the conditional test fails:

```
int iCount = 0;
while ( iCount < 10 ) {
  iCount += 2;
}
```

If the conditional test returns false the first time it is tested, then the body of the while loop is never executed.

do Loops

The do loop is like an upside-down while loop. A do loop executes a given statement or block of statements until a condition test returns false. The layout of the do loop looks like this:

```
do {
  statement;
} while (test)
```

You can see that the conditional test occurs after the body of the do loop. The statement or statements in the body of a do loop are always executed the first time your program encounters the loop. The body of the loop continues to be executed as long as the test at the end of the loop returns true. When false is returned, the do loop stops executing:

```
int iCount = 0;
do {
  iCount += 2;
} while ( iCount < 10 )
```

Summary

You reviewed C++ language syntax and the elements of C++ programming in this appendix. Most important, you reviewed the language's operators and execution flow control statements. Refer to this appendix as a reference. However, if you need a deeper understanding of the C++ language, you should consult a book devoted to the subject.

C++ is an object-oriented language, so knowing the language's syntax is only the first step in using it to write programs. When you write applications using Visual C++ you should understand what classes and objects are and understand the ideas behind object-oriented programming. In Appendix B, "C++ in a Flash: Object-Oriented Programming," you review object-oriented programming using the C++ language.

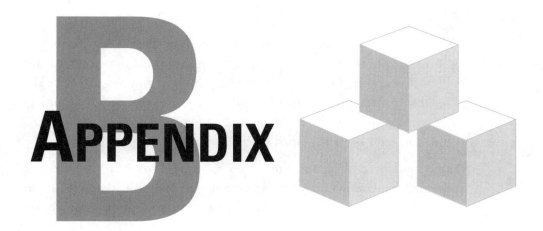

APPENDIX B

C++ in a Flash: Object-Oriented Programming

C++ is an object-oriented language. All of your C++ programs should be created from objects. In this appendix you learn how to create objects by writing classes. You also learn about the class library provided by Microsoft, known as the MFC (Microsoft Foundation Classes) library. The Visual C++ integrated development environment and the MFC library work together to provide you with extensive resources that provide all of the standard elements of your programs, especially the graphic user interface objects, so that you can focus on writing the code that makes your program special.

Note   Even if you already know object-oriented programming techniques, use this appendix as a handy reference to object-oriented programming in C++.

Objects

When you look around yourself you see objects. In fact, it may be impossible not to see things as objects around you. At first you may simply notice a table. On closer inspection, though, you might notice that the table is made up of other objects: the table top and perhaps four legs. The various parts of the table are made of particular materials, perhaps pine, and have specific colors, textures, and shapes.

Object-oriented programming takes advantage of how we mentally organize the world. The world is populated with objects that have attributes, such as color, and exhibit behaviors, such as a motionless table. You create software objects that display attributes and behaviors by writing classes.

Classes

A *class* is an object template, a kind of architectural blueprint for objects. You can write a class that encapsulates the features of all tables, for instance. Call it the Table class. The Table class is a kind of abstract table. It's a set of instructions on how to build a generic table in the same way that blueprints form a set of instructions on how to build a building. The Table class could specify a flat surface and four legs, and it could provide variables to hold attributes such as its color and the dimensions of its flat surface. In this case, all instances of the Table class would have flat surfaces and four legs. However, each instance of the class could display a different color and different dimensions.

Note	**An instance of a class is an object.**

A button for your application's graphic user interface is probably a more useful example than a table. You could create a Button class that provides button attributes such as a label, size, and color that can be set, and button behavior, such as giving the appearance of being depressed when a user clicks on it. Each instance of the Button class would take on all of the attributes and behaviors defined in the class but would use the particular values provided for the particular instance. Thus one Button object might display an OK label, whereas another Button object might display a Cancel label. By creating a Button class, you have reusable instructions for creating generic Button objects that you can individualize by providing unique values to their attributes.

Attributes

Attributes are the features or properties that make an object unique. An attribute can determine the appearance or state of an object. For instance, a Button object might have a label attribute and a pressed attribute. The label attribute would be assigned a string containing text, such as OK or Cancel, which would affect the appearance of the button. The pressed attribute would be assigned a Boolean value indicating whether or not the button was being pressed. This attribute would help determine the state of the Button object (whether or not the button is pressed).

You use class variables to hold attribute values. Typically these variables are private to the class. For instance, a pressed attribute would typically be declared as a variable similar to the one declared here:

```
private int bPressed = 0;   // initialized to false (0)
```

Attributes are typically set and accessed through special accessor functions. You learn about these later, in the section "Defining Classes."

Behavior

An object's behavior is determined by the object's state (is the button pressed?) and the things that the object does. An object typically contains, or encapsulates, functions that the object can carry out and that produce behavior. For instance, when a Button object is in its pressed state, a function might be triggered that causes an animation to run, creating the illusion that the button was physically pressed.

The Button object could also influence the behavior of other objects. For instance, in addition to running an animation when the Button object is pressed, a function encapsulated by the Button object could also launch a Web browser window and load it with a particular Web page.

Declaring Classes

Classes in C++ are user-defined data types that contain data elements (attributes) and procedural elements (functions, behaviors). Like all user defined data types in C++, classes must be declared before they can be used. You declare classes in header files that use the .h extension. For instance, the Button class declaration file might be named button.h.

A class declaration begins with the `class` keyword. The Button class is declared here:

```
class Button {
  private:
    int bPressed;
  public:
    void buttonPressed( void );
    void launchWebPage( void );
};
```

The Button class declaration includes three members: one variable and two functions. The variable, `bPressed`, is a property or attribute of the Button object and is declared as `private`. The two functions, `buttonPressed()` and `launchWebPage()`, are declared as `public`.

Note

Use the Calculator accessory provided with Windows to translate numbers between different bases. Switch to the scientific calculator by selecting the Scientific command in the View menu. A checkmark should appear next to the Scientific command. Switch between bases by selecting the different radio buttons in the upper-left area of the scientific calculator.

The public, private, and protected Keywords

The public and private keywords are access specifiers. They determine the level of access that other objects are allowed to this object's variables and functions. The public keyword specifies free access from other objects, whereas the private keyword specifies no access from other objects. A third access specifier provided by the protected keyword allows access from all objects derived from the class that the function or variable is declared in.

Defining Classes

Declaring a class is a first step. You can't create any objects from a declaration. A class declaration simply states the name of a class, its variables and their data types, and the headers of its functions. The next step is to define the class's member functions.

Functions

You define class functions in a C++ definition file, which has the .cpp extension. Add the #include preprocessor identifier followed by the header file name enclosed between a pair of double quote marks, as in the following example, to the top of the definition files.

```
#include "button.h"
```

The button.h header file contains the class declaration.

The following code is a definition of the Button class `buttonPressed()` member function:

```
void Button::buttonPressed( void )
{
  if ( bPressed )
    // carry out an animation
}
```

Note This function definition doesn't show much code. It's meant to show the general form of a function definition.

The header of the function is the first line. It begins with the `void` keyword, indicating that the function doesn't return any values. Next, the class name appears, followed by a pair of colons (`::`), which is followed by the function name. The pair of colons (`::`) is a scope resolution operator.

The scope resolution operator (`::`) lets you specify the scope of a function or variable. That is, you can explicitly state the context in which a function or variable exists. In the preceding case, the `buttonPressed()` function (the second operand) exists as part of a Button object (the first operand) as long as that object exists. The `buttonPressed()` function is a member of the Button class.

Inside the `buttonPressed()` function is an `if` statement that tests the value assigned to the `bPressed` variable even though this variable is `private`. Private variables can be accessed freely from within the class that they're declared in. They cannot be reached from objects created from other classes.

Constructors

A `constructor` is a member function that is automatically called and executed when an object is created. All objects in C++ call a constructor when they're created. A generic constructor is used if one isn't explicitly defined for the class. Constructors always have the same name as the class. For instance, a constructor for the Button class could be defined like this:

```
Button::Button( void ) {
  bPressed = 0; // initialize as false
}
```

Constructors never return a value, so their definitions begin right away with the class name, followed by the scope operator, and the constructor name, which is the same as the class name.

Constructors are an excellent place to initialize variables. The `Button` constructor initializes the `bPressed` variable to 0 (false).

You can provide a class with as many constructors as you like. They all must have the same name, the name of the class, but they each have different numbers and types of arguments. This provides a way to individualize each object during its creation by passing different values to class variables that determine the object's state or appearance.

The `Button` constructor listed previously has no arguments, as indicated by the void keyword. Suppose that you want to be able to set the size of a Button object, its width and height in pixels, when you create it. Add variables to the Button class declaration that can be assigned size property values. The modified Button class declaration should look something like the example here:

```
class Button {
  private:
    int bPressed;
    int iWidth;
    int iHeight;
  public:
    Button();
    void buttonPressed( void );
    void launchWebPage( void );
};
```

Declarations for the iWidth and iHeight variables were added to the declaration. Next, you can define another constructor for the Button class.

```
Button::Button( int width, int height ) {
  bPressed = 0; // initialize as false
  iWidth = width;
  iHeight = height;
}
```

This is known as overloading a constructor. Now when you create a new Button object, you have the option to set the size by passing this new constructor an integer determining the button's width and an integer determining the button's height. The values passed to the constructor are assigned to the private class variables iWidth and iHeight. If you don't pass two integer values when you create a Button object, then the previous constructor with no arguments is called. Shortly, in the "Creating Objects" section, you'll see how to go about creating an object from a class.

Destructors

A *destructor* is an opposite of a constructor. An object's destructor is called when the object is being destroyed. Objects are destroyed when they go out of scope, are purposely deleted, or the program is exited. Unlike with constructors, you can only write one destructor for each class.

Like when writing constructors, you begin writing class destructors with the name of the class followed by the scope operator and then the name of the destructor. The name of the destructor is always the class name with a tilde (~) prepended, as in the example destructor here:

```
Button::~Button( void ) {
  // cleanup statements
}
```

If you don't create your own class destructor, a default destructor is invoked. Write a class destructor when there is a specific action or group of actions that you want performed when an object created from the class is destroyed.

Creating Objects

Once you've both declared and defined a class, you're ready to create an instance of the class. To create an object, use the new keyword followed by a call to a class constructor. Create a new Button object by calling the Button class constructor.

```
Button btnClose = new Button();
```

You assign the new Button object to the btnClose variable declared as a Button class data type.

You can create an object from any of the constructors available in a class. For instance, you can create a Button object with a preset size of 30 pixels wide and 10 pixels high by using the earlier constructor example:

```
Button btnStart = new Button( 30, 10 );
```

Abstraction and Encapsulation

Abstraction is a description of concepts embodied by an object, the tasks the object can perform, and the interface used to access the object. *Encapsulation* is the establishment of boundaries around an object and managing its internal state. Abstraction and encapsulation are complementary aspects of an object's treatment. Abstraction treats the object's externally visible interface, whereas encapsulation treats the internal aspects of the object.

When you're designing your classes, you should first think about an abstract description of what you want objects created from the class to do. For instance, when you create a Button class, an abstraction of a Button object created from the class would include a visual representation of a button, a visual representation of the button being pressed when it is clicked on, and a button press resulting in some action.

Once you've decided on an abstraction, you move to designing the encapsulated aspects of the object. You decide the variables to create and which of them are public, which are protected, and which are private to the object. Access control with judicious application of these keywords is crucial to a well-designed object. Objects shouldn't always be able to change the properties of other objects at will. You can't change the color of a flower at will while walking through a garden. Nevertheless, there are some manipulations that might change the flower; for instance, adding food coloring to the water that you feed it. You might provide public functions to allow external objects to carry out operations that ultimately affect properties of an object.

You might also provide `public` functions that can be used by other objects to influence states of the object. For instance, the state of a flower can vary between wilted or even dead to fully hydrated. These states depend on the flower's water supply.

> **Note**
>
> **Variables should rarely be declared as** `public`**. Declare variables with either the** `private` **or** `protected` **keyword and use accessor functions to assign values to and get values from the variables.**

Once you've decided on your object's abstraction and encapsulation, it's time for its implementation. Write the class declaration on the basis of your object-oriented design and then create a definition for each of the functions that you planned using the techniques described earlier this appendix.

Inheritance

Inheritance is the ability of C++ classes to inherit features of other classes and is one of the features that makes object-oriented programming powerful. Use inheritance to express "is a" relationships or "kind of" relationships between classes.

Inheritance supposes a hierarchical relationship between classes. For example, you might start with a Flower class, representing all flowers. The Flower class could be considered the top of the flower hierarchy. The Flower class is an abstraction and encapsulation of all those features that apply to flowers in general. For instance, flowers typically have petals and color. An abbreviated Flower class is declared here:

```
class Flower {
  protected:
    int iPetals;  // number of petals
    int iColor;   // number representing color
    float fltCupWater;
  public:
    void water( float cupsWater );
};
```

Derive flower objects of all the various flower types from the Flower class, each of which will be lower in the flower hierarchy.

Deriving Classes

A rose is a flower. This is a clear expression of inheritance, the "is a" relationship. Create a rose by deriving it from the Flower class, the base class in the flower hierarchy. You derive a class from an already existing class by using the derived from operator (:) in the manner shown here:

```
class Rose : public Flower {
  protected:
    int iThorns; // number of thorns
};
```

The notation in the class header, `class Rose : public Flower`, reads "class Rose is publicly derived from Flower." It says that a Rose is a Flower but with some changes and additions that make roses a special kind of flower. These changes and additions are listed between the braces. In this case, the `iThorns` variable is added to account for the thorns found on roses but not all other flowers.

Member variables of Rose objects created from the Rose class include both the new iThorns variable and any public and protected members of the Flower class. They are inherited from the Flower class by the Rose class. A Rose object can access the iPetals, iColor, and fltCupWater variables declared in the Flower class just as if they were declared in the Rose class. The same thing is true of functions. The water() function declared in the Flower class is accessible from Rose objects just as if it was declared in the Rose class.

The rules of base class member accessibility for publicly derived classes are:

- Private members of the base class are inaccessible to objects created from the derived class.

- Protected members of the base class remain protected in the derived class.

- Public members of the base class remain public in the derived class.

You should derive your class publicly when you want to be able to use your derived class as the base class for another derived class. For instance, you might want to derive classes that represent different types of roses from the Rose class. You could do that by declaring the ClimbingRose class shown here:

```
class ClimbingRose : public Rose {
  // declarations specific to derived class
};
```

ClimbingRose objects have access to all of the protected and public members that are accessible by Rose objects. On the other hand, if you don't want anyone to be able to derive a class from your class or, at least, if you don't want objects instantiated from a class derived from your class to use any of the your class's variables and functions, privately derive your class. You could privately derive a RedChineseRose class from the Rose class with the declaration shown here:

```
class RedChineseRose : private Rose {
  // declarations specific to derived class
};
```

The rules of base class member accessibility for privately derived classes are:

- `Private` members of the base class are inaccessible to objects created from the derived class.
- `Protected` members of the base class are private in the derived class.
- `Public` members of the base class are private in the derived class.

Writing function definitions for derived classes is the same as for base classes. Write the derived class name followed by the scope operator and the function name.

Multiple Inheritance

In C++, you can derive classes from more than one base class. This is known as multiple inheritance. A class can inherit class members from more than one base class. You could create the FloweringTree class shown here, for instance, which is derived from the Flower class and a Tree class:

```
class FloweringTree : public Flower, public Tree {
   // declarations specific to derived class
};
```

Objects created from the FloweringTree class have access to all of the `public` and `protected` variables and functions declared in the Flower and Tree classes.

Polymorphism

Functions in C++ objects can take many forms; they can be polymorphic. Polymorphism is handy when you might derive classes from a base class for creating several kinds of a particular object. For instance, flowers all need water but different kinds of flowers have different water requirements. Polymorphism allows you to create a family of classes with common behaviors that vary in detail according to what's appropriate for each class.

Polymorphic member functions, also known as virtual member functions, are declared using the `virtual` keyword. You can modify the Flower class so that its `water()` function is a polymorphic member function. Recall that the Flower class declaration includes a `water()` function. The Flower class declaration is reproduced here:

```
class Flower {
  protected:
    int iPetals;   // number of petals
    int iColor;    // number representing color
    float fltCupWater;
  public:
    void water( float cupsWater );
};
```

This Flower class declaration includes the modified `water()` function so that it's polymorphic:

```
class Flower {
  protected:
    int iPetals;   // number of petals
    int iColor;    // number representing color
    float fltCupWater;
  public:
    virtual void water( float cupsWater );
};
```

Notice that the only change is the addition of the `virtual` keyword at the beginning of the function declaration. Classes derived from the Flower class can either define their own version of the `water()` function or use the version inherited from the Flower class.

The power of polymorphism comes out during run time. You can write code that, for instance, tells the program to water flowers. You could declare a variable of the Flower class data type, like the one here:

```
Flower anyFlower;
```

Then in the program, any kind of object created from a class derived from the Flower class can be assigned to the `anyFlower` variable. An object created from the Rose class, for instance:

```
anyFlower = new Rose( );
```

You run the `water()` function encapsulated by the object currently assigned to the `anyFlower` variable with this statement:

```
anyFlower.water( );
```

This is particularly powerful in code that can receive any number of different objects created from different classes derived from the `Flower` class. You could assign a ClimbingRose object or CactusFlower object to the `anyFlower` variable; the preceding statement will call the `water()` function appropriate to particular class derived from the Flower class that created the object.

Microsoft Foundation Classes (MFC)

The Visual C++ integrated development environment includes a large library of classes, known as the Microsoft Foundation Classes (MFC) library, which are already written for you. One of the major advantages of using an object-oriented programming language such as C++ is that once someone writes a class, the class can be used over and over again. The MFC library provides a vast resource that would be impossible for any one person to create. Visual C++ works closely with the MFC library through wizards and other tools to take care of most routine programming tasks so that you can focus on the code that makes your application special.

By convention, the names of all classes that are part of the MFC library begin with an uppercase C. For instance, the base class for the majority of the MFC library classes is the CObject class, and the base window class is named CWnd.

APPENDIX

Online Resources

The Visual C++ integrated development environment is integrated with an armload of tools that sit on your computer, but it is also integrated with important online resources. The Visual C++ programming environment extends across the computing enterprise and provides it all to you at your fingertips. This appendix presents a brief overview of these resources and goes beyond them to other sites that you might find useful in the course of your Visual C++ programming efforts.

Resources Integrated with Visual C++

Visual C++ uses the entire computing enterprise as a giant computer with vast resources. You have access to technical support and several other Microsoft Web sites through the Visual C++ Help menu and the MSDN Library.

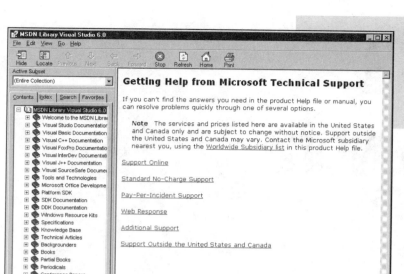

Figure C-1
The Getting Help from Microsoft Technical Support page in the MSDN Library

Microsoft Technical Support

Select the Technical Support command from the Help menu in Visual C++. The MSDN Library Visual Studio 6.0 window appears, displaying the Getting Help from Microsoft Technical Support page, as in Figure C-1.

This page presents several options for you to click on depending on what kind of technical help service you need. As an illustration of what to expect, click on the Standard No-Charge Support hyperlink. Another MSDN Library page displays, as in Figure C-2.

Information is presented on this page to make sure that you get the right service. Finally, you can click on the Standard No-Charge Support via e-mail hyperlink or you can call the telephone number provided for support. The hyperlink takes you to another MSDN Library page, where you can then click on a Web link that takes you to Microsoft Support Online, as in Figure C-3. Web pages are loaded directly into the MSDN Library window.

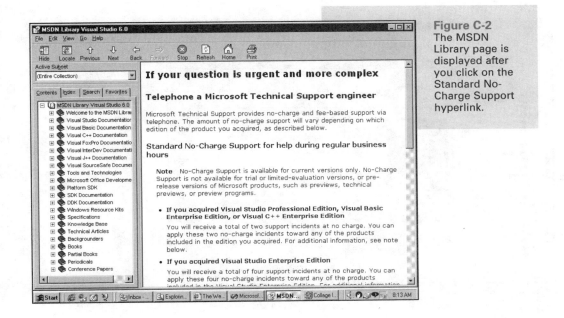

Visual C++ and the MSDN Library provide a wide range of links to the Web. You simply follow the information trail wherever it leads and don't worry about where the information is actually located.

Microsoft Web Sites

Several Microsoft Web sites are available to you through the Microsoft on the Web submenu on the Help menu in Visual C++. Simply click on one of the commands in that menu, such as MSDN Online. Your Web browser is launched and the Web site displayed, as in Figure C-4.

Web Resources

The enterprise is so vast that every useful link can't be provided on a menu in Visual C++. The following sections present a categorized list of Web sites that you might find useful while programming using Visual C++.

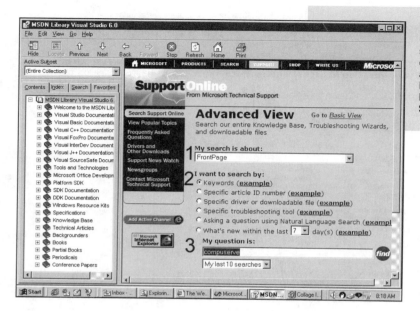

Figure C-3
Get technical support questions answered 24 hours a day on Microsoft Support Online.

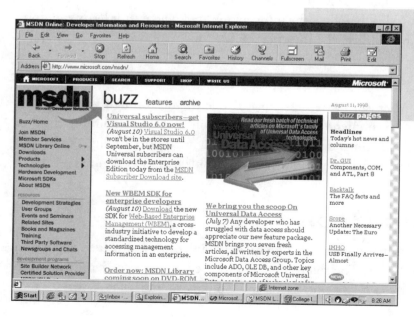

Figure C-4
MSDN Online is accessed directly from the Visual C++ integrated development environment.

Component Object Model (COM) and Distributed COM (DCOM)

Microsoft COM Technologies: **www.microsoft.com/com/**

Object News: **www.objectnews.com**

Digital Signing

VeriSign: **digitalid.verisign.com**

Microsoft Foundation Classes Library

The MFC Professional: **www.visionx.com/mfcpro/**

Standards Organizations

American National Standards Institute (ANSI): **web.ansi.org**

The Open Group. Formerly the Open Software Foundation (OSF): **www.opengroup.org**

Distributed Computing Environment: **www.camb.opengroup.org/tech/dce/**

International Organization for Standardization: **www.iso.ch**

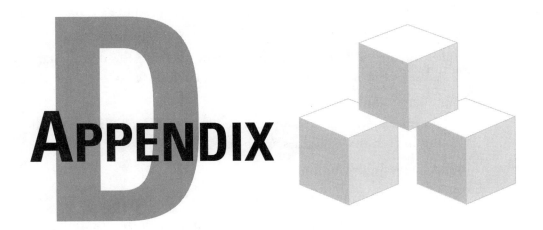

APPENDIX D

Glossary

Active Template Library: A library of template-based C++ classes that facilitate the creation of small, fast COM objects for your software components.

ActiveX: A set of technologies that enables software components to interact with one another in a networked environment. The ActiveX specification is built on COM and, like COM, is language independent.

ActiveX Control: An object created using Microsoft's ActiveX technology. ActiveX controls are built around the COM specification.

American National Standards Institute: An organization that sets standards for a variety of programming languages and systems.

ANSI: See *American National Standards Institute*.

ATL: See *Active Template Library*.

Automation: The COM facility that exposes application functionality for use by other programs.

Binding: When one object accesses another object and calls one of the methods, properties, or events in that object.

Class Factory: An object that implements the IClassFactory interface. Class factories create other objects from specific classes based on the class identifier (CLSID) specified.

Class Identifier: A universally unique identifier (UUID) for an application class that identifies an object.

CLSID: See *Class Identifier*.

COM: See *Component Object Model*.

Component Object Model: A software component specification that defines a binary standard for interfaces to COM objects. These interfaces must be used by the components for communicating to other objects and applications. The specification is programming-language neutral.

Custom Interface: A user-defined COM interface.

DCE: See *Distributed Computing Environment*.

DCOM: See *Distributed Component Object Model*.

Device-Independent Bitmap: Bitmap files that define the images' color and resolution without regard to the particular hardware device displaying them.

DIB: See *Device-Independent Bitmap*.

Dispatch Identifier: A number that identifies a COM object's member function, parameter, or data member. The number is known internally to the IDispatch interface.

DISPID: See *Dispatch Identifier*.

Distributed Component Object Model: The latest update of the COM specification, which realizes the location transparency goal that COM has been aiming at all along.

Distributed Computing Environment: An industry standard, vendor-neutral set of distributed computing technologies developed by the Open Software Foundation (OSF).

DLL: See *Dynamic-Link Library.*

Dual Interface: An interface that supports both IDispatch and custom binding.

Dynamic-Link Library: A routine that user applications access through ordinary procedure calls. The code for the routine is not included in the user's executable file. Instead, the code is dynamically linked with the code from the executable file during run time.

Encapsulation: Containing and hiding information about a software object, which results in isolating the internal complexity of an object's operation from other objects and applications.

Globally Unique Identifier: A Microsoft-specific implementation of the Universally Unique Identifier (UUID).

GUID: See *Globally Unique Identifier.*

IDL: See *Interface Description Language.*

Interface Description Language: A relatively generic programming language developed by the Distributed Computing Environment consortium, which is used to declare COM interfaces so that COM interface implementation remains language neutral. COM actually uses a Microsoft flavor of IDL known as Microsoft IDL, or MIDL.

International Organization for Standardization: A worldwide federation of national standards bodies from about 130 countries. A nongovernmental organization established to promote the development of standardization and related activities in the world with a view to furthering the international exchange of goods and services, and to develop cooperation in the spheres of intellectual, scientific, technological, and economic activity.

ISO: See *International Organization for Standardization.*

Lightweight Remote Procedure Calls: A Microsoft proprietary version of Remote Procedure Calls (RPC). It uses the same syntax as the run-time Distributed Computing Environment RPC but is optimized to reduce data copying and eliminate access to the networking code.

LRPC: See *Lightweight Remote Procedure Calls.*

Marshaling: Generally, marshaling is the ordering and packaging of procedure parameters in a particular format for sending across a network. COM-based objects pack data into a channel buffer in a well-defined format known as the Network Data Representation created for Distributed Computing Environment Remote Procedure Calls.

MFC: See *Microsoft Foundation Classes Library.*

Microsoft Foundation Classes Library: A C++ library that provides an application framework for C++ programming in Microsoft Windows.

Microsoft Interface Description Language: The Microsoft version of the Distributed Computing Environment Interface Description Language, known as MIDL. COM interfaces are implemented in MIDL, and the MIDL compiler compiles the implementation files.

MIDL: See *Microsoft Interface Description Language.*

MIDL Compiler: A compiler that takes files written in Microsoft Interface Description Language (MIDL) and produces stub routines for use in Remote Procedure Call (RPC) applications such as DCOM-based components.

NDR: See *Network Data Representation.*

Network Data Representation: An agreed marshaling format for the Distributed Computing Environment Remote Procedure Calls to transmit different data types between dissimilar machines so that the same data can be reconstructed exactly at the destination machine.

Object Description Language: A scripting language used to describe exposed libraries, objects, types, and interfaces.

Object RPC: The name often used for the DCOM network protocol, since DCOM has a close relationship with RPC.

ODL: See *Object Description Language*.

Open Software Foundation: A nonprofit research and development organization whose goal is to provide a software solution that enables computers from multiple vendors to work together in a true open-systems computing environment. Now known as The Open Group.

ORPC: See *Object RPC*.

OSF: See *Open Software Foundation*.

Parameterized types: See *Templates*.

Process: A logical division of labor in an operating system. In Windows a process comprises a virtual address space, an executable program, one or more threads of execution, some portion of the user's resource quotas, and the system resources that the operating system has allocated to the process's threads.

Property: A data member of an exposed object that is set or retrieved through put and get accessor functions.

Proxy: An interface-specific object that packages parameters for the interface in preparation for a remote method call. A proxy runs in the address space of a sending software component and communicates with a corresponding stub in the receiving component's address space.

Remote Procedure Call: A message-passing facility that allows a distributed application to call services available on various machines in a network without regard to their locations. Remote network operations are handled automatically. RPC provides a procedural view, rather than a transport-centered view, of networked operations.

RPC: See *Remote Procedure Call.*

Scripting Languages: One of several relatively lightweight languages that are often used for programming Web pages or for macros in applications such as those in Microsoft Office. VBScript and JavaScript are currently the most popular scripting languages.

Smart Pointers: Classes that encapsulate pointers and override pointer operators to add new functionality to pointer operations. Smart pointers are typically implemented using template classes.

Standard C++ Library: A library used in C++ programming that is included with all ANSI/ISO-compliant C++ compilers.

Standard Template Library: Part of the Standard C++ Library included with all ANSI/ISO-compliant C++ compilers. The design of the Microsoft Active Template Library (ATL) is based on the Standard Template Library (STL).

STL: See *Standard Template Library.*

Stub: An interface-specific object that unpackages the parameters for the interface and makes the requested method call after the parameters are marshaled across the process boundary. A stub runs in the address space of a receiving software component and communicates with a corresponding proxy in the sending component's address space.

Stub Procedure: A procedure in a dynamic-link library (DLL) that serves as an entry point for an application programming interface (API). When a client application calls the API routine, the stub procedure marshals the API parameters it receives into a message and sends them to either a local server (subsystem) or a remote server on the network.

Synchronization: The ability of one thread to pause during execution and wait until another thread performs an operation.

Templates: In C++, templates are a mechanism for generating functions and classes based on type parameters. Templates enable you to design a single class that operates on data of many types so that you don't need to create a different class for each data type that you want the class to operate on. Templates are sometimes referred to as parameterized types.

Thread: An executable entity that belongs to one, and only one, process. A thread comprises a program counter, a user-mode stack, a kernel-mode stack, and a set of register values.

Type Library: A file or component within another file that contains type information about exposed objects.

Unicode: A fixed-width, 16-bit character encoding standard capable of representing all scripts in the world.

Uniform Resource Locator: Identifies the full path of some data or location on the Internet or an intranet. In addition, it specifies the protocol to use.

Universally Unique Identifier: A unique 128-bit value used to identify objects such as interfaces and COM classes.

URL: See *Uniform Resource Locator.*

UUID: See *Universally Unique Identifier.*

Void Pointers: Used to allow functions to operate on data of unknown data types.

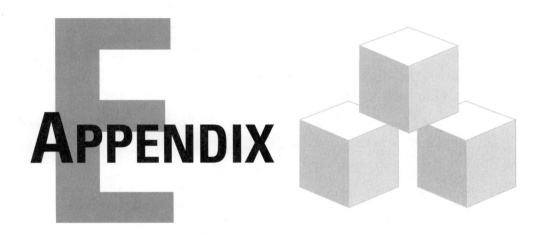

APPENDIX E

What's On the CD?

The CD that accompanies this book contains example projects and code from the book, as well as a large variety of Web tools and utilities to assist you in your Visual C++ development efforts.

Running the CD

To make the CD more user friendly and take up less of your disk space, no installation is required. This means that the only files transferred to your hard disk are the ones you choose to copy or install.

Caution

This CD has been designed to run under Windows 95/98 and Windows NT 4. While it will run under Windows 3.1, you may encounter unexpected problems. In addition, many of the software programs contained on the CD are 32 bit programs, and as such, will not run in Windows 3.1.

Windows 95/98/NT4

Because there is no install routine, running the CD in Windows 95/98/NT4 is a breeze, especially if you have autorun enabled. Simply insert the CD in the CD-ROM drive, close the tray, and wait for the CD to load.

If you have disabled autorun, place the CD in the CD-ROM drive and follow these steps:

1. From the Start menu, select Run.
2. Type **D:\prima.exe** (where D:\ is the CD-ROM drive).
3. Click on OK.

The Prima User Interface

Prima's user interface is designed to make viewing and using the CD contents quick and easy. The opening screen contains four category buttons, and a command bar with three navigational buttons. Click on a category button to jump to the associated page containing the available software titles or book examples. Once you reach a category page, click on a title button to display a pop-up menu with options for installing and viewing the software/examples.

Category/Title Buttons

Book Examples. Project files and source code from "Hands On Visual C++ for Web Development."

Developer Tools. An assortment of handy tools and utilities to aid in your development efforts.

Utilities. File compression, FTP, and assorted file managment utilities.

Web Tools. Here you'll find a variety of Web management tools that will enable you to monitor and maintain your Web sites with ease.

Command Bar Buttons

Exit. When you're finished using the CD, shut it down with this button.

Explore. Use this button to view the contents of the CD using the Windows Explorer.

Navigate. Click this button to display a pop-up menu containing links to the various category pages.

Next and Previous. The arrows located at either end of the command bar are Previous (left side) and Next (right side) buttons that will move you to the page before or after the current page.

Pop-up Menu Options

Install. If the selected title contains an install routine, choosing this option begins the installation process.

Explore. Selecting this option allows you to view the folder containing the program files, using Windows Explorer.

Information. Use this menu item to open the Readme file associated with the selected title. If no Readme file is present, the Help file will be opened.

Visit Web Site. If you're running Windows 95/98/NT4 and a recent version of Internet Explorer or Netscape Navigator, and have established an Internet connection, selecting this option will launch your browser and take you to the associated Web site.

The Software

This section gives you a brief description of some of the shareware and evaluation software you'll find on the CD. This is just a sampling. As you browse the CD you will find much more.

Any shareware distributed on this disk is for evaluation pur-poses only and should be registered with the shareware ven-dor if used beyond the trial period.

3D power pack. A collection of small ActiveX controls that Windows application developers can use to add true dynamic 3D graphics inter-faces to their applications.

CC-Rider. CC-Rider provides tools to develop, visualize and document software written in the C and C++ programming languages.

Browse And Zip. This handy plugin for Netscape and Internet Explorer will supercharge your Web browser's handling of Zip files.

Centura Team Developer. A 32-bit development tool set that allows you to create robust, scalable, and Internet-enabled applications that meet your strategic business needs.

Dameware Component Pack 4. A collection of ActiveX controls that can be used with VB, Visual C++, and HTML.

Genitor. Genitor is a next-generation, object-oriented editor for C/C++ programming that provides the most effective way to implement, docu-ment, and reuse C/C++ code.

Logiscope. A multifaceted application that enables improved program-ming quality, maintenance and test coverage through a comprehensive source code tool set.

StarTeam. StarTeam provides fast and efficient SCM tools which include project organization, defect tracking, topic discussion, view management, and support for parallel development.

WinZip. One of the most popular file compression utilities around.

Index

F

Favorites menu, 9

file compression utilities, 424

File menu, QuickBrowse, 120, 121

floating-point literals, C++, 364, 366

for loops, C++, 386-387

form <FORM> tag, 26

free-threaded marshaler support, 310

FrontPage Express, 286-287

FTP (file transfer protocol), 3, 4

    servers, 7

functions

    class functions, defining, 395-396

    MsgBox function, 27

G

Genitor, 424

GetDocument() functions, 111-112

GetObject() method, 341

GetTreeCtrl() function, 116

GetTreeCtrol() function, 88

GetWindowLong() function, 84-85

global variables, 73

glossary, 413-419

Go menu, QuickBrowse, 125-126

Gopher servers, 7

GUID (globally unique identifer), 205

    for InstantPostServer component, 348

H

headers

    CHeaderCtrl, 46

    of function, 396

head <HEAD> tags, 9

help, online resources, 407-411

helpstring attribute, 206

Hide command, Output window, hiding, 74, 157

HKEY_CLASSES_ROOT base key, 347

hot keys, 46

hottool.bmp, 130

HTML (Hypertext Markup Language), 6, 7-12

    display text, 10-12

    new document in, 7-9

HTML tags, 9

HTTP (Hypertext Transfer Protocol), 3, 4, 6

Hypertext Markup Language (HTML). *See* HTML (Hypertext Markup Language)

I

IBindStatusCallback interface, 220

_IClientManagerEvents interface, 318

IClientManager interface, 325

iCount variable, 117-118, 150

IDE (Integrated Development Environment), 30

    LogoMagic, running, 190-194

    QuickBrowse, running, 66-69

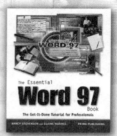

Title of this book: _____

Send Us
YOUR COMMENTS

Dear Reader:

Thank you for buying this book. In order to offer you more quality books on the topics *you* would like to see, we need your input. At Prima Publishing, we pride ourselves on timely responsiveness to our readers needs. If you'll complete and return this brief questionnaire, *we will listen!*

Name: (first) _____ (M.I.) _____ (last) _____

Company: _____ Type of business: _____

Address: _____ City: _____ State: _____ Zip: _____

Phone: _____ Fax: _____ E-mail address: _____

May we contact you for research purposes? ☐ Yes ☐ No

(If you participate in a research project, we will supply you with your choice of a book from Prima Tech)

❶ How would you rate this book, overall?

☐ Excellent   ☐ Fair
☐ Very Good   ☐ Below Average
☐ Good   ☐ Poor

❷ Why did you buy this book?

☐ Price of book   ☐ Content
☐ Author's reputation   ☐ Prima's reputation
☐ CD-ROM/disk included with book
☐ Information highlighted on cover
☐ Other (Please specify): _____

❸ How did you discover this book?

☐ Found it on bookstore shelf
☐ Saw it in Prima Publishing catalog
☐ Recommended by store personnel
☐ Recommended by friend or colleague
☐ Saw an advertisement in: _____
☐ Read book review in: _____
☐ Saw it on Web site: _____
☐ Other (Please specify): _____

❹ Where did you buy this book?

☐ Bookstore (name) _____
☐ Computer Store (name) _____
☐ Electronics Store (name) _____
☐ Wholesale Club (name) _____
☐ Mail Order (name) _____
☐ Direct from Prima Publishing
☐ Other (please specify): _____

❺ Which computer periodicals do you read regularly? _____

_____

_____

❻ Would you like to see your name in print?

May we use your name and quote you in future Prima Publishing books or promotional materials?

☐ Yes   ☐ No

P PRIMA TECH

❼ Comments & Suggestions: _____

_____

_____

⑧ Where do you use your computer?

	100%	75%	50%	25%
Work	☐	☐	☐	☐
Home	☐	☐	☐	☐
School	☐	☐	☐	☐

Other _____

⑨ How do you rate your level of computer skills?

☐ Beginner
☐ Advanced
☐ Intermediate

⑩ What is your age?

☐ Under 18
☐ 18-24   ☐ 40-49
☐ 25-29   ☐ 50-59
☐ 30-39   ☐ 60-over

⑪ I would be interested in computer books on these topics

☐ Word Processing   ☐ Database:
☐ Networking   ☐ Spreadsheets
☐ Desktop Publishing   ☐ Web site design

Other _____

PLEASE
PLACE
STAMP
HERE

PRIMA PUBLISHING
Prima Tech Division
3875 Atherton Rd.
Rocklin, CA 95765

Other Books from PRIMA TECH

ISBN	Title	Price
0-7615-1046-X	Hands On Visual Basic 5	$40.00
0-7615-1047-8	Hands On JavaBeans	$40.00
0-7615-1339-6	Hands On Access 97	$40.00
0-7615-0955-0	Hands On Visual Basic 5 for Web Development	$40.00
0-7615-1647-6	Hands On Visual Basic 6 for Web Development	$40.00
0-7615-1635-2	Hands On Visual Basic 6	$40.00
0-7615-1678-6	Hands On Visual InterDev 6	$40.00
0-7615-1392-2	Introduction to ABAP/4 Programming for SAP	$50.00
0-7615-0751-5	Windows NT Server 4 Administrator's Guide	$50.00
0-7615-1005-2	Internet Information Server 3 Administrator's Guide	$40.00
0-7615-1387-6	Internet Information Server 4 Administrator's Guide	$50.00
0-7615-1750-2	Supporting SAP R/3	$50.00
0-7615-1381-7	Visual FoxPro 6 Enterprise Development	$55.00

COMING SOON:

ISBN	Title	Price
0-7615-1514-3	Hands On Cold Fusion 4.0	$40.00
0-7615-1535-6	Hands On XML	$40.00
0-7615-1386-8	Hands On SQL Server 7 with Access	$40.00
0-7615-1385-X	Hands On SQL Server 7 with Visual Basic 6	$40.00
0-7615-1389-2	Microsoft SQL Server 7 Administrator's Guide	$50.00
0-7615-1390-6	Exchange Server 6 Administrator's Guide	$50.00
0-7615-1395-7	Windows NT Server 5 Administrator's Guide	$50.00

To Order Books

Please send me the following items:

Quantity	Title	Unit Price	Total
_____	_____	$ _____	$ _____
_____	_____	$ _____	$ _____
_____	_____	$ _____	$ _____
_____	_____	$ _____	$ _____
_____	_____	$ _____	$ _____

Subtotal	$ _____
Deduct 10% when ordering 3-5 books	$ _____
7.25% Sales Tax (CA only)	$ _____
8.25% Sales Tax (TN only)	$ _____
5.0% Sales Tax (MD and IN only)	$ _____
7.0% G.S.T. Tax (Canada only)	$ _____
Shipping and Handling*	$ _____
Total Order	$ _____

*Shipping and Handling depend on Subtotal.

Subtotal	Shipping/Handling
$0.00–$14.99	$3.00
$15.00–$29.99	$4.00
$30.00–$49.99	$6.00
$50.00–$99.99	$10.00
$100.00–$199.99	$13.50
$200.00+	Call for Quote

**Foreign and all Priority Request orders:
Call Order Entry department
for price quote at 916-632-4400**

This chart represents the total retail price of books only (before applicable discounts are taken).

By Telephone: With American Express, MC or Visa, call 800-632-8676 or 916-632-4400. Mon–Fri, 8:30-4:30.

www.prima-tech.com

By E-mail: sales@primapub.com

By Mail: Just fill out the information below and send with your remittance to:

**Prima Publishing
P.O. Box 1260BK
Rocklin, CA 95677**

My name is _____

I live at _____

City_____ State _____ ZIP _____

MC/Visa#_____ Exp._____

Check/money order enclosed for $ _____ Payable to Prima Publishing

Daytime telephone _____

Signature _____

Mountains
of
Wisdom ... in compact, portable form!

Using the very latest Windows-based technology, these CDs hold 6 full years of magazines, along with the PROFESSIONAL RESOURCE CD files from each issue.

Full-text search allows you to locate articles from all issues within seconds. See diagrams, figures, photos, and code as originally published—in full color. Copy and paste published routines right into your applications!

NEW!
The Complete
ACCESS-OFFICE-VB ADVISOR
1998 CD-ROM

Also Available:
THE COMPLETE ACCESS-OFFICE-VB ADVISOR 1997 CD-ROM
THE COMPLETE ACCESS/VISUAL BASIC ADVISOR 1996 CD-ROM
THE COMPLETE ACCESS/VISUAL BASIC ADVISOR 1995 CD-ROM
THE COMPLETE ACCESS ADVISOR 93-94 CD-ROM
EACH ANNUAL EDITION: U.S. $49, Other Countries $59

CALL TOLL FREE 800-336-6060
Outside U.S. (619)278-5600 · Fax (619)279-4728
order@advisor.com · www.advisor.com

System Requirements: 386 or 486 PC, 4MB RAM, VGA, 4MB disk space, CD-ROM drive, Microsoft Windows 3.1 or later

Build Databased Web Solutions with Microsoft Technology

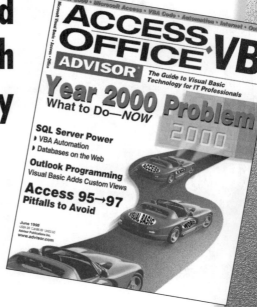

ACCESS-OFFICE-VB ADVISOR is the only independent technical magazine devoted to Microsoft database, Visual Basic, and web technology. Written by the leading experts, each monthly issue brings you the designs, tools, techniques, add-ons, RAD methods and management practices you need to implement the best custom enterprise solutions.

ACCESS-OFFICE-VB ADVISOR is packed with professional techniques using these Microsoft tools:

- Access
- Visual Basic
- SQL Server
- Visual InterDev
- Office
- Outlook
- Internet Information Server
- Exchange Server
- Excel
- Transaction Server
- Site Server
- ActiveX

"Thanks for all the great tips and techniques...they have saved me many, many times!"

ACCESS-OFFICE-VB ADVISOR

MAGAZINE ONLY
12 Issues: US $39, Canada $59, Other Countries $79

MAGAZINE + PROFESSIONAL RESOURCE CD
12 Issues + 12 CDs: US $129, Canada $169, Other Countries $199

ADVISOR Professional Resource CD

To Subscribe, Call Toll Free
800-336-6060

Outside U.S. call (619)278-5600 • Fax (619)279-4728
subscribe@advisor.com • www.advisor.com

License Agreement/Notice of Limited Warranty

By opening the sealed disk container in this book, you agree to the following terms and conditions. If, upon reading the following license agreement and notice of limited warranty, you cannot agree to the terms and conditions set forth, return the unused book with unopened disk to the place where you purchased it for a refund.

License:
The enclosed software is copyrighted by the copyright holder(s) indicated on the software disk. You are licensed to copy the software onto a single computer for use by a single concurrent user and to a backup disk. You may not reproduce, make copies, or distribute copies or rent or lease the software in whole or in part, except with written permission of the copyright holder(s). You may transfer the enclosed disk only together with this license, and only if you destroy all other copies of the software and the transferee agrees to the terms of the license. You may not decompile, reverse assemble, or reverse engineer the software.

Notice of Limited Warranty:
The enclosed disk is warranted by Prima Publishing to be free of physical defects in materials and workmanship for a period of sixty (60) days from end user's purchase of the book/disk combination. During the sixty-day term of the limited warranty, Prima will provide a replacement disk upon the return of a defective disk.

Limited Liability:
THE SOLE REMEDY FOR BREACH OF THIS LIMITED WARRANTY SHALL CONSIST ENTIRELY OF REPLACEMENT OF THE DEFECTIVE DISK. IN NO EVENT SHALL PRIMA OR THE AUTHORS BE LIABLE FOR ANY OTHER DAMAGES, INCLUDING LOSS OR CORRUPTION OF DATA, CHANGES IN THE FUNCTIONAL CHARACTERISTICS OF THE HARDWARE OR OPERATING SYSTEM, DELETERIOUS INTERACTION WITH OTHER SOFTWARE, OR ANY OTHER SPECIAL, INCIDENTAL, OR CONSEQUENTIAL DAMAGES THAT MAY ARISE, EVEN IF PRIMA AND/OR THE AUTHOR HAVE PREVIOUSLY BEEN NOTIFIED THAT THE POSSIBILITY OF SUCH DAMAGES EXISTS.

Disclaimer of Warranties:
PRIMA AND THE AUTHORS SPECIFICALLY DISCLAIM ANY AND ALL OTHER WARRANTIES, EITHER EXPRESS OR IMPLIED, INCLUDING WARRANTIES OF MERCHANTABILITY, SUITABILITY TO A PARTICULAR TASK OR PURPOSE, OR FREEDOM FROM ERRORS. SOME STATES DO NOT ALLOW FOR EXCLUSION OF IMPLIED WARRANTIES OR LIMITATION OF INCIDENTAL OR CONSEQUENTIAL DAMAGES, SO THESE LIMITATIONS MAY NOT APPLY TO YOU.

Other:
This Agreement is governed by the laws of the State of California without regard to choice of law principles. The United Convention of Contracts for the International Sale of Goods is specifically disclaimed. This Agreement constitutes the entire agreement between you and Prima Publishing regarding use of the software.